CW01663213

DOING A MASTER'S DISSERTATION IN TESOL AND APPLIED LINGUISTICS

Doing a Master's Dissertation in TESOL and Applied Linguistics is a practical guide for master's students tackling research and research writing for the first time. Structured for use in class or as part of an independent study, and divided into the four stages of designing, researching, writing up and submitting a dissertation, this book:

- carefully guides readers from the very beginning of producing a research proposal, all the way through to assessment procedures and the provisions for resubmission;
- covers publishing your dissertation and applying for higher research degrees, including funding;
- addresses all the most fundamental concerns students have about master's dissertations, including how to choose a topic and conducting a literature review;
- draws upon examples from master's dissertations from the UK, US and Australia and provides numerous 'how-to' tables and checklists; and
- includes activities and resources to facilitate master's research and dissertation writing, as well as FAQs and solutions at the end of each chapter.

Tailormade for MA students in TESOL or Applied Linguistics, this book is essential reading for students on these degrees around the world as well as for their supervisors and programme directors.

Lindy Woodrow is Honorary Senior Lecturer in TESOL at the University of Sydney, Australia.

DOING A MASTER'S DISSERTATION IN TESOL AND APPLIED LINGUISTICS

Lindy Woodrow

Routledge
Taylor & Francis Group
LONDON AND NEW YORK

First published 2020
by Routledge
2 Park Square, Milton Park, Abingdon, Oxon OX14 4RN

and by Routledge
52 Vanderbilt Avenue, New York, NY 10017

Routledge is an imprint of the Taylor & Francis Group, an informa business

© 2020 Lindy Woodrow

The right of Lindy Woodrow to be identified as author of this work has been asserted by her in accordance with sections 77 and 78 of the Copyright, Designs and Patents Act 1988.

All rights reserved. No part of this book may be reprinted or reproduced or utilised in any form or by any electronic, mechanical, or other means, now known or hereafter invented, including photocopying and recording, or in any information storage or retrieval system, without permission in writing from the publishers.

Trademark notice: Product or corporate names may be trademarks or registered trademarks, and are used only for identification and explanation without intent to infringe.

British Library Cataloguing-in-Publication Data
A catalogue record for this book is available from the British Library

Library of Congress Cataloging-in-Publication Data
Names: Woodrow, Lindy, 1954– author.
Title: Doing a master's dissertation in TESOL and applied linguistics / Lindy Woodrow.
Description: Abingdon, Oxon ; New York : Routledge, 2020. | Includes bibliographical references and index.
Identifiers: LCCN 2019032146 (print) | LCCN 2019032147 (ebook) | ISBN 9781138587281 (hardback) | ISBN 9781138587298 (paperback) | ISBN 9780429504068 (ebook)
Subjects: LCSH: Dissertations, Academic—Authorship. | Academic writing—Study and teaching. | Applied linguistics—Study and teaching. | English language—Study and teaching—Foreign speakers.
Classification: LCC LB2369 .W656 2020 (print) | LCC LB2369 (ebook) | DDC 808.06/6378—dc23
LC record available at https://lccn.loc.gov/2019032146
LC ebook record available at https://lccn.loc.gov/2019032147

ISBN: 978-1-138-58728-1 (hbk)
ISBN: 978-1-138-58729-8 (pbk)
ISBN: 978-0-429-50406-8 (ebk)

Typeset in Bembo
by Apex CoVantage, LLC

CONTENTS

List of Figures *xii*
List of Tables *xv*
Acknowledgements *xviii*

1 Introduction 1

1.1 What is a dissertation? 1
1.2 The purpose of the dissertation 3
1.3 Managing the dissertation process 4
1.4 How to use this book 6

PART I
Project design 9

2 Choosing a topic 11
2.1 How to choose a topic 11
2.1.1 Topics emerging from modules and assignments 11
2.1.2 Topics emerging from previous dissertations 12
2.1.3 Topics informed by personal interest 12
2.1.4 Topics informed by professional need 13
2.1.5 Topics based on supervisor expertise 13
2.1.6 Topics based on career trajectory 13
2.1.7 Reading 14
2.2 Researchable topics 14
2.3 Developing the topic 15
2.4 Changing topics 16
2.5 Dissertation title 16

3 Reviewing the literature 21
3.1 The purpose of the literature review 22
3.2 Stage one: broad review of the literature 22
3.2.1 Types of literature 24
3.3 Stage two: finding sources 25
3.3.1 Keeping track of reading 26
3.4 Stage three: reading skills 27
3.5 Role of theory and research 29
3.6 Avoiding plagiarism 29

4 Methodological approach 32
4.1 Research methodology 32
4.2 Research design 33
4.2.1 Quantitative methods 34
4.2.2 Qualitative methods 37
4.3 Types of research design 37
4.3.1 Survey research 37
4.3.2 Action research 38
4.3.3 Ethnography 38
4.3.4 Case study 39
4.4 Data collection methods 39
4.4.1 Questionnaires 39
4.4.2 Interviews 40
4.4.3 Focus groups 41
4.4.4 Observations 41
4.4.5 Corpus linguistics 42
4.4.6 Discourse analysis 42
4.5 Analysis 42
4.5.1 Quantitative analysis 43
4.5.2 Qualitative analysis 43
4.6 Sampling 45
4.7 Ethics 46
4.8 Validity and reliability 46

5 The dissertation proposal 51
5.1 The purpose of the proposal 51
5.2 Title/abstract 52
5.3 Proposal introduction 53
5.4 Purpose of the study 54
5.5 Background/literature review 54
5.6 Research questions 55
5.7 Methodology 57
5.8 Procedure/timeline 58

5.9 Appendix 59
5.10 Bibliography or references 59
5.11 Assessment and feedback 59
5.12 Using proposal feedback 60

6 Supervisors and supervision 63
6.1 Allocation of supervisors 63
6.2 Supervision by committee 64
6.3 Contact time 64
6.4 Roles of supervisor and student 65
6.5 Supervisory meetings 66
6.6 Problems with supervision 68

PART II
The research procedure 71

7 The data collection procedure 73
7.1 Participants 73
7.1.1 Using fellow students 73
7.1.2 Using participants from home institution 74
7.1.3 Using students from the university language centre 74
7.1.4 Using intact classes 74
7.2 Recruiting participants 75
7.3 Modes of data collection 76
7.3.1 Textual data 78
7.3.2 Questionnaire data 79
7.3.3 Interviews 82
7.4 Unforeseen circumstances 84
7.4.1 Not getting permission to access participants 85
7.4.2 Participants do not respond 85
7.4.3 Insufficient or incorrect materials 85
7.4.4 Research site is inadequate 85
7.4.5 Participants turn up late 85
7.4.6 Recording device fails 86

8 Data Analysis 89
8.1 Keeping a research diary 89
8.2 Preparing the data for analysis 92
8.3 Quantitative data 92
8.3.1 Preparing the codebook 93
8.3.2 Screening the data 95
8.3.3 Describing the data 95
8.3.4 Further analysis 96

8.4 *Qualitative data 98*
8.4.1 *Interviews and documents 98*
8.4.2 *Approaches to qualitative analysis 100*
8.5 *Getting help with research process 100*

PART III
Writing the dissertation 105

9 General writing guidelines 107
9.1 *When to start writing 107*
9.2 *Organisation of a dissertation 109*
9.3 *General requirements of a dissertation 111*
9.4 *Academic writing 112*
9.4.1 *Audience 112*
9.4.2 *Purpose 112*
9.4.3 *Expectations 112*
9.5 *Features of academic style 112*
9.5.1 *Vocabulary 113*
9.5.2 *Grammar 113*
9.5.3 *Punctuation 114*
9.6 *Use the marking scheme while writing 115*
9.7 *Process of writing 116*

10 Writing the literature review 119
10.1 *The purpose of the literature review 119*
10.2 *Organisation of the literature review 120*
10.3 *Sources to include in the review 123*
10.4 *Critical reading and writing 124*
10.5 *Referring to the gap in knowledge 125*
10.6 *Citing 126*

11 Writing the methodology chapter 131
11.1 *The purpose of the methodology chapter 131*
11.2 *Organisation of the methodology chapter 132*
11.2.1 *Research questions 132*
11.2.2 *Methodological approach 132*
11.2.3 *The role of the researcher 133*
11.2.4 *The research context 133*
11.2.5 *Participants 134*
11.2.6 *Methods of data collection 137*
11.2.7 *Methods of data analysis 137*

11.2.8 Reliability and validity 138
11.2.9 Ethics 140
11.3 Language in the methodology chapter 140

12 Writing the results and discussion chapters 144
12.1 The results chapter 144
12.1.1 The purpose of the results chapter 145
12.1.2 Organisation of results chapter 146
12.1.3 Reporting quantitative results 148
12.1.4 Using tables and graphics 148
12.1.5 Reporting qualitative results 149
12.2 The discussion chapter 152
12.2.1 The purpose of the discussion chapter 152
12.2.2 Organisation of the discussion chapter 155
12.2.3 Limitations of the study 156
12.2.4 Implications of the study 158
12.3 Language of results and discussion 158

13 Beginning and ending the dissertation 163
13.1 The introduction 163
13.2 The conclusion 166
13.3 The reference list 170
13.3.1 Digital object identifiers (DOIs) 172
13.3.2 Referencing software 172

PART IV
Dissertation submission 177

14 The finishing touches 179
14.1 Title page 179
14.2 The dissertation abstract 179
14.3 Acknowledgements 183
14.4 The table of contents 183
14.5 Declaration 186
14.6 List of terms and abbreviations 186
14.7 Appendices 186
14.8 Editing and proof-reading 189

15 The examination and beyond 193
15.1 Examination of the dissertation 193
15.1.1 Who marks the dissertation? 193

15.1.2 *Dissertation assessment criteria 194*
15.1.3 *Feedback on the dissertation 195*
15.2 *The viva 198*
15.2.1 *Before the viva 198*
15.2.2 *During the viva 199*
15.3 *Oral presentations 200*
15.4 *After the dissertation 201*
15.4.1 *Resubmission 201*
15.4.2 *Using the dissertation as a pathway 201*
15.4.3 *Disseminating knowledge 202*
15.4.4 *Giving a conference presentation 203*
15.4.5 *Publishing a journal article 203*
15.4.6 *Differences between a dissertation and an article 204*
15.4.7 *Dissertation awards 205*

16 Resources 208
16.1 *Dissertation guides 208*
16.2 *Proposal writing guides 209*
16.3 *List of Routledge Handbooks on TESOL and applied linguistics 209*
16.4 *List of academic journals in TESOL and applied linguistics 210*
16.5 *Sources for the literature review 212*
16.5.1 *Referencing software 212*
16.5.2 *Referencing guides 213*
16.5.3 *Guides to the literature review 213*
16.5.4 *Digital object identifiers (DOIs) 213*
16.6 *Sources for research methodology 213*
16.6.1 *Statistical analysis software 214*
16.7 *Finding dissertations 214*
16.8 *Setting up a writing group 215*
16.9 *Academic writing links 215*
16.10 *Example of a research proposal with analysis 216*
16.11 *Examples of dissertation abstracts 226*
16.11.1 *Study using ethnography, text analysis, observations, interviews 226*
16.11.2 *Study using existing quantitative questionnaires and interviews utilising descriptive and inferential statistics 227*
16.11.3 *Study using a case study design 227*
16.11.4 *Study based on classroom discourse and observations 228*

16.11.5 Action research study using an intervention 228
16.11.6 Study using existing textual data 229
16.11.7 Study trialling a pedagogical technique – story telling 229
16.11.8 In-depth qualitative study using a small sample 230
16.11.9 Study using a pre- and post-test design 231
16.12 Further weblinks 231
16.12.1 How to get published 231
16.12.2 The linguist list 232
16.12.3 Time management apps 232
16.12.4 Blogs 232
16.13 Dissertation checklist 232

Glossary 235
Index 240

FIGURES

2.1 Some examples of master's dissertation titles 17
3.1 The purposes of reviewing the literature 22
3.2 Types of literature 24
3.3 Some databases in TESOL and applied linguistics 26
3.4 Example of reference in APA 6th edition using DOI 29
4.1 The major characteristics of a quantitative approach to research 34
4.2 The major characteristics of a qualitative approach to research 35
4.3 Action research cycle 38
4.4 Types of questionnaire questions 40
5.1 Example of a summary of a project from a master's dissertation proposal 53
5.2 Example of background sections of a research proposal 55
5.3 Generic criteria for assessing a dissertation proposal 60
6.1 Examples from dissertation handbooks 64
6.2 Important stages of dissertation for discussion 67
6.3 Preparing for supervision meetings 68
7.1 Participant recruitment template 77
7.2 Example of a can-do scale with directions 80
7.3 Example of a five-point Likert scale with directions 81
8.1 What to include in a research diary 90
8.2 Strategies for organising data 92
8.3 Example of a five-point Likert scale used to measure in-class and out-of-class anxiety 93
8.4 Stages in quantitative analysis 97
8.5 Stages in analysis in a qualitative study 99

9.1	Dissertation organisation, example 1	109
9.2	Dissertation organisation, example 2	110
9.3	Dissertation organisation, example 3	110
9.4	General requirements of a dissertation	111
9.5	Process of writing	117
10.1	Organisation of the literature chapter using headings, example 1	121
10.2	Organisation of the literature chapter using headings, example 2	121
10.3	The structure of literature chapter introductions, example 1	122
10.4	The structure of literature chapter introductions, example 2	122
10.5	The structure of literature chapter introductions, example 3	123
10.6	Example of critical writing: combining views in literature review	124
10.7	Establishing a gap in knowledge, example 1	125
10.8	Establishing a gap in knowledge, example 2	125
10.9	Establishing a gap in knowledge, example 3	126
10.10	Synthesising studies	127
10.11	Author and research prominent citations	127
11.1	Organisation of the methodology chapter, example 1	133
11.2	Organisation of the methodology chapter, example 2	134
11.3	Organisation of the methodology chapter, example 3	135
11.4	Referring to methodological approach in a dissertation	135
11.5	Describing and selecting participants, example 1	136
11.6	Describing and selecting participants, example 2	136
11.7	Writing about analysis	137
11.8	Writing about reliability in a quantitative study	138
11.9	Writing about reliability and validity in a qualitative study	139
11.10	Example of referring to ethics approval	140
11.11	Tense in the methodology chapter	141
12.1	Criteria for selecting results	145
12.2	Examples of organisation of the results by research question	146
12.3	Organisation of results chapter by cases	147
12.4	Example of introduction to results by describing what will follow	147
12.5	Example of introduction to results chapter using summary of findings	148
12.6	Example of table and text reference in a quantitative study using correlations	150
12.7	List of tables and figures	150
12.8	Reporting interview results, example 1	151
12.9	Reporting interview results, example 2	151
12.10	Some examples of descriptors at a distinction level used in the assessment of discussion sections	153

12.11	Referring to previous research in the discussion chapter	153
12.12	The purposes of the discussion chapter	154
12.13	Introduction to the discussion chapter	155
12.14	Conclusion to the discussion chapter	156
12.15	Suggested structure of the discussion chapter	157
12.16	Example of the limitations section	157
12.17	Language used in making claims	159
13.1	Structure of a master's dissertation introduction	166
13.2	Examples of purpose statements	167
13.3	Examples of assessment criteria for a reference list	172
14.1	Sample title page	180
14.2	Typical structure of dissertation abstracts	181
14.3	Example of an acknowledgements section	184
14.4	Template for acknowledgements	184
14.5	Typical sections and ordering of a dissertation in the table of contents	185
14.6	Example of a declaration page	187
14.7	Example of a list of abbreviations	187
14.8	Examples of material that may be included in the appendix	188
14.9	Example of appendices	189
15.1	Example of a dissertation feedback form	196
15.2	Example of a dissertation examiner's report	197
15.3	Some typical questions asked during oral examinations	199
15.4	Example of a referee form	203

TABLES

1.1	The major differences between a master's course-work assignment and a dissertation	2
1.2	Time management diary template	4
2.1	Focusing the topic, example 1	15
2.2	Focusing the topic, example 2	16
3.1	Example of a broad literature review	23
3.2	Template for the initial literature review	24
3.3	Criteria for selecting literature sources	27
3.4	Some examples of citation management software	27
3.5	Template for reviewing the literature	27
3.6	Reading strategies	28
4.1	Comparison of steps in experimental and quasi-experimental research to examine vocabulary learning	36
4.2	Example of a qualitative research design to examine vocabulary learning	37
4.3	Some common types of analyses for quantitative data	44
4.4	Sampling in quantitative and qualitative research	45
4.5	Reliability and validity	47
5.1	Comparison of areas required in a research proposal from three universities	52
5.2	The Who? What? Where? and How? of introductory sections in a dissertation proposal	54
5.3	Some examples of types of research questions	56
5.4	Examples of poor research questions	56
5.5	Types of question words	57
5.6	Summarising research questions, methods and analysis	58
5.7	Sample timetable for research	58

5.8	Checklist for the research proposal	60
6.1	Some typical supervisor and student roles	66
6.2	Example of a summary of a supervision session in the research design stage of the dissertation	69
7.1	Examples of sources of participants in master's research projects	75
7.2	Guidelines for producing a participant information sheet	77
7.3	Examples of text-based research projects	79
7.4	Methods of administering questionnaires	82
7.5	Advice for interviewing	83
7.6	Example of general interview question and prompts	84
8.1	Example of a research diary from the analysis phase of research	91
8.2	Example of a codebook for an anxiety study based on the questionnaire in Figure 8.3	94
8.3	Descriptive statistics in a quantitative study	95
8.4	Example of descriptive statistics reporting number and percentage	96
8.5	Example of descriptive statistics using range	96
8.6	Example of mean (M) and standard deviation (SD)	96
8.7	Typical statistical analyses in master's research studies	97
8.8	Non-parametric equivalents to parametric tests	98
8.9	Acceptability of getting help with collecting and analysing data	101
9.1	Avoiding procrastination in writing	108
9.2	Example of a writing diary	108
9.3	Academic style: vocabulary	113
9.4	Academic grammar	113
9.5	Common types of punctuation	114
10.1	Characteristics of the dissertation literature review chapter	120
10.2	Verbs for referring to the literature	127
11.1	Characteristics of a dissertation methodology chapter	131
12.1	Example of a table showing descriptive statistics in a quantitative study	149
12.2	Template for relating results to literature	154
13.1	Example of a master's dissertation introduction	164
13.2	Example of a master's dissertation conclusion chapter	168
13.3	Example of a master's dissertation concluding paragraph	170
13.4	Example of an excerpt from a reference list in APA 6th edition	171
14.1	Dissertation abstract, example 1	181
14.2	Dissertation abstract, example 2	182
14.3	General editing checklist for organisation of the dissertation	190

14.4 General editing checklist for language in the dissertation 190
15.1 Broad assessment criteria for a master's dissertation 194
15.2 Breakdown of assessment criteria by dissertation section 195
15.3 Stages for viva oral examination 198
15.4 Some examples of positive and negative self-talk 200
15.5 Template for a short oral presentation about the dissertation 201
15.6 Publishing a journal article 204
15.7 Differences between a dissertation and journal article 205
16.1 Questions to ask when setting up a writing group 216
16.2 Sample proposal with comments 217
16.3 Checklist for editing the dissertation 232

ACKNOWLEDGEMENTS

The motivation for this book arose from many years teaching dissertation writing skills and my experience supervising with master's dissertation students in Australia and the UK. I hope that this book helps students demystify process of doing a master's dissertation. The book relies heavily on excerpts from master's dissertations taken from UK, Australian and US dissertations. I would like to thank these dissertation writers who have provided me with their dissertations and those publicly available.

I would like to thank the following writers for the use of extracts. Full bibliographic details are provided at the end of this section.

Chapter 5: Y. Guo (2018) for the summary of the project taken from a research proposal.

Chapter 7: J Anderson (2016) for interview questions and prompts.

Chapter 11: M. Spencer (2018) for subheadings in the methodology chapter and referring to the methodological approach. N. Mai (2018) for describing participants and selection. J. Anderson (2016) for writing about analysis. A. Steinhoff (2018) for writing about reliability and writing about ethics. Q. Lin (2018) for writing about validity and reliability.

Chapter 12: R. Forde (2018) for the introduction to results. R. Dry (2017) for interview results and the introduction to the discussion chapter. N. Mai (2018) for the conclusion to discussion chapter.

Chapter 13: J. Anderson (2016) for the dissertation introduction. M. Spencer (2018) for the dissertation conclusion.

Chapter 14: H. Zhou (2017) for the abstract and acknowledgements section. L. Da Silva (2016) for the dissertation abstract.

Chapter 16: M. Spencer (2018) for his master's research proposal. A. Turner (2012) for the dissertation abstract. A. Alzalam (2018) for the dissertation abstract. S. Jones (2011) for the dissertation abstract. S. Hazari (2014) for the dissertation abstract. Y. Chen (2018) for the dissertation abstract. W. Matsuoka (2009) for the dissertation abstract. R. Forde (2018) for the dissertation abstract. A. Steinhoff (2018) for the dissertation abstract.

My thanks also go to the following dissertation writers whose work I have consulted and quoted:

Alghamdy, S. (2016). *Motivational strategies in an EFL classroom: Students' Perceptions vs. Teachers' Practices*. (Master's Dissertation), Newcastle University.

Alzalam, A. (2018). *Culturally relevant materials: An inquiry into the role of faith*. (Master's Dissertation), University of Hull. Retrieved from https://englishagenda.britishcouncil.org/sites/default/files/attachments/alaa_dean_alzalam_university_of_hull_dissertation.pdf (Accessed 28 May, 2019)

Anderson, J. (2016). *A qualitative study into the role of initial teacher training courses in the professional development of experienced non-native speaker teachers of English*. (Master's Dissertation), Kings College, London. Retrieved from https://englishagenda.britishcouncil.org/sites/default/files/attachments/mda2017_winner_jason_anderson_king_s_college_london.pdf (Accessed 24 May, 2019)

Asada, A. (2013). *An investigation of the impact of bilingualism on the identity of a sample of bilingual English teachers*. (Master's Dissertation), Canterbury Christ Church University. Retrieved from www.asian-efl-journal.com/8681/thesis/an-investigation-of-the-impact-of-bilingualism-on-the-identity-of-a-sample-of-bilingual-english-teachers/ (Accessed 21 March, 2019).

Awder, R. A. (UD). *Investigating spelling errors of Kurd EFL learners in the eighth year of basic school*. (Master's Dissertation), Newcastle University.

Barrass, J. (2017). *The intelligibility of Korean English pronunciation from a Lingua Franca perspective*. (Master's Dissertation), University of Oxford. Retrieved from https://englishagenda.britishcouncil.org/sites/default/files/attachments/justin_barrass_university_of_oxford_dissertation.pdf (Accessed 24 May, 2019)

Campbell, E. (2016). *Up, up and away! Taking off with SFG: An investigation into the impact of selected Systemic Functional Grammar (SFG) concepts on students' writing of a film review*. (Master's Dissertation), Aston University. Retrieved from https://englishagenda.britishcouncil.org/sites/default/files/attachments/dissertation_design_for_publication_2016_aston_university.pdf (Accessed 24 May, 2019)

Cardiff, P. (2015). *Perspectives of EAP: Students' perspectives of pre-sessional English courses at Newcastle University English Language Centre*. (Master's Dissertation), Newcastle University.

Chen, S. (2011). *Genre features of personal statements by Chinese English-as-an-additional language writers: A corpus driven study*. (Master's Dissertation), University of Victoria.

Chen, Y. (2017). *The impact of storytelling on young learners' motivation in English classes in primary school in China*. (Master's Dissertation), Newcastle University.

Cooper, C. (2016). *Scaffolding during the initial reading of picture books in Japanese elementary school EFL classrooms: A qualitative study investigating how teachers and learners co-construct meaning during whole class picture book reading*. (Master's Dissertation), Sheffield Hallam University.

Crofton, B. (2011). *The usefulness of decision-forcing case studies in helping to prepare new and experienced English language teachers*. (Master's Dissertation), Concordia University, Portland.

Crofton-Martin, I. (2015). *Perceptions of pronunciation in the EFL classroom*. (Master's Dissertation), Canterbury Christchurch University. Retrieved from https://englishagenda.britishcouncil.org/sites/default/files/attachments/cantenbury_christ_church_university_isabel_crofton-martin_dissertation.pdf (Accessed 24 May, 2019)

Da Silva, L. (2016). *Academic vocabulary: A corpus linguistic study on how Brazilian students write academic English*. (Master's Dissertation), University of Warwick. Retrieved from https://englishagenda.britishcouncil.org/sites/default/files/attachments/mda2017_special_commendation_larissa_goulart_da_silva_university_of_warwick.pdf (Accessed 24 May, 2019)

Dickson, B. (2015). *Newspaper discourses on Andy Murray's performance at Wimbledon: A contrastive corpus driven investigation of successful and unsuccessful tennis match reports*. (Master's Dissertation), University of Stirling. Retrieved from https://englishagenda.britishcouncil.org/sites/default/files/attachments/dissertation_for_publication_stirling_university.pdf (Accessed 24 May, 2019)

Dore, C. (2016). *Perceptions of fluency*. (Master's Dissertation), University of Reading. Retrieved from https://englishagenda.britishcouncil.org/sites/default/files/attachments/dissertation_design_for_publication_2016_reading_university_cecilia_dore.pdf(Accessed24May, 2019)

Dry, R. (2017). *EAL in the mainstream: A Northumberland case study*. (Master's Dissertation), Newcastle University.

Ellman, M. (2017). *"You're more likely to pick up on stuff": Evaluating the impact of video evidence on English language teachers' post-observation reflections*. (Master's Dissertation), University of Birmingham. Retrieved from https://englishagenda.britishcouncil.org/research-publications/elt-masters-dissertations/2017-2018-winners (Accessed 24 May, 2019)

Fitriani, R. (2018). *EFL students' perceptions on translanguaging in the general English classroom at an Indonesian university*. (Master's Dissertation), University of Sydney.

Forde, R. (2018). *How can I teach this? Examining collaborative dialogic reflection and its impact on teacher learning*. (Master's Dissertation), Newcastle University.

Guo, Y. (2018). *A research proposal on teacher beliefs and the usage of online teaching websites in Chinese as a foreign language classrooms*. (Master's Dissertation), University of Sydney.

Hanisch, R. (2015). *The effect of the implementation of an Extensive Reading Programme (ERP) in English language teaching (ELT) on the reading abilities and reading habits of 12–13 year old students in an Austrian Secondary Modern School*. (Master's Dissertation), Norwich Institute for Language Education. Retrieved from https://englishagenda.britishcouncil.org/sites/default/files/attachments/dissertation_for_publication_nile.pdf (Accessed 30 April, 2019)

Hicking, R. (2015). *Subtitles in authentic video listening: An exploration of the benefits of captions in relation to sensory preference types*. (Master's Dissertation), University College, London. Retrieved from https://englishagenda.britishcouncil.org/sites/default/files/attachments/dissertation_for_publication_ucl.pdf (Accessed 24 May, 2019)

Iyer, P. (2013). *The effect of collaborative blogging on communicative skills in the writing of Thai EFL students*. (Master's Dissertation), University of Birmingham. Retrieved from http://asian-efl-journal.com/wp-content/uploads/2014/thesis/Purnima_Iyer_M_%20Dissertation.pdf (Accessed 24 May, 2019)

Jiang, J. (2015). *A survey of English teachers' ability to write reading comprehension questions in secondary schools in Beijing*. (Master's Dissertation), University of Warwick. Retrieved from https://englishagenda.britishcouncil.org/sites/default/files/attachments/dissertation_for_publication_warwick_university.pdf (Accessed 24 May, 2019)

Jones, S. (2011). *Investigating the F-move in teacher talk: A South Korean study on teachers' beliefs and classroom practices*. (Master's Dissertation), University of Birmingham.

Kelly, R. (2015). *An exploration of Instagram to develop ESL learners' writing proficiency*. (Master's Dissertation), Ulster University. Retrieved from https://englishagenda.britishcouncil.org/sites/default/files/attachments/dissertation_for_publication_ulster_university.pdf (Accessed 24 May, 2019)

Le, Q. K. (2017). *English final consonant clusters in the interlanguage of Northern Vietnamese young adult learners*. (Master's Dissertation), Newcastle University.

Lestari, S. B. (2014). *Paraphrasing in high-scoring and low-scoring L2 integrated writing test task responses*. (Master's Dissertation), University of Warwick. Retrieved from https://englishagenda.britishcouncil.org/sites/default/files/filefield_paths/paraphrasing_in_high_scoring_and_low_scoring_l2_integrated_writing_v2.pdf (Accessed 24 May, 2019)

Lin, Q. (2018). *Assessing teacher verbal feedback using the SETT framework: A case study on three English classes in a high school in China*. (Master's Dissertation), Newcastle University.

Liu, X. (2018). *The effects of indirect written corrective feedback on English learners at different proficiency levels: A qualitative research*. (Unpublished MEd research proposal), University of Sydney.

Mai, N. (2018). *Investigating the effects of code-mixed reading texts on vocabulary learning of Vietnamese adult learners*. (Master's Dissertation), Newcastle University.

Marsh, D. (2011). *Using critical discourse analysis to raise critical language awareness in Japanese medical students: An exploratory action research project*. (Master's Dissertation), University of Birmingham. Retrieved from http://asian-efl-journal.com/wp-content/uploads/mgm/downloads/64517300.pdf (Accessed 30 April, 2019)

Matsuoka, W. E. (2009). *Vocabulary learning opportunities in a commercial ELT coursebook*. (Master's Dissertation), University of Sydney.

Nazari, A. (2015). *English language lecturers' views on dynamic assessment and its potential in higher education: Challenging the current status quo*. (Master's Dissertation), London Metropolitan University. Retrieved from https://englishagenda.britishcouncil.org/sites/default/files/attachments/dissertation_design_for_publication_2016_londonmetropolianuniversity.pdf (Accessed 24 May, 2019)

Newnham, S.-A. (2013). *Text complexity in graded readers: A systemic functional look*. (Master's Dissertation), Marshal University. Retrieved from https://mds.marshall.edu/etd/498/ (Accessed 30 April, 2019)

O'Donovan, E. (2016). *Exploring culturally sensitive alternatives for the First Certificate in English*. (Master's Dissertation), University of Liverpool. Retrieved from https://englishagenda.britishcouncil.org/sites/default/files/attachments/dissertation_for_publication_2016_liverpool_university.pdf (Accessed 24 May, 2019)

Ohlrogge, A. C. (2009). *Academic vocabulary at the word and formula level: An examination of test-taker discourse*. (Master's Dissertation), Michigan State University.

Philip, C. (2017). *Positive and negative written corrective feedback: A mixed-method investigation of EAP teachers' word choices*. (Master's Dissertation), University of Stirling. Retrieved from https://englishagenda.britishcouncil.org/sites/default/files/attachments/claire_philip_university_of_stirling_dissertation.pdf (Accessed 1 March, 2019)

Ring, N. M. (2016). *My friend TED: Implementing effective listening strategies into academic listening using TED talks*. (Master's Dissertation), Sheffield Hallam University. Retrieved from https://englishagenda.britishcouncil.org/sites/default/files/attachments/dissertation_for_publication_sheffield_hallam_university.pdf (Accessed 24 May, 2019)

Spencer, M. (2018). *Synchronous online learning via Zoom Videoconferencing: A multimodal conversation analytic study of teacher-student interaction*. (Master's Dissertation), Newcastle University.

Steinhoff, A. (2018). *The influence of pre-writing strategies on the quality of essay structure and topic sentences in ESL academic writing*. (Master's Dissertation), University of Sydney.

Su, L. (2107). *Identifying dyslexia in children learning English as an additional language: Primary school teachers' perceptions of the main challenges: A Somerset study*. (Master's Dissertation), Bath Spa University. Retrieved from https://englishagenda.britishcouncil.org/sites/

default/files/attachments/laura_su_bath_spa_university_dissertation.pdf (Accessed 24 May, 2019)

Tu, W. (2010). *How universities in China introduce themselves in Chinese and English on the internet: A contrastive genre study*. (Master's Dissertation), University of Sydney.

Wilson, O. (2013). *Teachers' motivational strategies and students' motivated behaviour in the tertiary Australian ESL context*. (Master's Dissertation), University of Sydney.

Xie, Y. (2017). *Who do you hang out with? A mixed-methods study on how Chinese students' social networks relate to their oral proficiency gains during study abroad*. (Master's Dissertation), University of Cambridge. Retrieved from https://englishagenda.britishcouncil.org/sites/default/files/attachments/yushan_xie_university_of_cambridge_dissertation.pdf (Accessed 24 May, 2019)

Xu, J. (2013). *An investigation of differences in the levels and types of writing anxiety experienced by Chinese postgraduates in the UK and China*. (Master's Dissertation), Newcastle University.

Zhou, H. (2017). *An analysis of the misuse of English articles by Chinese University-level EFL students and its relationship to pedagogy*. (Master's Dissertation), Newcastle University.

Zhu, J. (2017). *The technical vocabulary of newspapers*. (Master's Dissertation), Western University. Retrieved from https://ir.lib.uwo.ca/etd/4872/ (Accessed 30 April, 2019)

1

INTRODUCTION

This chapter defines a dissertation and outlines the purposes of a dissertation from both the university and the student viewpoint. It covers reasons for the dissertation that students may not have considered, such as providing a pathway for future study and publication.

The chapter makes suggestions for using the book and an outline of the sections of this book.

1.1 What is a dissertation?

According to the Oxford Advanced Learner's dictionary a dissertation is "a long piece of writing on a particular subject especially one for a degree or diploma" (https://www.oxfordlearnersdictionaries.com/). In British and Australian English, a dissertation refers to the document produced for a master's degree, while a thesis refers to the document produced for doctoral degrees. In the US these terms are reversed, with a thesis referring to master's study and a dissertation referring to the result of doctoral programme.

At most universities a dissertation is required to qualify for a master's degree. The dissertation is a text of around 15,000 words and is usually based on a piece of original research. Although alternative tasks may be acceptable, such as a literature review or a body of work, the educational principal underlying these is the same. The dissertation is sometimes referred to as a 'capstone' activity because it should push the student's academic thinking to a higher level than is required for usual assignment work, thus allowing the student to reach his/her maximum potential. The time allowed for a dissertation is typically around six months to a year, including related research methodology course-work, and the dissertation is typically worth around one third of the total degree. At some universities the dissertation is the basis for 100% of the degree assessment.

Dissertation alternatives might include a literature review based on published works that reflect current thinking and research in a given area; a body of work, such as a needs analysis for a English course for a given group of learners; or a developed course and materials for a given group of learners. Students may choose the type of capstone activity they would like to do, and this decision would be informed by their personal and academic goals, such as using the work for professional purposes or progressing to a higher research degree. This book focuses on the research-based dissertation as this is the most common type of task for master's students in TESOL and applied linguistics.

A dissertation is very different from the other types of assessment tasks for a master's degree in TESOL or applied linguistics, and this is the main reason that students find the dissertation challenging. The main difference between an assignment and a dissertation is the level of freedom. In the dissertation component of the degree the student has a great deal of freedom concerning the content of the dissertation. Lecturer input is minimal because the student is expected to be independent; however, it must adhere to the recognised skills and norms expected in research. Table 1.1 presents a generalised view of the major differences between course-work assignments and dissertations. It should be remembered that course-work assignments can be extremely varied, this is especially true on master's degrees that have a strong professional focus.

TABLE 1.1 The major differences between a master's course-work assignment and a dissertation

Aspect	*Assignment*	*Dissertation*
Purpose	Demonstrate mastered course content.	Demonstrate independent study.
	Demonstrate that student has completed required reading.	Demonstrate ability to review literature in particular field.
	Reproduce knowledge about a given subject.	Make a contribution to knowledge in a subject.
	May be very similar to other students' assignments.	Needs to be original.
Type of task	Range of tasks, for example, essay, oral presentation, group project.	Written dissertation of around 15,000 words.
Task content	May have similar content for all students.	Different content for each student.
	Linked to professional practice.	May not be linked to professional practice.
	All students may complete same task.	Each student's dissertation will be different.
Lecturer input	Lectures, seminars. Large and small groups.	One-to- one, or one to small group.

(Continued)

TABLE 1.1 (Continued)

Aspect	*Assignment*	*Dissertation*
	General input supported by further reading.	Focused topic, procedural and skills advice.
	Exact task and content provided by lecturer.	No direct input from lecturer.
	Relevant reading lists and references.	Guidance on skills to find reading sources.
	Great deal of lecturer input.	Little lecturer input.
Assessment	Assessed by lecturer or tutor of course.	Assessed by more than one examiner, may use examiner from outside department.
	Happens during semester/term time.	Happens after end of semester/term time.
	Can be formative, linked to learning.	Always summative, although the proposal may be formative.
	Assessment criteria specific to task.	Assessment criteria specific to research projects /dissertation.

1.2 The purpose of the dissertation

The purpose of the dissertation may be viewed from two perspectives: that of the university and that of the student. From the university's perspective the master's dissertation is an essential part of the assessment of a master's degree; it is what distinguishes the master's degree from other qualifications. The dissertation is designed to meet higher learning objectives attributable to postgraduates. From the university's point of view the dissertation can be viewed as evidence of a student's capability to do research, it can therefore be viewed as a basic qualification to do research. The dissertation is a learning task designed to extend a student's knowledge and skills acquired through the taught element of the master's course.

From the student's perspective the dissertation is typically worth around one third of the total marks of a master's degree, so it is necessary not to fail the dissertation in order to pass the degree. The dissertation may be important to a student for career purposes. If a student wishes to pursue further studies, such as a higher research degree like a PhD or Master's by Research, then the grade on the dissertation is extremely important as it demonstrates the student's research capability. It is also worth mentioning that funding for research is largely informed by course grades, in particular, the research component of the degree.

The dissertation can be important to students who wish to implement change in the teaching and learning of languages in their own setting. Action research plays a vital role in developing knowledge and the application of research into language learning. From a more psychological viewpoint doing a dissertation can be a very challenging but satisfying. Most students experience a great sense of achievement upon completion of this research component of the master's degree.

TASK 1.1

What do you think are the purposes of a dissertation?
What does the dissertation mean to you personally?
What attributes do you think master's graduates should possess?

1.3 Managing the dissertation process

For most master's students, the dissertation process is a new type of learning activity. Most students have experience of the process of completing academic assignments. While there are many different types of academic assignments, students are very familiar with written essay type assignments. Most students have written such academic texts since their schooldays. Typically, a course-work assignment involves answering a question or discussing a topic presented by the lecturer, completing reading based on a set reading list, taking notes and constructing a written account including a critical perspective. With the dissertation the student needs to choose the literature and construct an argument based on topic of his/her own choice. The student needs to select and use research methods to collect data.

Many students underestimate the demands of the dissertation component of the master's degree. It is important to remember that the dissertation is usually the equivalent of three master's modules or units and is typically worth 60 credits. This amounts to 600 hours of study time, with most of this time being independent study (www.postgrad.com/uk_student_schedule/).

Time management is often an issue with the dissertation. Students may decide to put off work on the dissertation until after they have completed all their course-work assignments. Some decide to take a holiday at the end of the taught component. This can be disastrous for the dissertation as there is insufficient time left to complete the study and make a good job of writing the dissertation. The best way to deal with time management is to plan academic tasks on a calendar. Table 1.2

TABLE 1.2 Time management diary template

Month	*Supervision*	*Activities*	*Deadlines*	*Feeling*	✓
January					
February					
March					
April					
May					
June					
July					
August					
September					
October					
November					
December					

presents an example of a template that can help with time management for the dissertation. The table can be used to plan stages of the dissertation and list deadlines. There is also a column for recording how the student is feeling, which can be informative. In the supervision column, as well as dates and tasks, it is a good idea to list outcomes and agreed tasks after each meeting. This is discussed more fully in Chapter 6 on Supervision.

For those that prefer to work electronically there are several apps available for phones that can help with time management by having to do lists, diaries and reminders. Some examples of these are given at the end of this chapter.

Managing the dissertation from a psychological point of view is important too. Nearly every student will experience a certain level of stress, as there is usually too much work for the time available. Some students experience a lack of confidence believing independent study and a dissertation is beyond their capabilities. This is referred to as 'imposter syndrome', where the students fear they may be discovered as being inadequate to the job in hand. This can lead to anxiety, which interferes with cognitive processes. Another issue is perfectionism. In this case the student wants the dissertation to be perfect and believes it can never be good enough; this can lead to procrastination.

One activity that can be very helpful with research and writing the dissertation is keeping a research diary. This is a private diary that records thoughts and activities related to the research process. This is discussed in more detail in Chapter 8. Cabraal (2013) has an excellent blog on the reasons to keep a research diary and how to go about it.

Completing a dissertation can be a rewarding experience with students experiencing a great sense of achievement at the end of the process. This satisfaction is increased because of the independent element, which promotes ownership of the study and text. However, there are bound to be low points during the dissertation process; it is worth remembering these will be matched by high points, therefore it is useful to record mood and psychological states during the dissertation process. The dissertation should be set as a goal that is systematically completed and duly celebrated upon completion.

This book offers advice on designing and executing a master's research project and provides guidelines on how to write a dissertation. The book uses examples taken from recent TESOL and applied linguistics master's dissertations in the UK, Australia and USA. The advice in this book is not intended to be prescriptive, as it is important to remember that requirements and expectations for academic work vary between universities and academic departments, so it is essential that the dissertation is informed by institutional norms. To achieve this the student must read the dissertation guidelines thoroughly, understand the assessment criteria used and examine past dissertations. Gaining a deep understanding of the requirements of the dissertation and asking questions about the norms and expectations of the dissertation is frequently referred to in this book. This approach is based on an academic literacies view (Lea and Street, 1998) common in current English for Academic Purposes (EAP) research. This theoretical perspective is based on the notion that excellence in academic writing is based on context and that literacy is plural rather than unitary. So, for example, an essay written for a chemistry assignment and one written for a TESOL assignment are very different.

TASK 1.2

Find the guidelines for the dissertation from your department.
What are the objectives of the dissertation?
How is the dissertation assessed?
Looking at some examples of good dissertations, what do you think makes a good dissertation?

1.4 How to use this book

This book follows the process of producing a dissertation from generating an idea, to writing the dissertation and options after examination. Part I addresses the design of the research; Part II is concerned with the process of collecting and analysing data; Part III focuses on the writing of the dissertation and Part IV discusses the examination of the dissertation. For this reason the chapters are able to stand alone. Some issues, such as assessment criteria, editing checklists and useful websites, are referred to in several chapters so it is not necessary to start at the beginning and read to the end. This book includes a great number of tables and figures designed to help with the thinking and execution of research and writing, such as the time management template in this chapter.

Each chapter includes tasks to highlight points and advice given. These can be completed with a partner or individually. Working with others is always a valuable experience, and it is a good idea to set up a peer group to discuss aspects of the dissertation research and writing. This can be done quite informally by collaborating with a few friends enrolled in the same master's programme or more formally as is presented in Chapter 16 about setting up a writing group. The advantages of participating in a writing group usually far outweigh the drawbacks in terms of time.

Part I focuses on the design of a master's research project and has five chapters. Chapter 2 looks at the process of developing and refining a worthwhile research topic. Chapter 3 is about reviewing the literature, an essential step in developing a research topic worth researching. This chapter focuses on how resources are selected and the process of reading and recording information. Chapter 4 covers the choice of methodological approach and research methods used in the study. The chapter looks at quantitative and qualitative approaches to research and describes the most common methods used to collect data in TESOL and applied linguistics research. Chapter 5 focuses on developing and writing a research proposal. This is an essential step in the research project process and is often an assessed component. An example of an annotated research proposal is presented in Chapter 16. Chapter 6 addresses the very important issue of supervision: how supervisors are allocated and what supervision entails. It provides advice on how to optimize this method of instruction.

Part II of the book focuses on the procedure of the research: the process of collecting and analysing data. Chapter 7 examines how to select participants and how to access and elicit different types of data. Chapter 8 concerns data analysis, both qualitative and quantitative. The chapter stresses the importance of keeping a research diary and outlines how this can be done.

Part III of the book addresses issues in writing the dissertation. Chapter 9 provides general writing guidelines for completing the dissertation. Chapter 10 focuses on how the literature chapter can be written by focusing on the purpose and typical organisation of the chapter. It also has a section on being critical in reading and writing. Chapter 11 employs the same approach to writing about the methodology used in the study. This chapter includes a section on the characteristics of high and low scoring chapters. Chapter 12 shows how the results and discussion chapters can be presented. Qualitative and quantitative studies are considered; the chapter also considers the inclusion of limitations of the study and implications for practice and further research. Chapter 13 looks at beginning and ending dissertations by focusing on the introduction, the conclusion and the reference list.

Part IV comprises two chapters. Chapter 14 presents the finishing touches to the dissertation and looks at how to construct a dissertation abstract, acknowledgements, table of contents and appendices. The chapter also has section on editing and proofreading. Chapter 15 examines issues of examinations and beyond the submission. The chapter includes marking criteria and the inclusion of a viva component to the examination. The chapter then discusses options beyond the dissertation, which include applying for higher research degrees and publishing from the dissertation.

Chapter 16 provides a list of resources that can be useful in writing a dissertation. These includes lists of academic journals, sources of literature, links to dissertations and other useful web pages.

The book uses authentic example of dissertations to provide examples. Many of these dissertations are accessible online. Every chapter in this book has a similar format. The chapter addresses the important information on the topic, this is accompanied by tasks. This book relies heavily on tables and figures that highlight the steps and organisation of tasks and texts that can be used in the student's own project. Each chapter includes guidance for further reading about the topic, a section on some of the most common mistakes and a list of frequently asked questions about doing a dissertation. The book concludes with a glossary of common terms used in this book.

References

Cabraal, A. (2013). *Keep a research journal: It's important*. Retrieved from https://anujacabraal.wordpress.com/2013/07/03/keep-a-research-journal-it-is-important/

Lea, M., & Street, B. (1998). Student writing in higher education: An academic literacies approach. *Higher Education, 23*(2): 157–172.

Time management applications

Any.do www.any.do/
Get it done https://getitdoneapp.com/
Trello https://trello.com/?truid=trbf098b-f460-2c5b-205a-931be112039c

PART I
Project design

2

CHOOSING A TOPIC

Choosing a research topic for a dissertation is often difficult for students, and the wrong choice can have serious implications for success. This chapter addresses how to find a topic, issues in topic selection and what makes a topic researchable. The chapter then discusses focusing the topic and investigates the structure of dissertation titles.

2.1 How to choose a topic

Many students find the selection of a topic quite daunting. This is quite understandable as the dissertation commands a lot of effort and thinking time – around 600 hours of study time for a 60 credit point dissertation. So, the topic needs to be interesting, have good advice available and be reasonably easy to research in the given time frame. The best approach is to invest a great deal of thought about a suitable topic at the very beginning of the dissertation process. While topics develop and may change during the process of research, major changes to the topic can have serious outcomes as the time spent on the original topic probably does not contribute to the recommended study hours for the dissertation. There are a number of methods that can be used to select a topic for a dissertation. Obviously, the more prior knowledge a student has of the subject, the easier the project will be. This is because it takes wide reading to gain a base level knowledge in a given area. Good topics build on prior knowledge and prior experience. The following section provides some ideas for finding a suitable researchable topic for a master's dissertation.

2.1.1 Topics emerging from modules and assignments

The dissertation is set to push students to an intellectual ceiling, so ideally it should be based on the work and tasks included in the taught component of the master's degree. It is useful to think about the modules or units of study that are most interesting. Perhaps the student particularly enjoyed one of the assignments and got a high grade or positive feedback. This would be a good area for a dissertation topic. Another idea is to go through the notes and materials for each module and make a list of areas that stimulate interest. One problem with using modules and assignments to inform the development of a dissertation topic is that the selection of the dissertation topic probably needs to be made before the module is taught completely. Often in master's degrees up to 50% of course assignments will be due at the end of the term, and by this stage the dissertation needs to be well underway.

2.1.2 Topics emerging from previous dissertations

Another useful method of identifying topics is to look at dissertations from previous cohorts of master's students. However, it is important to remember that each dissertation needs to have an element of originality, so the topic cannot be exactly the same as previous dissertations. One method of achieving this is to read the conclusions or implications section of a dissertation and look at the recommendations for further research, using this as a basis for the dissertation topic.

TASK 2.1

Identify key subject areas that occur in your modules.
Identify key areas of expertise of the academic staff on your master's course.
Identify common topics in previous dissertations.

2.1.3 Topics informed by personal interest

Some students are passionate in their choice of dissertation topic, so the choice of topic is an easy choice. For example, MA student Susan is an English teacher and felt she was discriminated against in terms of employment opportunities because she is a non-native English speaker. She believes that preference is given to native English speakers when recruiting teachers. So, she decided to investigate attitudes toward native and non-native English speaker teachers (NNESTs) at a number of language centres.

In this case Susan needs to be aware of personal bias. Research questions need to have more than one possible answer and the researcher needs to understand that the answer may not align with their expectations. So, Susan needs to be prepared for there to be no evidence of discrimination in the centres she investigates.

A topic needs to be researchable. To start with, Susan needs to have a suitable supervisor, so there would have to be a member of the staff who knows about NNESTs or has expertise in attitude research. She would also need to have access to several language centres.

2.1.4 Topics informed by professional need

Some students choose topics based on a professional need. For example, David from Thailand decided to design and conduct a needs analysis of the English language students at his university as a preamble to designing a more relevant university English for Academic Purposes (EAP) course. The dissertation is an excellent opportunity for practitioners to devote time and research to pedagogical aspects. In this approach it may be possible to implement an action research project trialling a new method and approaches and making an evaluation of these. Such projects are valuable in instigating change for the better in language teaching settings.

2.1.5 Topics based on supervisor expertise

Sometimes students look at the expertise of their lecturers and choose a topic they may have published on. Initially this seems like a good idea. The lecturer could provide excellent supervision because they are knowledgeable about the topic and familiar with the research methods associated with this topic. However, it must be remembered that the dissertation is an independent task. Students usually do not have more than 4–6 hours supervision time and supervisors often have many supervisees. If the topic does not fall within the master's degree curriculum then it is not a good idea to choose it. For example, I have published widely on language learning anxiety; however, this was not included in the MA applied linguistics course on which I taught. Thus, the students do not have any background in the area and it would not be a good choice of topic for any students on this degree course.

Some students want to have the most well-known academic in their department as their supervisor. There can be issues with this, as senior academics often have a varied and intensive work load; they also may travel a lot so they may not be able to spend as much time providing feedback to students as their more junior colleagues.

2.1.6 Topics based on career trajectory

Some students may have a very clear career trajectory. For example, Fiona wants to become head of the testing unit in her department. So, she chose an important area in testing which would stand her in good stead for developing the testing unit and subsequently being promoted. To this end, she might aim to publish a journal article based on her master's research, which would further enhance her career.

Some students have the goal of doing a higher research degree such as a PhD after the master's course and use the dissertation as a vehicle for gaining research experience. In this case it would be a good idea to choose a topic related to the intended PhD. One method is to use the master's as a pilot or preliminary study for the future PhD project. However, it needs to be remembered that the research in the master's dissertation cannot be included as part of the PhD as each degree needs to have its own unique data set.

TASK 2.2 Topic selection

Decide on three possible topics you could choose for your master's dissertation. List the broad topic and why you would want to conduct research into this topic.

Topic	*Motivation*
Topic 1	
Topic 2	
Topic 3	

Motivation: assignments/modules
personal interest/passion
professional interest/need
supervisor expertise
career trajectory

2.1.7 Reading

The basis of all good research projects is reading. The importance of a strong theoretical and research base for projects cannot be overemphasised. Looking at recent journal articles from reputable academic journals can highlight current interest and trends in research. Chapter 16 provides a list of journals in TESOL and applied linguistics. One way of finding suitable topics, like with dissertations, is to look at the final section of the journal article where it refers to recommendations for further research. Every article has such a section.

2.2 Researchable topics

Topics need to be researchable or doable. The time available for a master's dissertation is short, so research projects need to be small. This should be reflected in all aspects of the study: literature review, data collection and data analysis. In the literature review the sources need to be available in the university library or online. Relying on the interlibrary loan service can be time consuming and sometimes unavailable. In terms of reviewing the literature, the area needs to be reasonably accessible. A totally new and complex theoretical perspective would present too many challenges for a master's project. The data for a master's project needs to be easily gathered. Familiar sources easily accessible are best, for example, using participants from the student's university or language school. Students should also consider the nature of ethics approval when considering data collection methods. All research projects need ethics approval if using people in the study. Some universities make this easy by having departmental approval while others have complex and time-consuming central ethics approval procedures. In this case students may prefer to conduct a text-based study that does not need ethics approval, for example, discourse analysis of texts. The data analysis techniques need to be relatively simple too. So, a complex quantitative study using, for example, structural equation modelling would be too time consuming unless the student is already familiar with this statistical technique. Similarly, the software used to analyse data needs to be thought about. There are software programmes that greatly help with the analysis of data – for example, SPSS for quantitative data and NVivo for qualitative data – but these programmes need to be mastered and this may take too long.

Sometimes students decide to research a topic because it has not been done before. This alone is not sufficient, there may be a good reason why the area has not been researched. For example, the data may be too difficult to get or there is no answer to the question. A research topic needs to be worthy of investigation, if you know the answer to the research question there is no point researching the topic.

Some students worry about originality and the contribution to knowledge their dissertation will make. While both are necessary, they may be very modest. For example, this can be achieved simply by changing the setting or participants of a previous study. Of course if the student intends the master's dissertation to be treated as a preliminary study of a future PhD in the field, more consideration needs to be given to significance and originality.

2.3 Developing the topic

After choosing a broad topic area the topic needs to be focused until a specific title for the dissertation emerges. Deciding on the dissertation topic will be based on the limitations discussed previously, that is, access to the literature, to the research site and to the participants. Being specific is the easiest way to narrow the focus of the topic. Too broad a topic can lead to a lack of focus in reading the literature. Table 2.1 and Table 2.2 provide examples of how topics can be focused. Refinement is achieved by considering variables, participants, setting, the gap in knowledge and data. Included in this refinement are the strengths the researcher can bring to the study; for example, in Table 2.1 Peng is a native Chinese speaker, thus giving her an advantage in talking with her participants about sensitive issues.

TABLE 2.1 Focusing the topic, example 1 (Peng)

Topic	*Focus*
Anxiety	Broad
Language anxiety	Broad
Speaking anxiety of English language learners	Refine based on variable
Speaking anxiety of Chinese English language learners	Refine based on participants
Speaking anxiety of Chinese English language learners at Newcastle University Language Centre	Refine based on setting
Speaking anxiety of Chinese English language learners at Tyne University Language Centre during oral presentation classes	Refine based on context
Want to know why students are anxious; as a cause and effect this is too difficult, the focus should be on why the students think they are anxious	Refine aspect
Reading indicates not many studies using qualitative methods	Gap in knowledge
Use qualitative rather than quantitative methods	Refine according to methodology/data
Use Chinese to uncover deep perspective on speaking anxiety of this group	Strengths

TABLE 2.2 Focusing the topic, example 2 (Phil)

Topic	*Focus*
Vocabulary learning	Broad
University of Bangkok English Department	Refine based on setting
EAP course	Refine based on context
Generate specific wordlist	Refine based on outcome/aspect
Of local value – University in Thailand	Gap in knowledge
Create a corpus of all reading texts from EAP course, which will be the basis of a corpus analysis	Refine based on data
Access to materials at home university	Strengths

Peng is very interested in anxiety. In particular, she would like to investigate why some of her students seem to get very anxious when speaking in English. After refining her topic, she decided to conduct a qualitative study on why students think they get anxious when speaking in English.

Phil is interested in helping his EAP students with vocabulary in his home university in Thailand. After his reading he decided to develop a specific wordlist that students could use to help with academic writing.

TASK 2.3 Focusing the dissertation topic

Using the template in either Table 2.1 or Table 2.2 and the topics you identified in Task 2.2, narrow the focus of your chosen topics.

2.4 Changing topics

It is important to make the final decision about the dissertation topic as soon as possible. Changing topics in the dissertation process is not a good idea. The time allocation for completion of a research-based dissertation in most master's degrees is very short, so if a student decides to change his/her topic then this time can be greatly reduced, and the time invested in the original topic is lost.

2.5 Dissertation title

The title of a master's dissertation may change throughout the research process. However, an initial title should be drafted very early on in the research process because it provides focus for the study and is required for the proposal. The title is usually the basis for the allocation of dissertation supervisors. Titles usually can be refined based on feedback from the research proposal or refined before submitting the final dissertation.

Titles typically contain information about the key concepts of the study. A good title should capture the essence of the study. Titles are best thought about in terms of descriptors that can be searched. Some titles include a snazzy first clause intended to grab the reader's attention. This is usually followed by further detail after a hyphen. Titles can include information about the purpose of the study, variables, theory, methodology, participants and the context of the study.

Figure 2.1 lists the titles of highly ranked master's dissertations from the British Council master's dissertation competition in 2016.

1. Perceptions of fluency. (Dore, 2016)
2. Exploring culturally sensitive alternatives for the first certificate in English. (O'Donovan, 2016)
3. My friend TED: Implementing effective listening strategies into academic listening using TED talks. (Ring, 2016)
4. English language lecturers' views on dynamic assessment and its potential in higher education: Challenging the current status quo. (Nazari, 2015)
5. Up, up and away! Taking off with SFG: An investigation into the impact of selected Systemic Functional Grammar (SFG) concepts on students' writing of a film review. (Campbell, 2016)
6. The effects of the implementation of an extensive reading programme in ELT on the reading abilities and reading habits of 12– 13 year old students. in an Austrian secondary modern school. (Hanisch, 2015)
7. An exploration of Instagram to develop ESL learners writing proficiency. (Kelly, 2015)
8. Subtitles in authentic video listening: An exploration of the benefits of captions in relation to sensory preference types. (Hicking, 2015)
9. Newspaper discourses on Andy Murray's performance at Wimbledon: A contrastive corpus-driven investigation of successful and unsuccessful tennis match reports. (Dickson, 2015)
10. A survey of English teachers' ability to write reading comprehension questions in classroom teaching in secondary schools in Beijing. (Jiang, 2015)

FIGURE 2.1 Some examples of master's dissertation titles

TASK 2.4 Title construction

Looking at Figure 2.1, do you have a clear idea about the topic from the title?
Make comments about the titles in terms of the following aspects:

- Level of detail
- Use of hyphen
- Methodology
- Type of study, eg exploratory study
- Theory
- Variables
- Creativity

Based on your discussion, draft some possible titles for your study.

Summary

This chapter has discussed the selection of a suitable topic for a master's dissertation. The chapter proposed starting points for topic selection such as interest, previous assignments, supervisor expertise and career objectives. The chapter examined how to refine a topic based on particular foci, such as variables and context. The chapter concluded with a section on developing a dissertation title.

Common mistakes in choosing a topic

- Choosing a topic that is too broad
- Choosing a topic that is too complex
- Changing topic during dissertation course
- Choosing an unfamiliar topic, for example, one not referred to during taught component
- Choosing a topic that requires a lengthy ethics approval process
- Choosing a topic with inaccessible data or participants

FAQs

1. *How do I choose a topic?*
   The most common ways to help choose a topic are assignments, reading, personal interest, professional need and supervisor expertise.
2. *Should I choose a topic that relates to a well-known name in the department?*
   This is a common motivator for choice of topic because the input from this person will be cutting edge. But of course, the professor in question can only supervise a finite number of students. It may be the case that the professor in question has many other commitments, which means the amount of supervision input may suffer.
3. *Can I get my supervisor to choose my topic?*
   Usually, no. The dissertation is designed to demonstrate independent study, so the topic must be chosen by the student. However, sometimes academics may

recruit students to help with a large-scale research project, and this section of the project may be used for the dissertation. This is quite rare at a master's level in TESOL and applied linguistics.

4 *Should I choose a topic that is popular in current publications?*
This is a good idea in principle; however, it is important that the amount of research and the prevailing research perspective in that area is considered in light of the contribution the dissertation will make to knowledge.

5 *Should I choose a topic many people have done before or a very unusual topic?*
There is no right answer to this question. The topic needs to reflect an element of originality, which may be difficult with widely researched projects. It also needs to be important; it is possible that an unusual topic has not been investigated because it is not important or it is impossible to research.

6 *Should I choose a topic related to my highest scoring assignment?*
This is a good starting point for choosing a topic, as the initial reading will have been done and assessment of the assignments will include valuable feedback.

Further reading

Wray and Bloomer's (2012) book has some very good suggestions for researchable topics in linguistics and language, although not many suggestions in TESOL. Each chapter addresses a broad topic and lists sources, themes and research in the area.

Bui's (2014) book *How to write a master's thesis* has a chapter devoted to selecting a research topic. This also includes advice on generating research questions and would be a useful source when writing the dissertation proposal.

References

Bui, Y. N. (2014). *How to write a master's thesis* (2nd ed.). Los Angeles, CA: Sage.

Campbell, E. (2016). *Up, up and away! Taking off with SFG: An investigation into the impact of selected Systemic Functional Grammar (SFG) concepts on students' writing of a film review.* (Master's Dissertation), Aston University. Retrieved from https://englishagenda.britishcouncil.org/sites/default/files/attachments/dissertation_design_for_publication_2016_aston_university.pdf (Accessed 30 April, 2019)

Dickson, B. (2015). *Newspaper discourses on Andy Murray's performance at Wimbledon: A contrastive corpus-driven investigation of successful and unsuccessful tennis match reports.* (Master's Dissertation), Stirling University. Retrieved from https://englishagenda.britishcouncil.org/sites/default/files/attachments/dissertation_for_publication_stirling_university.pdf (Accessed 15 May, 2019)

Dore, C. (2016). *Perceptions of fluency.* (Master's Dissertation), University of Reading. Retrieved from https://englishagenda.britishcouncil.org/sites/default/files/attachments/dissertation_design_for_publication_2016_reading_university_cecilia_dore.pdf (Accessed 30 April, 2019)

Hanisch, R. (2015). *The effect of the implementation of an Extensive Reading Programme (ERP) in English language teaching (ELT) on the reading abilities and reading habits of 12–13 year old students in an Austrian Secondary Modern School.* (Master's Dissertation), Norwich Institute for Language Education. Retrieved from https://englishagenda.britishcouncil.org/sites/default/files/attachments/dissertation_for_publication_nile.pdf (Accessed 30 April, 2019)

Hicking, R. (2015). *Subtitles in authentic video listening: An exploration of the benefits of captions in relation to sensory preference types.* (Master's Dissertation), University College, London. Retrieved from https://englishagenda.britishcouncil.org/sites/default/files/attachments/dissertation_for_publication_ucl.pdf (Accessed 30 April, 2019)

Jiang, J. (2015). *A survey of English teachers' ability to write reading comprehension questions in secondary schools in Beijing.* (Master's Dissertation), University of Warwick. Retrieved from https://englishagenda.britishcouncil.org/sites/default/files/attachments/dissertation_for_publication_warwick_university.pdf (Accessed 30 April, 2019)

Kelly, R. (2015). *An exploration of Instagram to develop ESL learners' writing proficiency.* (Master's Dissertation), Ulster University. Retrieved from https://englishagenda.britishcouncil.org/sites/default/files/attachments/dissertation_for_publication_ulster_university.pdf (Accessed 30 April, 2019)

Nazari, A. (2015). *English language lecturers' views on dynamic assessment and its potential in higher education: Challenging the current status quo.* (Master's Dissertation), London Metropolitan University. Retrieved from https://englishagenda.britishcouncil.org/sites/default/files/attachments/dissertation_design_for_publication_2016_londonmetropolianuniversity.pdf (Accessed 30 April, 2019)

O'Donovan, E. (2016). *Exploring culturally sensitive alternatives for the First Certificate in English.* (Master's degree), University of Liverpool. Retrieved from https://englishagenda.britishcouncil.org/sites/default/files/attachments/dissertation_for_publication_2016_liverpool_university.pdf (Accessed 30 April, 2019)

Ring, N. M. (2016). *My friend TED: Implementing effective listening strategies into academic listening using TED talks.* (Master's Dissertation), Sheffield Hallam University. Retrieved from https://englishagenda.britishcouncil.org/sites/default/files/attachments/dissertation_for_publication_sheffield_hallam_university.pdf (Accessed 30 April, 2019)

Wray, A., & Bloomer, A. (2012). *Projects in linguistics and language studies: A practical guide to researching language.* London: Hodder Education.

3

REVIEWING THE LITERATURE

A good dissertation topic arises from reviewing the literature in the field. Reviewing the literature starts at the very beginning of the dissertation process and continues until the final, submission of the dissertation.

The term 'literature' in academic parlance refers to the body of work about an academic subject. This literature is made up of textbooks, journal articles, reports, corpora etc. During the taught component of a master's degree, reading lists of appropriate literature are usually available; however, with the dissertation, students need to devise a reading list themselves based on a literature search. It can be a difficult task to select what to read, how to find sources and how to read the sources efficiently and critically.

The literature review in a dissertation should be viewed from two perspectives: First, as a process, searching for the literature, recording and critiquing sources. Second, as a product that reflects the organisation of an argument and the writing of the literature review chapter in the dissertation. This chapter is about the process, Chapter 10 refers to writing the literature review chapter.

This chapter divides reviewing the literature into three stages: stage one refers to broad reading to identify a topic using sources such as dictionaries and online sources, stage two refers to the process of finding and selecting the sources and stage three refers to reading and recording information. The chapter examines the skills needed to find the literature to support a topic from theoretical and research perspectives. It addresses decisions concerning what to review and how to review it, and includes discussion of using internet sources and how to avoid plagiarism.

TASK 3.1

What do you think is the purpose of reviewing the literature in your field?
What skills are needed to review the literature?

- Provide researcher with a grounding in topic
- Provide an overview of the topic
- Identify key scholars in field
- Identify main research studies
- Identify key theories
- Identify main methodology and methods
- Find gap in knowledge

FIGURE 3.1 The purposes of reviewing the literature

3.1 The purpose of the literature review

In the initial project design stage of the dissertation it is valuable to consider the general purpose of reviewing the literature. Figure 3.1 lists some of the purposes the literature review fulfils.

3.2 Stage one: broad review of the literature

In the first instance it is a good idea to conduct a broad review of the literature to become familiar with the topic. Introductory textbooks, general edited books, Wikipedia and subject dictionaries are useful starting points. This background reading should be for information purposes and are usually not referred to in the final dissertation because they do not match the criteria for selected literature (see Table 3.3). From there, chapters from edited books, subject encyclopaedias, chapters from handbooks and published reviews are valuable resources. Routledge published an excellent range of handbooks in applied linguistics. Each of these handbooks contains a large selection of chapters on specific topics, these are state-of-the-art papers written by experts in the field. The series covers a wide range of topics in TESOL and applied linguistics, but a good starting point would be the *Routledge handbook of applied linguistics* (Simpson, 2011) or the *Routledge handbook of English language teaching* (Hall, 2016). A list of titles of these with links to the contents is in Chapter 16. Another useful source is *Language Teaching*, an academic journal that frequently publishes literature reviews. They include two types of articles valuable to dissertation writers at this stage: state-of-the-art articles and research timelines. With the literature review at this stage it is best to choose very recent publications as this will present current thinking in the area and relevant references to further reading.

Table 3.1 outlines the types of literature that can be useful in the preliminary stages of reviewing the literature. The procedure for the first stage of the literature review has been applied to the topic of academic writing of international students.

In stage one of the literature review, the aim should be to identify the major arguments, theories and methods concerned with the topic. Table 3.2 provides a template for the broad literature review. It is useful to think about the gap in knowledge between what you know and what you need to know, and then move on to the major characteristics of the topic in terms of theory, research and methodology.

TABLE 3.1 Example of a broad literature review

Area and type of source	*Source*
Definitions of academic writing	www.yourdictionary.com/academic-writing
Introductory textbook – Good for major scholars, main theoretical perspectives and links to further readings	Charles, M., & Pecorari, D. (2016). *Introducing English for academic purposes.* Abingdon: Routledge.
Introductory textbook on teaching academic writing – To identify what academic writing is and considerations in teaching	Paltridge, B., Harbon, L., Hirsh, D., Shen, H., Stevenson, M., Phakiti, A., & Woodrow, L. (2009). *Teaching academic writing.* Ann Arbor: University of Michigan Press.
Encyclopaedia entry (Wikipedia) – For overview	https://en.wikipedia.org/wiki/Academic_writing
Handbook articles – Good for major perspectives, theories and research	Starfield, S. (2016). English for specific purposes. In G. Hall (Ed.), *Handbook of English language teaching.* Abingdon: Routledge. Basturkmen, H., & Wette, R. (2016). English for academic purposes. In Hall, G. (Ed.), *Routledge handbook of English language teaching.* Charles, M. (2013). English for academic purposes. In B. Paltridge & S. Starfield (Eds.), *The handbook of English for specific purposes.* Oxford: Wiley-Blackwell.
Literature review	Paltridge, B. (2004). Academic writing. *Language Teaching, 37*(2), 87–105.

TABLE 3.2 Template for the initial literature review

Task	*Notes*
What do I know about the subject?	
What do I need to know?	
Definitions of major terms	1.
	2.
	3.
Main scholars in field	1.
	2.
	3.
Major theories in field	
Main research methodology and methods in the field	
List of further readings:	
research	
theory	
methodology	
methods	

TASK 3.2

Using Table 3.1 and Table 3.2, conduct a broad literature review of your topic.

3.2.1 Types of literature

There are many possible types of literature that may be relevant to a research project. Figure 3.2 lists some of these. While this seems very large, in practice the majority of sources come from academic journals and books.

encyclopaedias	dictionaries	handbooks	statistics
textbooks	monographs		books
reports	conference papers	journal articles	
newspaper articles	archives	blogs	
corpora	wordlists	dissertations	theses

FIGURE 3.2 Types of literature

It is important to be aware of the top journals in the field. The Institute for Scientific Information (ISI) publishes yearly impact factors based on citations for high ranking journals. For example, the top-ranking journal in linguistics is *Applied Linguistics* with an impact factor of 3.593 in 2017. While it is useful to identify top journals, not all journals subscribe to the list and in some fields there are very few ISI journals.

TASK 3.3

Make a list of the top journals in your field.
Are they ISI journals?
Using the list, conduct a search of each journal for your topic.

3.3 Stage two: finding sources

There are a few ways that sources can be found. The internet is the first place most students will look. Searching using Google will produce a very long list of sources, such as Wikipedia, books, articles and blogs, however, not all of these are suitable. After the initial broad review, reliable sources need to be selected.

The best place to begin searching for literature is the university library. The first search should be of the catalogue, then the library's databases. A database is a large collection of academic materials such as abstracts, citations, reports, articles, books and theses. Many of the databases have full-text access. Databases are very useful because the quality of the sources is assured, unlike a Google search. In TESOL and applied linguistics the databases listed in Figure 3.3 may be useful.

TASK 3.4

What databases do you have access to through your university library?
Experiment with search terms from your topic. What sources are available?

When deciding what to read it is important to assess the reliability of the sources. The essential quality of a source is that it is peer reviewed. Peer review means that text has been evaluated by others. So, journal articles, for example, are usually reviewed by two or more experts in the field before being accepted for publication. Material on the internet – for example, Wikipedia, blogs and lecture notes – may not be peer reviewed.

Consideration should be given to the authority of the source. Is the author an established expert in the field? Sometimes sources available online do not have an obvious author, these sources should not be used as there is no way of knowing whether the author is an expert in the field. The focus of the source needs to be considered: Is the source a research paper? A theoretical discussion? Sources also need to reflect current thinking in the field, so they need to be recent. Of course, seminal works – that is, very important articles – may not be recent. For example, Vygotsky's notion of the zone of proximal development was put forward in the 1970s and is still widely referred to today (Vygotsky, 1978).

- ERIC Educational Resources Information Center (US) has an educational focus

  https://eric.ed.gov/

- ProQuest offers LLBA Language and Linguistics behaviour abstracts and has a linguistics focus

  http://proquest.libguides.com/llba/fields

- ProQuest also has a database of dissertations and theses

  https://www.proquest.com/products-services/proquest-dissertation-publishing.html

- JSTOR is a database with sources from humanities and social sciences

  https://www.jstor.org/

- Scopus is a multi-disciplinary database

  https://www.elsevier.com/solutions/scopus

- PsycInfo is a database with a psychology focus

  https://www.apa.org/pubs/databases/psycinfo/index.aspx

FIGURE 3.3 Some databases in TESOL and applied linguistics

A further distinction can be made between primary and secondary sources. In the field of TESOL and applied linguistics, a primary source refers to an original research article or report and a secondary source refers to a description of the area. So, for example, Lamb (2015) *A self-system perspective on young adolescents motivation to learn English in urban and rural settings* is a research article, while Dörnyei and Ushoida (2011) *Teaching and researching motivation* is a secondary source providing an overview of the area. Table 3.3 lists some of the criteria for selecting publications to review.

3.3.1 Keeping track of reading

During the literature review decisions need to be made about how to record and store sources. There are many methods for doing this, but every source needs to be accurately recorded. There are a number of software packages designed to keep track of references and generate citations and reference lists while writing. Most of these programmes allow users to store PDFs and notes. This is very useful, as it keeps all the information in one place and makes writing a reference list effortless. Table 3.4 lists some popular referencing software packages. Before deciding

TABLE 3.3 Criteria for selecting literature sources

Criteria	*Question*
Authority	Is the author an authority in the field? Is the author the researcher?
Focus	Is the publication a research report? Is the publication a theoretical discussion? Seminal work?
Date	Does the publication reflect current thinking in the area?
Primary/secondary	Is the publication a primary source?
Availability	Is the source easily available through your university?

TABLE 3.4 Some examples of citation management software

Name	*Availability*	*Link*
EndNote	Usually available through university, otherwise $200 +	http://endnote.com
Zotero	Free	www.zotero.org
RefWorks	Free	www.proquest.com/products-services/refworks.html
Mendeley	Free	www.mendeley.com

TABLE 3.5 Template for reviewing the literature

Reference	*Problem/ issue*	*Theoretical framework*	*Research design*	*Findings*	*Comments*

on a programme, you should check on the preferences of your department. Some university libraries provide software to students.

One method of keeping track of reading is to use a MS word or Excel template like that shown in Table 3.5. This template facilitates critically reviewing the literature. However, it would still be worthwhile using citation software to store PDFs and to generate reference lists when writing.

3.4 Stage three: reading skills

One of the biggest challenges facing graduate students is getting through the required reading. When writing a dissertation, the need for a wide range of reading is essential, and this requires a range of reading skills – from reading to get the gist to critical reading. The most important aspect of any academic reading is purpose.

You should ask yourself why you are reading a text, otherwise it is very easy to lose focus and end up reading a lot of material that will not be used.

Choosing what to read is the first stage, this should be a speedy process. Looking at the introduction, table of contents and headings will give a good idea of whether the text is relevant. After this, two strategies are useful: scanning and skimming. Scanning refers to getting the gist of the text by looking at parts of the text; skimming involves looking over the text for key terms.

Perhaps the most difficult reading skill for students is critical reading. In the early stages of research it is very easy to think that academic texts cannot be questioned because they are written by experts. Being critical does not mean taking an opposite standpoint, it means evaluating the content of the text based on the evidence provided and comparing this to other texts. Critical reading gets easier once the reader has a grounding in the topic.

After selecting a source, critical reading involves asking questions of the text, looking at conclusions and deciding whether these are sound based on the evidence in the article.

Table 3.6 summarises these different reading skills and strategies. Andy Gillet (2018) has an excellent blog about academic English, which includes a section on academic reading strategies with exercises.

It is very important that a record is kept of reading. The most efficient way of doing this is to use a referencing software programme or the template in Table 3.5 right from the beginning. The record should include as much information as possible and reflect the department's requirements. For example, some referencing styles

TABLE 3.6 Reading strategies

	Books	*Articles*
Choosing what to read	Read back cover Look at contents Look at references	Read abstract Final conclusions
Scanning texts	Read introduction Read first and last paragraphs of chapters Look at index	Read introduction Read findings Read first and last sentence of each section
Skimming texts	Look very quickly over text Look for specific terms	
Critical reading	Identify main argument What evidence is there for this argument? Is the evidence appropriate? Read and highlight Annotate with comments Annotate with questions Compare to other scholars in the field for similar and different conclusions	

Macaro, E., Curle, S., Pun, J, An, J., & Searden, J. (2018). A systematic review of English medium instruction in higher education: State-of-the-art article. *Language Teaching, 51*(1), 36–76. doi:10.1017/S0261444817000350

FIGURE 3.4 Example of reference in APA 6th edition using DOI

require author first names rather than initials; some departments and publishers want to have Digital Object Identifier (DOI) numbers included and page numbers may need to be included. Inserting this information after the dissertation is completed is very time consuming. Figure 3.4 shows an example of a reference that includes the DOI.

3.5 Role of theory and research

There are two main types of texts that inform dissertations: theory and research. Theory related texts are often book sources and may not be recent. Research focused sources such as journal articles should be recent.

One question students are often concerned about is how much reading should be done. This depends very much on the field. Some fields have a vast literature, and some may have very little. As a rule of thumb, the literature chapter should be about 20% of the dissertation. It should be remembered that not all sources read will be included in the final dissertation. However, it is important in the early stages of project design to identify the gap in knowledge for the project. This may be minimal, but one of the aims of reviewing the literature is to identify this gap.

3.6 Avoiding plagiarism

Plagiarism refers to the use of a source without acknowledging the author. This may be deliberate or accidental. In the early stages of a dissertation it is important that bibliographic details are recorded fully. It is also important to identify in notes which words and phrases belong to the author so that accidental plagiarism is avoided.

Summary

This chapter has covered aspects of reviewing the literature in the early stages of a research project. It has addressed finding and choosing appropriate sources. Types of literature sources are discussed, as well as how to read these using reading strategies with particular reference to critical reading. The chapter stresses the importance of recording references fully at this stage and suggests methods of doing this.

Common mistakes in reviewing the literature

- Not starting early enough
- Not keeping a record of sources
- Not identifying author's words and phrases
- Using sources that are too old
- Using sources that lack authority
- Using too few sources
- Using too many sources
- Using sources not directly related to the topic
- Not being focused in reading
- Relying solely on internet sources
- Not reading critically

FAQs

1 *How many sources do I need to read for my dissertation?*
There is no clear answer to this because each study has a different literature. In some research areas there is very little literature and in others there is a vast amount.

2 *Where can I get my sources?*
The best place to start with finding sources is in the university library, in particular the library's databases will be a rich source of material. A second way is to do an electronic search for your topic in major journals in your field. The most popular method of finding materials is by using internet search engines such as Google; however, these sources need to be evaluated for suitability and reliability.

3 *My sources take too long to read, what should I do?*
You do not need to read every word of every source. Over time you can develop reading strategies that enable you to read quickly and efficiently. Start by reading the abstract, the introduction and the first line of every paragraph. Then look at the findings and the conclusion of the article or source.

4 *Should I be reading mostly books or journal articles?*
Literature reviews in dissertations should be up to date. This means recent books and journal articles are the best sources to use. By reading several of the most recent sources you will be able to identify the major scholars in the area through their literature sections.

5 *Can I use secondary sources for my review?*
A secondary source is a source that refers to another source. In some general TESOL and applied linguistics books, the work of leading scholars is summarised. These are useful in the initial stages of reviewing the literature, but it is a good idea to also go to the original source too.

Further reading

Chris Hart's (2001)book *Doing a literature search* is very useful for finding sources, although some techniques for searching are a bit outdated. Diana Ridley's (2008) book *The literature guide: A step-by-step guide for students* covers all aspects of searching and writing the review, she includes chapters on reading strategies and being critical. Andy Gillet has an excellent resource with exercises focusing on academic reading: http://www.uefap.net/

References

Basturkmen, H., & Wette, R. (2016). English for academic purposes. In G. Hall (Ed.), *Handbook of English language teaching* (pp. 162–176). Abingdon: Routledge.

Charles, M. (2013). English for academic purposes. In B. Paltridge & S. Starfield (Eds.), *The handbook of English for specific purposes* (pp. 137–154). Oxford: Wiley-Blackwell.

Charles, M., & Pecorari, D. (2016). *Introducing English for academic purposes*. Abingdon: Routledge.

Dörnyei, Z., & Ushoida, E. (2011). *Teaching and researching motivation*. Harlow: Longman.

Gillet, A. (2018). Using English for academic purposes for students in higher education: Reading for academic study. Retrieved from www.uefap.com/reading/readfram.htm (Accessed 1 May, 2019)

Hall, G. (Ed.). *Handbook of English language teaching*. Abingdon: Routledge.

Hart, C. (2001). *Doing a literature search: A comprehensive guide for the social sciences*. London: Sage Publications.

Lamb, M. (2015). A self-system perspective on young adolescents motivation to learn English in urban and rural settings. *Language Learning*, *62*(4),

Paltridge, B. (2004). Academic writing. *Language Teaching*, *37*(2), 87–105.

Paltridge, B., Harbon, L., Hirsh, D., Chen, H., Stevenson, M., Phakiti, A., & Woodrow, L. (2009). *Teaching academic writing*. Ann Arbor, MI: University of Michigan Press.

Ridley, D. (2008). *The literature review: A step-by-step guide for students*. London: Sage Publications.

Simpson, J. (2011). *The Routledge handbook of applied linguistics*. Abingdon: Routledge.

Starfield, S. (2016). English for specific purposes. In G. Hall (Ed.), *The Routledge handbook of English language teaching*. Abingdon: Routledge.

Vygotsky, L. S. (1978). *Mind in society: The development of higher psychological processes*. Cambridge, MA: Harvard University Press.

4

METHODOLOGICAL APPROACH

This chapter provides an overview of the methodology and methods used in the early stages of designing a research project for a master's dissertation; however, it is assumed that readers have some understanding of research methods as this is usually part of the master's course for those intending to write a dissertation. A research project cannot be completed without a good understanding of relevant research methods in TESOL and applied linguistics. There are a large range of research methods available to collect data for a project, so in this chapter I attempt to identify the most popular methods for master's dissertations. These methods are selected based on constraints of time and the typical availability of data for a master's project.

The chapter addresses the methodological approach to research, then examines some common research methods. The advantages and disadvantages of these methods for dissertation purposes are discussed. Resources to help with the use of methods are presented in Chapter 16. The themes explored in this chapter are those that need consideration in the design of the project, research methods are discussed in further detail in subsequent chapters; for example, Chapter 8 examines data analysis.

4.1 Research methodology

There is a difference between the methodology of a study and the research methods used. The research methodology represents the research paradigm informing the study. It reflects an approach to reality (ontology) and knowledge (epistemology). Paltridge and Phakiti (2015) provide an excellent discussion of this and include a table contrasting research paradigms (p. 15–21). The methodology in turn informs the research perspective. There are three main approaches to methodology: a quantitative approach, a qualitative approach and a mixed methods approach.

At a basic level a quantitative approach to research aligns with a positivist or post-positivist paradigm that views knowledge as scientific facts that can be measured objectively mainly through the use of mathematical models. A qualitative approach to research aligns with a constructivist paradigm that assumes knowledge is less distinct. This approach is subjective and informed by people and contexts. A mixed methods approach aligns with a pragmatist paradigm that attempts to combine both approaches, accepting both objective and subjective approaches depending on the problem. For a more in-depth discussion about mixed methods research in second language acquisition (SLA) see Deifell and Shimanskaya (2013).

Generally, there will be a dominance of one approach in particular research topic areas. For example, until recently, much of the research done in language learning motivation was based on a quantitative perspective. It is useful to identify the main methodological trends in the topic area by reading recent journal articles, and the earlier this is done in the dissertation process, the better. A decision to use methods not usually used in the field may seem like a good idea because it could add a dimension of originality to the study; however, there may be good reasons why these methods were not chosen.

It is not always necessary to include a long and detailed discussion of the methodological paradigm as described previously, but it is important that this is thought through prior to designing the study. Demonstrating an awareness of the methodological approach informing the study is one of the qualities of a high scoring dissertation.

TASK 4.1

Look at five past dissertations from your department.
Do they include a discussion of the methodological paradigm informing the study?
How are these paradigms discussed?

4.2 Research design

This section addressed the most common types of research design used in TESOL and applied linguistics research. It is important to remember that unless the student has previous research experience the methods will need to be modest. For example, designing a model that uses structural equation modelling may be an excellent method to address a research problem; however, it takes a long time to be proficient in the skills needed to conduct such analyses.

A quantitative approach to research is rigorous and pre-determined. It seeks to be objective by controlling variables and sampling. This approach uses descriptive statistics to order the data and inferential statistics to make generalisations of the results beyond the sample used. Figure 4.1 summarises the main characteristics of a quantitative approach to research.

A qualitative approach to research investigates the 'why' of a problem and accepts subjectivity in the research. The investigation is emergent and may change during the project. It relies on detailed investigation of data. The researcher plays a central role in qualitative research. Qualitative data is described and discussed and rarely relies on statistics. Figure 4.2 summarises the major characteristics of a qualitative approach to research.

Research is deductive
Data collection very controlled
Data is categorised before data collection (a-priori)
Data is in numerical form
May have hypotheses (H1, H0)
Can generalise beyond sample
Sampling is controlled
Size of sample is important
Uses variables
Independent variables
Dependent variables
Uses statistical analyses
Aims for objectivity
Researcher neutral

FIGURE 4.1 The major characteristics of a quantitative approach to research

4.2.1 Quantitative methods

Quantitative methods are techniques used to collect and analyse data that is numerical in format. These methods examine the relationship between variables. This may be exploratory (that is, investigating an issue to get new information), or it may be confirmatory (that is, providing further evidence for a previously made claim).

Research is inductive

Emergent research design

Naturalistic

Data detailed (rich)

Research is context sensitive

Data is textual

In-depth investigation

Small sample

Sampling is focused

Uses content analysis

Accepts subjectivity

Researcher agent in research

Researcher reflexive

FIGURE 4.2 The major characteristics of a qualitative approach to research

Research designs using quantitative methods may be descriptive, experimental, quasi-experimental or correlational. A descriptive study uses basic statistics to count and produce frequency scores and averages, and thus identify trends in data from a sample. But claims beyond the sample cannot be made. For this, a research design that includes inferential statistical analysis must be used.

In an experimental design all aspects of the study are controlled. Typically, this type of research involves a pre-test, a treatment group, a control group and a post-test. These are analysed to see whether the treatment produces the results anticipated. Such a design would have at least one independent variable (IV), a variable expected to exert influence on the dependent variable (DV). So, for example, a particular teaching method would be an IV, and the language performance of the learners would be the DV. In an experimental design, the IV can be manipulated with one group of students receiving the treatment (teaching method) and a control group who do not. The defining feature of an experimental design is random sampling. This means the participants are randomly assigned to the treatment and control groups. This is often quite hard to do in TESOL and applied linguistics research, as students come in naturally occurring groups. To solve this problem, a quasi-experimental design has all the same characteristics as an experimental design but the sample does not need to be random and can be used with intact groups such as classes of students. Table 4.1 compares an experimental study and a quasi-experimental study. The sampling issue is addressed in the quasi-experimental study by ensuring there are no significant differences between the groups in terms of vocabulary knowledge.

Experimental and quasi-experimental studies are not very common in MA dissertations, as there needs to be a time for the treatment to be applied in order to see its effect. In Table 4.1 the time lag is five weeks, this is a significant chunk of time, especially if the research is conducted off-shore.

TABLE 4.1 Comparison of steps in experimental and quasi-experimental research to examine vocabulary learning

Research question: Are vocabulary learning strategies effective?	
Experimental	*Quasi-experimental*
Pre-test: Vocabulary test	Pre-test: Vocabulary test
Questionnaire about vocabulary	Questionnaire about vocabulary
Random allocation to two groups	In-tact class groups
	Statistically compare two groups to ensure no significant differences (t-tests (p = <.05)
Treatment (5-week programme)	Treatment (5-week programme)
Group 1 vocabulary learning strategies included in language lessons	Class 1 vocabulary learning strategies included in language lessons
Group 2 usual vocabulary included in language lessons	Class 2 usual vocabulary included in language lessons
Post-test	Post- test
Vocabulary test	Vocabulary test
Questionnaire about vocabulary	Questionnaire about vocabulary
Analysis: compare two groups for significant differences	Analysis: compare two groups for significant differences
Eg. t- tests (repeated measures)	Eg. t- tests (repeated measures)
Attribute this to treatment	Attribute this to treatment

TABLE 4.2 Example of a qualitative research design to examine vocabulary learning

Research question: How do learners in class 3 learn vocabulary?
Select sample – sub-group of students from class 3
Interview participants about vocabulary learning strategies used
Transcribe and analyse interview data
Observe language class for focus on vocabulary
Transcribe and analyse observational data
Analyse vocabulary activities in course-book and supplementary materials
Textual analysis
Combine results

Correlational studies seek to examine relationships between variables, for example, course grades and interest in English. This is done statistically and can indicate whether two or more variables are likely to be influenced by each other. For example, a study might investigate whether language proficiency and vocabulary knowledge are related. Measures on both these tests are analysed using correlational analysis. However, with correlational studies it is not possible to ascertain the direction of the relationship, whether vocabulary knowledge influences language proficiency or whether language proficiency influences vocabulary knowledge.

4.2.2 Qualitative methods

Qualitative methods are used to investigate language and learning in natural settings and seek to investigate these in a broad manner. Qualitative research is often described as being able to provide a rich description of data from a given setting (Mackay & Gass, 2005). Qualitative projects are likely to yield a lot of data and usually have far fewer participants than quantitative projects. Table 4.2 illustrates an example from vocabulary learning.

4.3 Types of research design

The following types of research design may use either quantitative or qualitative methods or a combination of both.

4.3.1 Survey research

This term is commonly attributed to quantitative methods using a questionnaire, but this does not have to be the case. Surveys can be quantitative, qualitative or a mixture of both. Surveys can rely on paper or electronic questionnaires or interviews. They may include multiple choice types of questions, which generate quantitative data, or open ended questions, which generate qualitative data. Surveys are used to provide a snapshot of conditions, views or events of a group at a given time, such a design is referred to as cross-sectional. Survey research is widely used in MA dissertations because data collection is often very quick, and the method can be used in a variety of situations with a range of research questions. (Wagner has a chapter on survey research in Paltridge and Phakiti [2015]).

4.3.2 Action research

A common research design in MA projects is one informed by action research, sometimes referred to as classroom research. The aim of action research is to bring about a positive pedagogical change. This is a useful approach because it is very practical. Action research is conceptualised as a cycle. Action research is a practical version of experimental research applicable to a very narrow field, the sample used. The cycle of action research is plan, act, observe and reflect. Figure 4.3 summarises this cycle. However, like an experimental study, action research usually requires time. For example, trialling a vocabulary strategy learning programme takes several lessons. Ann Burns has a chapter in Paltridge and Phakiti (2015) on action research that includes an example of a study.

4.3.3 Ethnography

This approach to research refers to research conducted in a naturalistic setting by a researcher who is involved in the setting. It has its origins in anthropology where researchers would live in the communities they were researching. In TESOL and

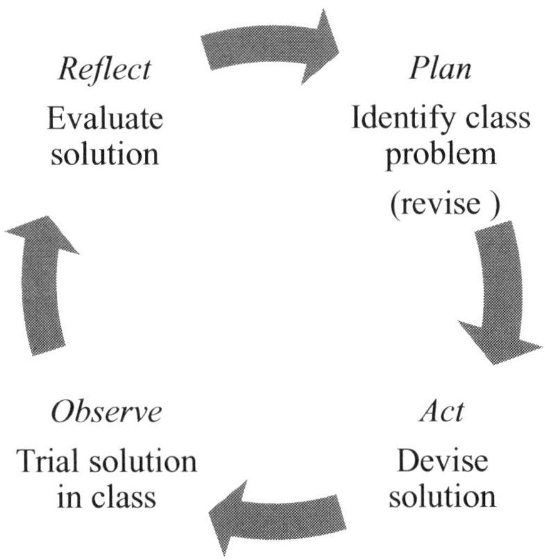

FIGURE 4.3 Action research cycle

applied linguistics, researchers are investigating language learning. Many have experience being learners of English themselves, so this approach is quite appropriate. The role of the researcher in ethnographic research is central to the research design. Ethnographic studies typically involve fieldwork, interviews and participant observations. Dörnyei (2007) has a very succinct and accessible description of ethnography in applied linguistics research (pp. 129–133).

4.3.4 Case study

The case study approach to research is another popular approach to research for master's students. A case study is an in-depth investigation of individuals, groups or organisations. The central aspect of this approach is the identification of the case. This is commonly a person but could also be an institution, an organisation or a group of people– for example, a class. In case studies, different methods can be used to explore a given case. Typically, multiple cases are investigated, for example, a case study of three English language learners that involves questionnaires and interviews.

4.4 Data collection methods

After the methodological approach, consideration needs to be given to the data collection methods or techniques. Quantitative methods use data that can be counted or translated into numbers, such as questionnaires or interviews. Qualitative methods use spoken or written data from interviews, focus groups ad observations. Often a master's research project will use more than one method to get a better picture of the situation. This is usually a mixed methods project, discussed further here.

4.4.1 Questionnaires

One of the most widely used methods to collect data in master's research projects is a questionnaire. Questionnaires are quick to administer and can be circulated electronically. The data analysis is also quick. When choosing a questionnaire, it is usually possible to use another researcher's questionnaire and adapt to the sample if necessary. Writing questionnaires is not easy, and ideally the instrument should be trialled.

One of the most common types of questionnaire is the Likert scale. This questionnaire is made up of closed questions that present a number of choices, often the extent to which the respondent agrees or disagrees. Other types of questionnaire questions are can-do scales, semantic differential scales and true/false questions. Dörnyei and Csizér (2012) have a chapter on designing questionnaire. Questionnaires often include open ended questions which add a qualitative dimension generating textual data that can be analysed qualitatively. The use of questionnaires is discussed further in Chapter 7 about the procedure of research. Figure 4.4 shows some examples of different types of questions that can be used in a questionnaire.

Likert scale

I get anxious when speaking in English

5	4	3	2	1
Strongly agree	*Agree*	*Neither agree nor disagree*	*Disagree*	*Strongly disagree*

Semantic differential scale

When speaking in English I feel:

anxious ------:------:------:------:------:------:------: not at all anxious

Can-do scale

How certain are you that you can give a 2-minute talk in English to your class about your weekend?

Certain cannot | *Certain can do*

0% 10 20 30 40 50 60 70 80 90 100%

True/False

I would describe myself as an anxious person. True/ False

Open ended questions

In what situations do you feel anxious when speaking in English?

____

____

____

FIGURE 4.4 Types of questionnaire questions

4.4.2 Interviews

The next most popular method in master's dissertations is the interview. These can be tightly controlled using structured interviews. This is essentially like giving a questionnaire, as there is little room for deviation from the questions. This type of interview can be done very quickly with a large number of participants and does not provide a lot of data, making it suitable for quantitative analysis. Semi-structured interviews are less structured and allow the researcher to investigate any interesting aspects that arise. The interview has a set of questions, but the interviewee is encouraged to provide in-depth answers to the questions. Because of its versatility, the semi-structured interview is the most common type in master's dissertations.

In unstructured interviews the session is informal, and the interviewer has one or two topics to guide the interview but makes few interruptions. This method takes a long time and typically involves few participants. Unstructured interviews yield a large amount of data. Whichever method is used, interviews are usually recorded and then transcribed and, if necessary, translated. The analysis is then done on the written text.

4.4.3 Focus groups

The focus group technique is essentially a group interview. The interviewer asks questions and encourages discussion amongst the group. In a focus group the interviewer acts as a moderator, ensuring the topic is adhered to and to ensure no one dominates the discussion. Focus groups typically have between six and ten participants to provide a wide discussion of the topic. This method can take a long time (at least one hour) and generates a lot of data. Focus groups are usually recorded using video or audio. The transcription can be challenging because there are a number of people and there may be overlaps and interruptions. One of the issues to bear in mind when conducting focus groups is peer pressure with a dominant subgroup dictating views that others are afraid to challenge. Edley and Litosseliti (2010) have a good chapter on interviews including focus groups and provide a step-by-step guide to conducting focus groups.

4.4.4 Observations

Using observations is a common technique in TESOL. Classroom interaction can be videoed or otherwise recorded to investigate pedagogic, linguistic and interactional occurrences in the language classroom. Typically, researchers use a checklist for observation to formalise the data collection process. There are two types of observations: participant observations and non-participant observations. In participant observations, the researcher is a member of the class community and takes part in the lesson; this method is common in ethnographic studies. In non-participant observations the researcher does not take part in the classroom activities but records activities and interaction without contributing to the session. Observations vary in the level of structure imposed on the data collection techniques. In an unstructured approach observation may be recorded through video, audio and field notes, and the researcher reflects on the raw data. This is more common in ethnographic participant observations. A structured approach involves the use of an observational schedule that can be used to record instances of language and interaction at regular intervals. This can be highly detailed and can result in data that can be analysed quantitatively. Richards (2003) has a good chapter on using observations.

4.4.5 Corpus linguistics

Corpus linguistics is an increasingly popular methodological choice for master's dissertations and often features as a module/unit of study on master's courses. A corpus is a collection of electronic authentic texts that are analysed for a given trends, for example, collocations. Because available corpora are very large, and the analytical software available very powerful, significant trends can be identified relatively easily. A study can use an existent corpus or can build a new corpus. An example of an existent corpus is the British National Corps (BNC). This is a 100 million word corpus of written and spoken English. For an example of building a corpus, Ben Dickson's (2015) dissertation reports on texts about the Scottish tennis player Andy Murray as published in newspapers.

4.4.6 Discourse analysis

Discourse analysis (DA) can focus on written or spoken text and is used to examine language in depth. This includes conversation analysis, genre analysis, critical discourse analysis and multimodal discourse analysis. Conversation analysis examines small sections of interactions, such as chat, in depth to provide insight on cultural issues such as gender and race. Genre analysis examines structural and linguistic features of texts to identify similarities and differences. Critical discourse analysis seeks to capture how discourse is informed by issues of identity and power relations of writers, readers, speakers and listeners. Multi-modal discourse analysis includes a variety of modes of communication such as images, videos and gestures.

Discourse analysis that focuses on written text or internet sources is a popular methodological approach for master's dissertation writers, as there is no need to recruit participants. This is particularly useful in settings where getting ethics approval is centralised, time consuming and complex. This is discussed in the following section on the ethics of conducting research.

Another popular approach in discourse analysis is the analysis of classroom discourse. This aims to provide insights into communication, relationships and learning within the classroom setting. For an excellent overview of discourse analysis see Paltridge (2012).

TASK 4.2

Look at the methods section of some academic journal articles in your chosen topic area.
What methodological approach is typically used?
What are some of the methods used?

4.5 Analysis

This section covers a very brief discussion of types of analyses typical of master's dissertations, as is needed at the design stage of a study. The procedural aspects of data analysis are discussed further in Chapter 8. It is important to consider the analysis of data before the data is collected to avoid possible problems, for example, matching the available sample size with that required by the method used. So, an overview of this should be included in the research design.

4.5.1 Quantitative analysis

There are two main types of statistical analyses associated with quantitative methods: descriptive and inferential. Descriptive statistics are used to count responses in order to get a picture of the characteristics of the data, for example, responses to factual questions, such as age, occupation, opinions and how much do you like X? The data is analysed using percentages, frequencies of scores and mean (average) scores. With descriptive statistics it is not possible to make claims beyond the sample used. Inferential statistical analysis enables the researcher to generalise beyond the sample by using appropriate sampling and statistical techniques, for example, t-tests. In most statistical reports both inferential and descriptive statistics are included. More information about this is included in Chapter 5 concerning writing a research proposal and in Chapter 11 on writing about methodology.

There are many inferential tests available to analyse quantitative data, and it is important to pick the correct test. Generally speaking, because of the time constraints of master's dissertations, univariate statistics are used; typically a researcher might use t-tests, correlation analysis, ANOVA or Chi square analysis. Table 4.3 lists some common statistical analyses used in master's research projects.

4.5.2 Qualitative analysis

Qualitative data analysis relies on the analysis of text. Data is transformed into text: Interviews and observations are transcribed, annotated videos and photographs may be included in the data along with field notes about the setting and participants. The data set for qualitative analyses can be very large, and the task of the researcher is to systematically reduce this to a manageable set of categories. The biggest problem with qualitative analysis in a master's project is time, as qualitative designs can yield a great deal of data that needs to be transcribed and analysed. This should be considered at the design phase.

In qualitative data analysis the researcher needs to be very close to the data. For this reason, it is best if the researcher carries out the data collection and analysis rather than using research assistants. The analysis, often referred to as content analysis, is iterative, which means the researcher goes through the data several times. In the first instance for a general sense of themes, then codes need to be developed and the data coded accordingly. The data then needs to be displayed in some way – for example, in table form – so that the results of the research can be easily accessed. For qualitative analysis, NVivo is a computer programme that can be used to facilitate analysis; however, this is not commonly used for master's dissertations because it takes time to learn how to use the programme and is not necessary for a small project. Many researchers find using Microsoft Excel or Word sufficient for analysis. The analysis of qualitative data is discussed further in Chapter 8.

TABLE 4.3 Some common types of analyses for quantitative data

Statistics	*Description*	*Use*
Descriptive statistics		
Mean	Average score	One or more of these needs to be reported for all statistical projects
Mode	Most frequent score	
Median	Middle level score	
Standard deviation	Difference between score and mean	Always reported in all quantitative studies
Distribution	Range of scores	Good for demographic data
Percentages, number	Percentages of respondents, numbers of respondents	Ages, gender, language
Frequencies	How many of a given response	
Cronbach's alpha	Reliability score	Conducted on questionnaire subscales
Inferential statistics		
t-tests	To compare two sets of data for significant differences To test hypotheses	Used in experimental and quasi-experimental research Identifies significant differences between two data sets
Chi square	To compare two sets of data Uses independent and dependent variables Dependent variable may be categorical	Identifies significant differences between two sets of data
Correlations	To look at relationship between variables	Used to find out relatedness between variables, for example, language test scores and self-study
ANOVA	To compare two or more sets of data	Different types of ANOVA, one-way, repeated measures Used with experiments and to test hypotheses
Regression	Used to predict scores Uses independent variables and a dependent variable	Good for predictive studies, such as years of study predicting language performance
Factor analysis	Used to investigate possible relationships between variables Used to reduce data set to factors of related variables	Used to establish validity of latent variables Used to validate questionnaires

TASK 4.3

What is your methodological stance for the study?
What methods will you use in the study?
What techniques will you use for collecting data?

4.6 Sampling

Choosing sources of data is very important in developing a research project. The idea behind sampling is that the sources selected to use for data are representative of the conclusions to be drawn; that is, from a small sample some inferences can be drawn that apply to a larger group even though this may be quite tentative. Sampling is important in both qualitative and quantitative research and needs to be carefully planned. For a master's research project perhaps one of the most important considerations is access to the data. Sources need to be easily and quickly accessible. Another consideration in sampling is the requirements of the analysis. Statistical analyses usually have sample assumptions; for example, the sample should be random and of a minimum size. This needs to be checked before embarking on the research project.

Table 4.4 lists some methods of sampling that can be used in quantitative and qualitative research. Quantitative sampling usually uses probability sampling, which is based on randomness. However, some statistical texts can use non-probabilistic sampling provided this falls within the assumptions of the statistical analysis. For many parametric tests there exists non-parametric tests that can be used if the sample is not random.

TABLE 4.4 Sampling in quantitative and qualitative research

Sampling	*How this is done*
Quantitative – probability sampling	
Random sampling	Participants are included in the sample on a random basis. This is a requirement of many parametric statistical tests.
Stratified random sampling	Random samples collected from groups formed based on one or more variables, for example, using two groups based on gender then randomly select participants.
Cluster	Randomly selected larger groups that use all participants in that group, for example, TESOL classes in a selected number of universities.
Qualitative and non- probability sampling	
Quota sampling	Groups showing same characteristics, for example, learners from Chinese speaking backgrounds.
Purposive sampling	Selecting participants or sites that can provide specific knowledge based on the judgement of the researcher, for example, English for Academic Purposes learners.
Convenience sampling	Participants selected from those available, for example, a class of language learners.
Snowball sampling	A small group of participants suggest others they know to participate in the research.

TASK 4.4

Look at some dissertations from your department or the dissertations available online*.
Is sampling discussed?
What type of sampling is used?
*https://englishagenda.britishcouncil.org/research-publications/elt-masters-dissertations

4.7 Ethics

All research that involves participants should be based on the notion of informed consent. This means the participants know what is involved in the study, how their data will be used and, most importantly, can choose whether to participate in the study. Most universities will have a formal process for ethics approval, this may be a department level process or a central university process. Getting ethics approval can be an extremely bureaucratic process taking six weeks or more, this applies particularly if approval is awarded at a central university level. This has implications for master's student research design because allocated time for the study is so limited. In these situations, students may choose a research topic that does not require ethics approval. Such a project would not involve participants, for example, textual analysis. It is important that students are familiar with ethics requirement of their department.

For almost all participant research, formal written permission from the participant needs to be given. This is usually done using a participant information and consent form. The participant information sheet explains, in terms the participant will understand, what the research is about and how data will be used. This is accompanied by a consent form that the participant needs to sign. The issue of confidentiality is central to ethical research. It should not be possible to identify participants from the research report. This means using pseudonyms and anonymising data. For example, consider referring to a 60-year-old Chinese female teacher of English, teaching a particular class, at a specific university in a province in China. In this example it would be easy to identify the participant, so steps would need to be taken to protect her identity.

TASK 4.5

What is the ethics procedure for your department?
What are the requirements?
Does your department have templates that can be used in an ethics application?

4.8 Validity and reliability

When planning a master's research project, thought needs to be given to validity and reliability. These terms refer to the quality and rigour of the research. Validity refers to whether the research measures what it purports to measure – that is, the extent to which the research can be trusted. Reliability refers to whether the research is replicable – that is, whether similar results would be achieved if the research was repeated. Claims about validity and reliability need to be supported with evidence.

In qualitative research the notions of reliability and validity need to be considered, but these are not so clear, as such research is subjective in nature. The role of the researcher needs to be discussed. In qualitative research there are a range of terms used to address the issues. Lincoln and Guba (1985) suggested the term 'trustworthiness' to refer to reliability and validity. Table 4.5 lists the major types of

TABLE 4.5 Reliability and validity

Type		*Explanation*	*Example of threat*
Quantitative	Internal reliability	Consistency of data collection and analysis	Poor questionnaire design with variables not being clearly operationalised, too few questions measuring variables.
Qualitative	Dependability	Extent to which similar results would be achieved if study repeated	Vague study design. Insufficient planning.
Quantitative	External reliability	Can be replicated	The questions produce very different results when given to another group with no apparent explanation.
Quantitative	Internal validity	Interpretability of the research	The data produces different results when analysed by other researchers.
Qualitative	Credibility	Truth and accuracy of data	
Quantitative	External validity	Extent to which results can be generalised	Using too few participants and inadequate inferential statistics to be able to generalise beyond study
Qualitative	Transferability	Can be applied to other contexts	Making claims based on too few respondents
Quantitative	Construct validity	Construct is defined and measured accurately	Questions in questionnaire do not clearly measure construct, for example, questions about motivation that measure attitudes.

reliability and validity and some threats to these. Both quantitative and qualitative perspectives are presented, as well as the qualitative counterparts.

There is a large literature on reliability in research, and every research methods book will have a section on this. Every research method has ways of addressing this. At the planning stage the researcher is advised to look at how these notions are usually addressed in similar studies reported in dissertations and journal articles, then go to the literature for this. For example, when checking the reliability in research using quantitative questionnaire, the data are often analysed using a reliability analysis such as Cronbach's Alpha. This results in a coefficient, for example, alpha = .85. This can then be interpreted in levels of reliability.

TASK 4.6

Look at some sample dissertations.
How is validity and reliability or trustworthiness addressed?

Summary

This chapter has discussed aspects of methodology, methods and analysis that are important to consider in the design phase of a research project. The chapter addresses the methodological approach to research and the methods commonly used to collect data in quantitative and qualitative research projects. Many of the areas discussed in this chapter are revisited in Chapter 8 concerning the procedure of the research and in Chapter 11 about writing of the methodology chapter of a dissertation. Chapter 16 includes resources that can be used in the design, execution and analysis of data.

Common mistakes in research design

- A naïve research design showing a lack of understanding of research methods
- Research design not doable, for example, sample may be too large
- Research not well informed by literature
- Not enough participants in study to support claims
- Inappropriate methods for research questions asked
- Inappropriate analyses of data
- Assumptions of analysis violated, for example, using a statistical text with a small intact group

FAQs

1 *Is qualitative research easier that quantitative research?*
No. Both approaches can be easy or difficult depending on the nature of the research design and the researcher's expertise. Quantitative research is much easier for those students who have experience with statistics, while some qualitative approaches such as conversation analysis are easier for students who have a linguistics background. The choice of approach should be based on the research design first, and then the expertise of the researcher and the available time for the study.

2 *I want to use statistics, but I have no experience. What should I do?*
Basic descriptive statistics are straightforward and require little more than mastering the processes in the computer software. Inferential statistics require an understanding of the concepts of the analyses, and this can be more time consuming. It is a good idea to think about the approach early in the master's course, so study choices that include quantitative methods are chosen. Very complex analyses such as structural equation modelling should be avoided by novices.

3 *How many participants do I need?*
Different methods have different sample sizes. In quantitative research the minimum sample sizes are usually stated in the assumptions of the analyses. In qualitative research it is up to the researcher to justify why the sample size is adequate.

4 *Must I always get signed consent from my participants or can I just collect data from my classes without doing this?*
It is necessary to get participant consent in any research project under the auspices of the academic institution. This is usually a condition of gaining ethics approval. The participants need to be able to decide to participate or not based on a description of the project.

5 *Should I design my own questionnaire to collect data?*
It is a good idea to use tried and tested questionnaires if possible. Designing a questionnaire is difficult and may not provide the information expected. One compromise is to use an existing questionnaire and adapt this to your purposes.

Further reading

A good starting point for research methods in TESOL and applied linguistics is Dörnyei (2007). This is a widely used textbook for research methods courses and is very accessible. However, this is an introductory textbook covering a wide range of methods, and researchers are advised to consult specific literature for the methods chosen. Paltridge and Phakiti (2015) have an excellent handbook of research methods in different areas of applied linguistics, with each chapter written by an expert in the field, for example, survey research (Wagner, 2015) and action research (Burns, 2015). Litosseliti (2010) deals with quantitative and qualitative methods including corpus linguistics. Richards (2003) has an excellent book on qualitative enquiry in TESOL and also a state-of-the-art article in *Language Teaching* (2009).

References

Burns, A. (2015). Action research. In B. Paltridge & A. Phakiti (Eds.), *Research methods in applied linguistics* (pp. 187–204). London: Bloomsbury.

Deifell, E., & Shimanskaya, E. (2013). Symposium: Methodologies in SLA. *Language Teaching, 46*(3), 427–431. doi:10.1017/S026144481300013X

Dickson, B. (2015). *Newspaper discourses on Andy Murray's performance at Wimbledon: A contrastive corpus-driven investigation of successful and unsuccessful tennis match reports.* (Master's dissertation), Stirling University. Retrieved from https://englishagenda.britishcouncil.

org/sites/default/files/attachments/dissertation_for_publication_stirling_university.pdf (Accessed 15 May, 2019).
Dörnyei, Z. (2007). *Research methods in applied linguistics*. Oxford: Oxford University Press.
Dörnyei, Z., & Csizér, K. (2012). How to design and analyze surveys in SLA research. In A. Mackay & S. Gass (Eds.), *Research methods in second language acquisition: A practical guide* (pp. 74–94). Malden, MA: Wiley-Blackwell.
Edley, N., & Litosseliti, L. (2010). Contemplating interviews and focus groups. In L. Litosseliti (Ed.), *Research methods in applied linguistics* (pp. 155–179). London: Continuum.
Lincoln, Y. S., & Guba, E. G. (1985). *Naturalistic inquiry*. Newbury Park, CA: Sage Publications.
Litosseliti, L. (Ed.). (2010). *Research methods in linguistics*. London: Continuum.
Mackay, A., & Gass, S. (2005). *Second language research: Methodology and design*. Mahwah, NJ: Lawrence Erlbaum.
Paltridge, B. (2012). *Discourse analysis: An introduction* (2nd ed.). London: Continuum.
Paltridge, B., & Phakiti, A. (Eds.). (2015). *Research methods in applied linguistics*. London: Bloomsbury.
Richards, K. (2003). *Qualitative inquiry in TESOL*. Basingstoke: Macmillan.
Richards, K. (2009). Trends in qualitative research in language teaching: State-of-the-art article. *Language Teaching*, *42*(2), 147–180.
Wagner, E. (2015). Survey research. In B. Paltridge & A. Phakiti (Eds.), *Research methods in applied linguistics* (pp. 83–100). London: Bloomsbury.

5
THE DISSERTATION PROPOSAL

It is usual for dissertation students to write a research proposal prior to starting the research. This normally needs to be approved by the department and it is at this stage that supervisors are usually allocated. This chapter outlines the stages of a proposal development. It analyses the genre of the research proposal with implications for writing a good proposal. Chapter 16 includes an example of a good master's research proposal with comments, this proposal was written for assessment and received a high grade.

5.1 The purpose of the proposal

Departments vary in their requirements for dissertation proposals; however, in most cases a proposal is required before a research project can progress. Students sometimes view the proposal task as coming too early, often six months or more before the dissertation is due. Dissertations are often set to come at the end of a research methods course and are part of the course formal assessment. Preparing a proposal is an extremely valuable activity. It forces the student to get organised early, and the proposal acts as a blueprint for the whole project reflecting the who, what, where, and how of the research project. It should provide background to the proposed study, the research design and procedure for collecting and analysing the data.

Different departments have different requirements for the dissertation proposal. Proposals vary in length requirements from 1000–3000 words. Some departments use the proposal as a wholly formative task with no grades involved; however, most departments use the proposal as a formal summative assessment task that contributes to the degree result. The areas covered in research proposals are generally similar and usually represent sections or headings in the proposal. Table 5.1 outlines the required proposal sections (headings) from three university MA TESOL/applied linguistics programmes. These sections will be discussed in turn.

TABLE 5.1 Comparison of areas required in a research proposal from three universities

University 1	*University 2*	*University 3*
Provisional title	Title	Working title
Rationale and focus of research	Summary of project	Introduction to topic
	Definition of key terms	Aims
	Purpose of project	Objectives
Review of relevant literature	Relevant background literature	Preliminary literature review
Research questions	Research questions	Research questions
Methodology	Methodology	Detailed methodology
Procedure		
Data analysis	Data analysis	
	Significance of project	
	Anticipated problems	
	Ethical considerations	
Timeline	Timetable for project	Timetable
	Resources for project	
References	References	
Appendix: instruments and techniques	Appendix: instruments and techniques	

TASK 5.1

Look at your department's guidelines for the dissertation.
Do you have to write a proposal?
How long does it need to be?
Is it assessed?
What are the recommended sections of the proposal?

5.2 Title/abstract

The title of the dissertation is usually tentative at the proposal stage, although it may remain the same. Often after feedback and more reading the final dissertation title will be refined.

Some departments demand an abstract at the proposal stage. An abstract is a brief summary of the project giving an overview of the important aspects of the research. This makes it easy to find potential supervisors for the project.

The abstract produced for the final dissertation will differ and is usually written shortly before submitting the dissertation as this section of the dissertation is read by more people. Examiners for the research may be allocated based on the final abstract. This should include major searchable keywords so the research can be easily accessed by others. Examination of the dissertation is discussed in Chapter 15.

5.3 Proposal introduction

All texts need introductions, and the dissertation proposal is no exception. This may be labelled as the rationale or purpose of the project. The introduction occurs at the beginning of the proposal and provides an overview of the project. This differs from a dissertation abstract as it leads the reader into the main body of the text, whereas an abstract summarises the whole project; however, some of the generic moves are the same. Genre analysis can be helpful for writers, as it provides a possible structure for the writing text, but it should be remembered that text structures can vary. Figure 5.1 presents an example of an introductory summary from a master's dissertation proposal and a generic analysis of this. The summary is direct and succinctly reflects the aim, background and methodology to the study. The first sentence of the introduction in a proposal usually addresses the importance of the area, often providing some general background. This is followed by more detail about the project and in this case finishes with a timetable for the research. The generic structure listed in Figure 5.1 can be applied to abstracts, summaries and introductions to the dissertation proposal. The introductory section usually presents the who, what,

Summary of project

This project is aiming to investigate the relationship between teachers' beliefs and the usage of online learning websites in Chinese as a foreign language classrooms.[1] The project is based on the finding of previous relevant literature which claims that the relationship between teachers' beliefs and integration of ICT in classrooms are mostly positive.[2] By focusing specifically on a CFL setting with a close look on three major online learning websites, this project will collect and analyse data from an online questionnaire and a follow-up small scale interview within Chinese teacher's association members.[3] Possible anticipated problems, limitations and ethical considerations are discussed. A detailed timetable and required resources of the project are proposed in this article.[4]

Generic structure of summary

1. Broad and direct statement of aim of project
2. Background to project
3. Description of methodology and methods
4. Reference to contents of proposal

FIGURE 5.1 Example of a summary of a project from a master's dissertation proposal

Source: Guo (2018)

TABLE 5.2 The Who? What? Where? and How? of introductory sections in a dissertation proposal. The analysis below is based on Figure 5.1.

Who?	Chinese Teacher's Association members
What?	Investigate the relationship between teachers' beliefs and the usage of online websites in Chinese as a foreign language classrooms
Where?	Chinese foreign language classrooms
How?	Examination of 3 major online websites, participant questionnaires and interviews

TASK 5.2 Complete the chart for your own study

Who?	
What?	
Where?	
How?	

where and how of a research project. Table 5.2 summarises this information for the introduction in Figure 5.1.

5.4 Purpose of the study

Usually in the introductory section of the proposal there will be a description of the aims, objectives and purpose of the study. The aim of the study should be clear in the proposal and is best expressed in one sentence, sometimes referred to as the statement of purpose. In Figure 5.1 the aim is expressed as "This project is aiming to investigate the relationship between teachers' beliefs and the usage of online learning websites in Chinese as a foreign language classrooms".

The rationale of the research should be stated in the research proposal. The rationale refers to why the study is being conducted and why it is important. In some dissertations this is presented under a separate heading, as is the case in the sample proposal in Chapter 16.

TASK 5.3

Write a purpose statement for your intended study.

5.5 Background/literature review

The proposal must contain a background section that includes a review of the literature upon which the study has emerged. At the proposal stage this is brief and focused. The aim of this section is to convince the reader that the project is based on research and theory. It is also important that very recent work is reflected in this section. This includes recent books and journal articles. It is important that this section is a structured argument that leads to the purpose of the study rather than a list of sources. So, the literature review may start by outlining the major findings in the topic area, then move on to the deficiencies in current research, finally identifying a gap in the literature that the current research will fill. Figure 5.2 presents a summary of the background sections in a proposal including the literature review.

5.6 Research questions

The research questions in a dissertation arise from the statement of purpose and are often placed at the end of the introduction, the statement of purpose or the literature review. It is usual to include research questions in the proposal although the questions may change. Research questions should be worth asking and answerable; they should be clear and unambiguous; and the answer to the question should not be obvious or biased.

There are three main types of research questions: descriptive, relational and causal. Descriptive research questions describe the existing situation. This type

Topic: Anxiety of Chinese University English EFL students giving oral presentations

Statement of purpose/Aim: This study aims to identify whether Chinese University EFL students experience anxiety when giving an oral presentation and whether this influences oral performance.

Objectives: Determine whether participants experience foreign language anxiety (FLA), compare this to performance on oral presentation, conclusions to help with lowering anxiety and improving performance

Literature review plan:

Overview of theorising and research into foreign language anxiety

FLA and speaking

FLA and Chinese students

Oral presentations in EFL courses in China, in target university

Gap: No research into anxiety and giving oral presentations on a specific EFL university English course

FIGURE 5.2 Example of background sections of a research proposal

of question is usual in qualitative studies. Relational questions compare two or more variables or groupings. Causal research questions look at cause and effect. Causal questions are rather difficult in any research outside the field of science. It is impossible to claim emphatically that X causes Y in the field because research does not take place in a laboratory where all influences can be controlled; however, this type of question is used with experiments and quasi-experiments. Often a research project may have more than one type of research question. In the field of applied linguistics and TESOL, evaluative questions are often asked. This can ascertain how effective a given project has been or is perceived to be. Some examples of research questions for a study that investigates listening comprehension strategies of students at the ECL language school are presented in Table 5.3.

Table 5.4 presents some examples of poorly constructed research questions. These would be very hard to answer. The basis of assessment of a dissertation is the answer to the research questions so it is important to devote a great deal of thought to the construction of these. The questions should be detailed and precise.

When crafting research questions it is important to consider the question word. So for example, a question with is/are/do/does requires a yes/no answer. This may be insufficient for a research project, as more detail would be required. This type of question can be combined with other types of question, for example, 'RQ1: Do

TABLE 5.3 Some examples of types of research questions

Research question	*Type*
Do intermediate ECL students use listening strategies?	Descriptive
How effective do ECL students think instruction in listening strategies is?	Evaluative
To what extent do teachers at ECL focus on listening strategies in class?	Descriptive
Which listening strategies do participants report using?	Descriptive
To what extent do listening strategies help with listening skills?	Relational
Is there a difference between listening strategy use of intermediate and advanced ECL students?	Relational
Is there an effect for gender in listening strategy use of ECL students?	Relational
Does instruction in listening strategies improve listening skills?	Causal

TABLE 5.4 Examples of poor research questions

Research question	*Problem*
Are listening strategies important?	This question is too broad and general
Do listening and reading strategies help with learning?	This contains two questions, one relating to listening and one to reading
Does the programme at ECL neglect listening strategy instruction?	This is a biased questions. It suggests the researcher believes this to be the case. The answer to this question is not very useful.
How do students learn listening strategies	This question is too broad. It is also impossible to answer.

TABLE 5.5 Types of question words

Question	*Example*
Do listening strategies help comprehension?	Yes/no question
Are listening strategies useful for listening comprehension?	Yes/no question
To what extent do listening strategies help listening comprehension?	Will provide more detail than a yes/no question
How do listening strategies help listening comprehension?	Requires a detailed answer
Which listening strategies help with listening comprehension?	Requires detailed answer

TASK 5.4

Based on your research topic, practice writing different types of research questions. What makes one question better than another?

the students of class X feel anxious when speaking in English? RQ2: In which situations do they report the highest level of anxiety?' In applied linguistics and TESOL, research questions may often use 'to what extent', which will provide a more detailed answer. Table 5.5 shows some examples of questions using different question words.

5.7 Methodology

The methodology section of the proposal should be succinct but should show a good understanding of research methods with reference to research methods literature. This is particularly important if the research proposal is the final assignment in a research methods module or unit of study. One of the most important aspects at the research design stage is choosing the most appropriate methods for the study.

Typically, the methodology/methods section of the proposal starts with the methodological approach and justification. This may be followed by information about the participants and the sampling strategy used. The data collection methods need to be described and justified. The techniques or instruments that will be used to elicit data may be required in the proposal and there also needs to be a section on how the data will be analysed, for example, content analysis or t-tests. This section will also include a section for the timetable of the study or a description of the procedure for data collection. This is discussed in section 5.8.

Summarising the methodology and analysis information of the study can be presented as a table that matches the research questions. A useful example of a table that links research questions, data collection methods and analysis is presented in Table 5.6. Using such a table clarifies thinking and makes it easy for the reader to understand the study at a glance.

TABLE 5.6 Summarising research questions, methods and analysis

Research question	*Data collection*	*Analysis*
RQ1: Do College English students experience language anxiety when giving oral presentations?	FL Oral presentation Language anxiety questionnaire Interview questions	Descriptive statistics Content analysis
RQ2: Does language anxiety affect performance in oral presentation of College English students?	Oral presentation grades FL oral presentation anxiety questionnaire Interview questions	Correlational analysis Content analysis

TASK 5.5

Make a table for the research questions, data collection methods and analysis in your project using the template provided in Table 5.6.

5.8 Procedure/timeline

All proposals need a section on the timetable or procedure. This can show that the project is achievable within the time frame available; it is also a useful time management tool. The timetable should be thought about very early in the research design process, with some aspects of the timetable firmly in place before the proposal is written. For example, it is important that access to the participants is possible. This means the research site should be contacted well in advance to assess the feasibility of collecting data. Table 5.7 provides an example of a research timetable from a master's student at a UK university.

TABLE 5.7 Sample timetable for research

Task	*Deadline*
Submit research proposal.	30 March
Make revisions to research design based on proposal feedback.	10 April
On-going literature review.	
Contact possible participants from UCL.	15 April
Finalise sample:	22 April
Participants for questionnaire.	
Two classes for class observation.	
Administer questionnaire.	1 May
Class observations.	10 May
Transcribe data.	20 May
Analyse quantitative data.	5 June
Code and analyse qualitative data.	10 June
Draft dissertation.	10 July
Editing dissertation.	10 August
Submit dissertation.	15 August

TASK 5.6

Draft a possible timetable for your research project.

5.9 Appendix

The appendix should contain all the data collection methods and instruments, for example, a questionnaire or interview questions. The appendix also should include evidence of ethics approval if required; this procedure is necessary to prevent problems with collecting data. The data collected from participants should be provided voluntarily to protect the participants. In applied linguistics and TESOL, participants come from diverse groups, which may include vulnerable people such as children and young people. The ethics approval procedure also serves to protect the university's reputation that research is sound and honest. To get ethics approval students need to describe the project briefly and identify possible risks to participants. A participant information sheet and consent form should be included. If data is to be collected from children, permission needs to be collected from parents or guardians and sometimes the local education authority. If data is to be collected from institutions such as a school or university, then evidence of permission should be included. An example of a participant information sheet is provided in Chapter 7. Departments usually have their own ethics procedures and forms. This application process may be centralized, whereby a university committee examines all ethics applications. In this case the application for approval can be time consuming. Often ethics approval is done at a departmental level based on university standards.

5.10 Bibliography or references

This section of the proposal should be a list of sources presented in the style required by the department, for example, APA 6th edition. Some departments require a bibliography, which is a list of all the sources consulted during the process of drafting the proposal, while some departments require a reference list that includes only those sources referred to in the proposal.

5.11 Assessment and feedback

Some departments use the proposal as a purely formative task. This means the proposal does not contribute to the overall degree grade. It is used solely to gain feedback and advice for the project. However, other master's programmes use the proposal as part of the overall assessment. Often this is the final assignment of a research methods course, in this case, it is important to be familiar with the assessment criteria. Sometimes these are generic criteria that are used for all course-work assignments, sometimes the criteria mirror those used for the assessment of the dissertation and sometimes the criteria are tailored to the proposal task. Figure 5.3 presents the generic assessment criteria that proposals are assessed by; however, it is very important that students are familiar with the assessment criteria before writing the proposal.

Based on understanding of current literature relevant to project

Includes a critique of literature

The research is feasible

Shows an understanding of research methods

Appropriate research methods are used for the project

Shows a sound argument

Writing adheres to department standards

FIGURE 5.3 Generic criteria for assessing a dissertation proposal

5.12 Using proposal feedback

Getting feedback on the research proposal is very useful, as this provides the student with ways to improve the project. Feedback should not be ignored, as this could lead to problems with the research procedure or execution.

Some students are disillusioned with the feedback on their proposal and decide to change their project completely. Changing the study at this stage is not a good idea, as the legwork for the project has already been completed and the time allocated for this used up, so a complete project change in topic after the proposal assessment should be avoided. It would be hard to complete a research project to an acceptable level in the remaining allocated time, this is assuming students only have a few months for the dissertation from beginning to end.

Based on the advice provided in this chapter and the general assessment criteria, Table 5.8 presents a checklist that can be used when writing a research proposal for a master's dissertation in applied linguistics and TESOL.

TABLE 5.8 Checklist for the research proposal

		✓
Title	Does the title reflect the topic, approach and variables?	
	Does the topic include keywords?	
Introductory section	Does this reflect department requirements?	
	Is it well organised?	
	Is the overall study clear from this section?	
Statement of purpose	Is the purpose clearly defined?	
	Is this statement purpose located in the correct position in the proposal based on department requirements?	

(*Continued*)

TABLE 5.8 (Continued)

		✓
Research questions	Are the questions answerable?	
	Are the questions worth asking?	
	Do the questions reflect the methodology?	
Literature review	Is the literature review the correct length? (not too long)	
	Are most of the sources recent?	
	Have the major works been included?	
	Is the review critical?	
	Is the gap in knowledge stated?	
	Is the literature review structured as an argument?	
	Are the citations correct?	
	Do your citations and reference list match?	
	Have you used the department style for your reference list?	
Ethics	Is an ethics application included if necessary?	
	Has your supervisor checked the ethics forms?	
Methodology	Have you referred to the methodological approach?	
	Are the methods appropriate for the research questions?	
	Have you included instrumentation if required? (questionnaire, interview questions)	
	Have you included reference to analysis of data?	
Timeline	Is your timeline reasonable?	
Feasibility	Can you access your data sources?	
	Do you have the skills necessary to collect the data?	
	Do you have the skills necessary to analyse the data?	

Summary

This chapter has discussed the purpose and the typical sections found in a master's dissertation proposal. The chapter stressed the importance of producing a well-developed proposal, as this can serve as a blueprint for the rest of the research. The research proposal is further explored in Chapter 16, with a sample of a good proposal together with comments.

Common mistakes in the research proposal

- The proposal is underdeveloped.
- The proposed project is not supported by sufficient reading.
- The project lacks significance.
- The outcome of the research is known already.
- The project is too ambitious.
- The proposal reflects a poor understanding of research methods.
- The Who? What? Where? How? are not clear.

FAQs

1 *Do I have to write a proposal for my study?*
Usually yes. The proposal is usually a department requirement. Aside from this a proposal is a good idea because it forces you to think clearly about the study and its execution. It serves as a blueprint for the research.

2 *Can I change my study after the proposal?*
Yes. It is not necessary to adhere to every detail laid out in the proposal, but it is a good idea to have the proposal as developed as possible and to stick to it so time is not wasted.

3 *I really want Professor B to be my supervisor. Should I write my proposal to reflect her research interests and use lots of quotations from her work?*
This represents one possible motivation for researching a topic. Choosing a field that can be supervised by an expert is a good idea, but it is important that the topic holds interest for you and that the project is doable.

4 *Can I change my study completely after the proposal?*
Yes, if this is necessary, perhaps because the original idea was not practical; however, it is a bad idea to depart completely from the original topic, as this means a lot of study time will have been wasted. It's possible but not a good idea.

5 *Can I use my proposal in my final dissertation?*
The proposal will be very useful when writing the dissertation, but it is not recommended to cut and paste from the proposal. The literature and methodology will probably be similar in both documents, but it is important that the dissertation is written as such. The dissertation has greater detail and may use different grammar; for example, the proposal is usually written referring to the future.

Further reading

There are no available sources that focus exclusively on master's dissertation proposals in TESOL and applied linguistics. Many of the sources on research proposals focus on PhD and grant proposals. Master's proposals are often shorter than these and much less detailed. Biggam (2016) has a good section (Chapter 4) on proposals that focuses on the background, aims, objectives, methods and ethics in master's dissertations. Hart (2005) also has a chapter (Chapter 11) on writing a proposal, which includes an analysis of a proposal. Punch (2016) and Locke et al. (2016) focus on PhD and grant proposals. Chapter 16 in this book provides a sample master's dissertation proposal with comments.

References

Biggam, J. (2016). *Succeeding with your master's dissertation: A step-by-step handbook*. Maidenhead: Open University Press.

Guo, Y. (2018). *A research proposal on teacher beliefs and the usage of online teaching websites in Chinese as a foreign language classrooms*. (Unpublished research proposal). University of Sydney.

Hart, C. (2005). *Doing your masters dissertation*. London: Sage Publications.

Locke, L., Spirduso, W. W., & Silverman, S. (2016). *Proposals that work: A guide for planning dissertations and grant proposals* (6th ed.). Thousand Oaks, CA: Sage Publications.

Punch, K. (2016). *Developing effective research proposals* (3rd ed.). London: Sage Publications.

6

SUPERVISORS AND SUPERVISION

Master's dissertations are supervised by a member of academic staff who has some expertise in the topic area. The supervision is usually a one-to-one meeting to discuss the dissertation. This method of teaching probably will be new to a lot of students, as the supervisor has a very different role from course-work sessions. Problems can emerge when the understanding of the roles and responsibilities of the supervisor and student do not match, which in turn can adversely affect the academic outcome. Unlike higher research degrees, supervision hours for dissertation students are usually very limited due to the staff–student ratio. This chapter addresses some of the issues common in research supervision.

6.1 Allocation of supervisors

In a research degree such as a PhD, the selection of a supervisor often lies with the student. The student researches possible supervisors for his/her project and approaches them directly. On taught master's courses this is usually not the case. Students may be asked to suggest possible supervisors for their project, but the allocation will be made by the department. In the UK almost all TESOL and applied linguistics master's students do a dissertation and therefore need a supervisor. Finding supervision for a large number of students is always challenging for an academic department. Sometimes in this situation, academic staff could be responsible for supervising many students, over ten is quite common. Sometimes staff manage this by supervising in groups; sometimes extra staff are recruited to supervise the projects. Students should be prepared for supervisors who are very busy or supervisors who are not readily accessible in the department as would be the case in part-time staff hired for the dissertation.

As far as possible supervisors are allocated based on their expertise in the student's topic, but this does not always happen. It may be that there are too many students interested in a topic for the resident expert to supervise, or that there is not an expert available. If the student intends to continue to a higher research degree, then it would be very valuable to have an expert in the research area comment on the proposal. However, students should not worry if their supervisor is not an expert in their field, as supervisors are usually experts in research methods and processes; expertise in the literature rests with the student, and one of the roles of the supervisor is to facilitate independent learning.

6.2 Supervision by committee

Some departments may have a system that involves a dissertation committee. This is common in US universities but is less usual in UK and Australian universities at a taught master's level. In the committee system the student usually has a primary advisor/supervisor and possibly a secondary advisor or reader. The supervision committee tends to focus on assessment with readers and a committee chair responsible for the assessment outcome for each dissertation. The dissertation process may reflect more than one assessment procedure, for example, a proposal, a proposal defence and the dissertation itself. Some departments require an oral component, a viva, to the dissertation. This is discussed in Chapter 15.

6.3 Contact time

Institutions vary in the amount of contact time available for master's dissertations. Usually the requirements are laid out in the degree handbook. Some departments are more flexible than others and provide help when needed rather than adhering to a strict number of hours. Figure 6.1 reflects some current practice at universities in the UK. These requirements refer to face-to-face supervisions. In some departments and in certain situations, online supervisions may be conducted using FaceTime or Skype, particularly if the student is collecting data away from the university.

University A: The usual supervision time is two to three 3 hours

University B: You will have three to four meetings with your supervisor all before the end of July

University C: You will have three hours of supervision.

FIGURE 6.1 Examples from dissertation handbooks

TASK 6.1

How are supervisors allocated in your department?
How many hours or meetings with your supervisor can you expect?
Will you have group sessions?

In addition to supervision sessions, a large proportion of the supervisor–student communication may be via email. This will include feedback on drafts, written tasks and answers to questions. For students, there are two golden rules with emails. The first is the 24-hour rule. Supervisors are very busy and often have to deal with a vast amount of email. It is not reasonable to expect an answer to an email query within a couple of hours; a 24-hour turnaround is the minimum for responses. The second rule is never to email at the weekend. Supervisors have lives outside of academia, and while many do work at the weekend it is polite to refrain from emailing requests over the weekend unless this is a prior agreement.

In some departments supervisions may occur in groups. In this case groups of students researching similar topics are grouped together. This is common in the early stages of the dissertation as questions about process and research design tend to be similar across topics. If group supervisions are not the norm in the department it is a good idea to set up an informal system of peer discussions about the dissertation. Such discussions can be less intimidating without the supervisor present and can provide a great deal of support. Chapter 16 has a section on setting up a writing group.

6.4 Roles of supervisor and student

The roles supervisors play in the dissertation process can be confusing for students. There are no set procedures for supervising students. Supervisors are informed by experience and department requirements, but of course supervisory practices vary tremendously. Some supervisors are very hands on, others involve themselves very little in the process, leaving students to sort things out for themselves. For this reason, it is very important for students to clarify the roles and responsibilities for both the student and the supervisor. Table 6.1 presents some possible roles for students and supervisors, but these will vary across institutions and, of course, personalities.

TASK 6.2

What is your opinion on the roles of a supervisor?
Make a list.
Does your supervisor agree with these roles?

In general, many students expect and would prefer supervisors to play a more directive role in their project, telling them what to do in detail. However, the main aim of the dissertation is to demonstrate independence in terms of study, so this tends not to happen. For example, students may think it should be the supervisor who chooses the topic. One area of mismatch, particularly for international

TABLE 6.1 Some typical supervisor and student roles

Supervisor roles	*Student roles*
Give guidance on developing the research project	
Advise on suitability of topic	Decide on topic
Advise on feasibility of project	Plan a feasible project
Advise on suitability of title	Draft title
Advise on suitability and phrasing of research questions	Draft research questions
Mark research proposal	Write research proposal
Approve research proposal	Act on feedback on proposal
Advise on suitable data collection methods	Develop a suitable research design for the study
Direct student to literature sources	Find, read and record literature sources
Help with ethics application	Fill in ethics forms and write participant information sheet and consent forms
Approve data collection methods and instrumentation	Decide on most suitable data collection methods and instruments
Provide feedback on drafts	Act on feedback
Discuss drafts in meetings	Complete drafts on time
Assess dissertation	

students whose first language is not English, is the extent to which the supervisor will correct the language in dissertation drafts. While there are exceptions, supervisors tend not to provide feedback on language nor proof-read drafts for the final dissertation.

6.5 Supervisory meetings

Students need to find out who sets the supervisory sessions – is it the student or the supervisor? In some settings students can contact their supervisor whenever they need. However, in a lot of cases, especially in UK universities where time is tight, meetings are set out in advance and are usually scheduled to correspond with important stages in the dissertation process. Figure 6.2 lists the stages of the dissertation process where feedback and discussion are very important.

TASK 6.3

What types of questions might arise in each of the stages of the dissertation?

It is advisable for students to be well prepared for supervisory meetings, especially where face-to-face contact time is limited, so as to maximise the advice given. Some students feel anxious in supervisory meetings. They may feel vulnerable because of the one-to-one nature of the interaction and the power imbalance, but experiencing anxiety during a meeting leads to a reduction in cognitive

1. Topic and initial project design and literature
2. Developed project design
3. Research proposal
4. Instrumentation and procedure
5. Dissertation writing
6. Assessment feedback

FIGURE 6.2 Important stages of dissertation for discussion

capacity due to worry, and this results in difficulty in absorbing information and advice. There are some methods to overcome anxiety in this context. One is by being very well prepared for the meeting, and the other is positive self-talk. It is important for the student to remember that he/she is not an expert, and this is perfectly acceptable – this is the reason they are consulting the supervisor. Figure 6.3 identifies some important areas that a student can prepare to get the most out of the meeting. It is very important that any task set by the supervisor is sent in by the due date, otherwise the supervisor will not be able to give the work the attention it deserves. The supervisor needs time to look at work and comment on it. It is impossible to do this if a draft is brought to the meeting. Sometimes the supervisor will send the draft back to the student before the meeting with written feedback. This can be then discussed in the meeting. One way of beating anxiety is to have a list of prepared questions to ask. It is important that students ask any questions about issues that worry may worry them regardless of how small. So for example, "I do not understand what a theoretical framework is". It is better to raise these issues and get advice on how to resolve them rather than have problems discovered at the examination stage.

During the supervisory session, taking clear and well organised notes is very important, writing quick notes without looking at the page is likely to result in a faulty recall later. Some students find recording the session using a mobile phone is useful; this needs to be cleared with the supervisor. However, this means that the whole session needs to be listened to again, and this can be quite time consuming. Figure 6.3 presents some strategies students can use to maximise the supervision experience.

One method of ensuring both supervisor and student have the same understanding of the decisions made in the meetings is to write a summary of the meeting focusing on action points. This summary can then be emailed to the

Send in draft on due date before the meeting.

Do not bring revised drafts to the meeting.

Make a list of questions to ask.

Raise any points that you do not understand about feedback.

Do not be embarrassed to ask questions.

Go through supervisor feedback point by point.

Take complete and ordered notes during the supervisory session.

Repeat to your supervisor any action points.

Send a summary of the meeting and action points after the meeting.

Raise any worries you have.

FIGURE 6.3 Preparing for supervision meetings

supervisor. Table 6.2 is an example of such a summary. This student is planning to design a needs analysis for English for Academic Purposes (EAP) in a university in Hong Kong.

6.6 Problems with supervision

The supervisor–student relationship can be a very emotional and intense one. The research project is very important to the student, and the supervisor is responsible to assist the student in completing this project. This relationship should always be strictly professional and focused on the dissertation; unless personal matters are impacting on the progress of the study these should not arise in a supervisory meeting.

Problems with supervision are the most frequently reported worry for students on PhD programmes (Paltridge & Woodrow, 2012). While supervision at a master's level is much shorter and arguably less intense, it is very important to make the relationship work. However, sometimes it does not. The student and supervisor may have different views about how the dissertation should progress, the student may feel they are not getting enough input from the supervisor or there may be a personality clash. It is important to identify the root cause of the discord and to try to solve the situation as quickly as possible to minimise the effect on the student's academic outcome. There are usually university guidelines for dealing with this problem and a procedure to follow. In the first instance the problem can be discussed with the dissertation module leader.

TABLE 6.2 Example of a summary of a supervision session in the research design stage of the dissertation

Point	*Action*	*Date*
Literature is based on old material.	Do a search for needs analysis in English for Specific Purposes and Journal of EAP. Look at Routledge Introduction series 206–218, particularly Brown 2017. Revise literature section.	10 May
The argument of dissertation not clear from literature.	Redraft literature reflecting a structured argument	10 May
The instrumentation needs developing.	Look at similar studies and examples of needs analysis instruments and questions. Draft questionnaire and interview questions. Send to supervisor.	30 May
A rather limited range of participants.	Think about including a range of participants in analysis, students, teachers, employers and previous students. Send with needs analysis. Think about whether want to use same instrumentation for all stakeholders. Send sampling in with instrumentation.	30 May
Ethics form incomplete and needs signature.	Complete storage section and participant information sheet. Send to supervisor for signature. After signed send to Brenda for approval. Cannot collect data before ethics approved.	ASAP
Next meeting	5th June, 3:00pm, Room 3.3	

Summary

This chapter has addressed some issues in MA dissertation supervision. The supervision experience is very different from the usual method of teaching found on MA courses. The sessions are usually, but not always, conducted one-to-one with the student expected to be independent. The chapter has discussed how supervisors are allocated and what students can expect from this method of teaching.

Common mistakes in supervision

- Expectations of the supervision of supervisors and students are not the same.
- Supervisors are away a lot.
- Students do not complete work on time.
- Students do not ask for clarification when unsure.
- Students are late or miss appointments.

FAQs

1 *I do not know what topic to choose for my research. Will my supervisor allocate me a topic?*
It is very unusual for a supervisor to choose a topic. Usually the student needs to choose the topic first and then supervisors are allocated based on their expertise. This is the first step toward independent study.

2 *Will my supervisor give me reading lists and tell me what to read?*
No. The supervisor will advise the student on good articles and possible sources, but it is up to the student to conduct the literature review relevant to the topic.

3 *Will my supervisor correct my English in my writing?*
No. If English is not your first language then you may need the help of a proof-reader in the final stages of the dissertation. This might be a professional editor or a critical friend.

4 *My supervisor is away a lot and is very busy, can I get the supervision I need?*
This can be a problem, but usually supervisors will inform their students when they will be away so the submission of drafts can be scheduled efficiently. If this is not the case, then advice from the dissertation module co-ordinator should be sought.

5 *Can I pop into my supervisor's office with any questions I may have?*
Usually not, unless this arrangement has been set in place. Supervision represents only one aspect of an academic's job description, so unscheduled interruptions are not usually welcome.

Further reading

Furseth and Everett (2013) have a chapter on support networks (Chapter 4, pp. 39–46). Paltridge and Starfield (2007) include a role-perception scale that can be used by students and supervisors to highlight the responsibility for aspects of the supervision and dissertation (p. 38). Harwood and Petric (2017) present a qualitative study about the experiences of master's students and their supervisors that also reflects the supervisor–student relationship.

References

Furseth, I., & Everett, E. L. (2013). *Doing your master's dissertation*. London: Sage Publications.

Harwood, N., & Petric, B. (2017). *Experiencing master's supervision: Perspectives of international students and their supervisors*. Oxford: Routledge.

Paltridge, B., & Starfield, S. (2007). *Thesis and dissertation writing in a second language: A handbook for supervisors*. Abingdon: Routledge.

Paltridge, B., & Woodrow, L. (2012). Dissertation writing: Moving beyond the text. In R. Tang (Ed.), *Academic writing in a second or foreign language: Issues and challenges facing ESL/EFL academic writers in higher education contexts* (pp. 88–104). London: Continuum.

PART II

The research procedure

7

THE DATA COLLECTION PROCEDURE

This chapter concerns the nuts and bolts of doing research. It looks at getting participants for research and collecting data. Two methods of data collection are addressed: questionnaires and interviews, as these are probably the two most common methods used in master's research. The chapter discusses methods of conducting the research and how to deal with unforeseen events during this period of the research.

7.1 Participants

Not all research involves the use of people; some projects rely on textual data. This is discussed in section 7.2. Recruiting participants can be difficult and can have a significant influence of the success of the project. If the study uses too few participants for a statistical technique, then the whole project is invalidated. New researchers often make the mistake of thinking people are keen to take part in research, but this is not the case. In the current climate of businesses requesting feedback on purchases and services, buyers are frequently asked to provide reviews and fill in questionnaires. Participating in research can be tedious. So, it is perhaps a good idea to think nobody is interested in the research and to think of ways to attract participants. An added constraint in terms of recruiting participants is the requirement for informed consent. From an ethical standpoint the researcher needs permission to participate in the research from all the participants. Despite these constraints there are some strategies that can be used to get the sample size required. These are addressed here.

7.1.1 Using fellow students

Strictly speaking this strategy can influence the outcomes of the research because the participants may have too many similarities, but it is still widely used and considered acceptable for a master's dissertation. Because every student needs to complete a dissertation on the master's programme, fellow students will understand the difficulty of recruiting participants and are more likely to volunteer to take part. This strategy depends upon the topic of the research being relevant; that is, the research must be about postgraduate TESOL/applied linguistics students.

Some students use their friends as a starting point, for example, Chinese postgraduate students at Tyne University. Using friends as participants can be problematic because they may provide the responses they think researcher wants rather than reveal their true feelings. However, using a snowball technique, which uses friends to introduce participants, is quite acceptable.

7.1.2 Using participants from home institution

Most master's TESOL/applied linguistics students have educational links prior to their studies. They may already have a job at a school or university, or they may have just completed their undergraduate studies and thus have links to their university. Some students decide to use this setting to recruit participants as they have an established relationship with the staff and students. Some students, particularly part-time students who work, have more time to complete their dissertation and may conduct action research with their own class over a period of time.

7.1.3 Using students from the university language centre

Most universities have English language centres or programmes that help students with English both prior to their studies (pre-sessional) and during their studies (in-sessional). This is an excellent place to recruit participants. The centre may be very keen to take part in research, as many of the students studying English will need to conduct master's research themselves during their academic studies. Promising to share the results of the research with staff and students at the centre is a further incentive for the language centre to participate in the research. However, permission from the centre's management must be sought prior to collecting data from these students if the topic is related to learning experiences in the centre.

7.1.4 Using intact classes

Some research projects rely upon using intact classes, perhaps it is an action research project or a quasi- experimental study. This is a relatively easy way of recruiting participants, as the data collection happens with a large group and people are inclined to take part. However, as voluntary participation in the research is essential, provision needs to be made for those who do not want to take part, for example, by providing an alternative activity or allowing those participants to be absent for the period of the data collection. This can pose problems if the project involves fee paying students, who may perceive the research project deters from their study goals. Table 7.1 shows some master's research projects and the sources of participants. Some of these examples use texts as data sources rather than recruiting participants.

TABLE 7.1 Examples of sources of participants in master's research projects

Title of dissertation	*Source of data*
Investigating spelling errors of Kurd EFL learners in the eighth year of basic school (Awder, UD)	Used sample from school where participant worked in home country.
An investigation of differences in the levels and types of writing anxiety experienced by Chinese postgraduates in the UK and China (Xu, 2013)	This study used a sample from the student's home university and from the current university.
Perspectives of EAP: Students' perspectives of pre-sessional English courses at Newcastle University English Language Centre (Cardiff, 2015)	This study used students at the English language centre attached to the university.
Teachers' feedback as a space for learning (Jiang, 2017)	This dissertation was based on an analysis of existing classroom videos used on a teacher training course.
Using critical discourse analysis to raise critical language awareness in Japanese medical students: An exploratory action research project (Marsh, 2011)	This dissertation analysed published medical related pamphlets and used these in an action research project with the researcher's class.
Newspaper discourses on Andy Murray's performance at Wimbledon: A contrastive corpus driven investigation of successful and unsuccessful tennis match reports (Dickson, 2015)	This study used published newspaper reports for analysis.

TASK 7.1

What do you think are the advantages and disadvantages of using the following participants?

Fellow master's students
University students from other departments
Participants from home institution
Students from university language centre
Intact classes

7.2 Recruiting participants

Once the target sample has been chosen potential participants need to be invited to take part in the study. There are several methods of recruiting participants. The easiest way is to ask acquaintances and friends, for example, fellow students, face-to-face. As mentioned previously this can also utilise the snowballing effect. This means that an initial group of participants is recruited, and they in turn suggest other participants, perhaps their fellow students.

Another popular way to recruit participants is to approach classes of students in person and ask them to take part; this needs to be done with permission from the class teacher. Usually the researcher would go to these classes either at the beginning or end of the session and explain the research, answer questions and then distribute the participant information sheets and consent forms. The actual data collection session could take place at a later date. An example of this procedure in a questionnaire study would be as follows: The researcher goes to the class, explains the research and the nature of participation and hands out information sheets, consent forms and also the study questionnaire. The researcher then returns to the next session of the class to collect the completed forms and questionnaire. It usually may take more than one return visit to the class to collect these, as participants may forget to return the forms.

Collecting data face-to-face is always more likely to get responses than research relying solely on online methods. However, face-to-face contact is not always possible, so in some circumstances an alternative is to put up flyers in prominent places to attract participants. Figure 7.1 shows an example of a template for recruiting participants. One technique used to assist recruitment is to include tear off contact details and/or a quick response (QR) code that can be scanned with a mobile phone. Similarly, potential participants can be contacted by email or social media such as Facebook. It should be noted that some universities and departments do not allow student access to email lists. Some studies offer an incentive to participate, perhaps a lucky draw with a gift voucher as the prize. This needs to be cleared by the ethics committee, as some rewards may be viewed as coercion. Figure 7.1 presents a template than can be used to invite participants to take part in a research project.

TASK 7.2

What data will you use for your study?
Where will your sample come from?
How will you recruit your participants?

At the proposal stage most students will need to have submitted an ethics application. The central notion of this is that students participate voluntarily and are fully informed of the research and its implications for them. Usually a student information sheet is drawn up. The department may have a template that can be used. Table 7.2 shows the areas of focus required in a participant information form with an example of a study.

7.3 Modes of data collection

Following are some of the main types of data collection in master's projects. Some studies will use multiple methods.

Official University Headed Paper/logo

Department of *(............)* University ....

PARTICIPANTS NEEDED FOR RESEARCH IN *(specify topic/area)*

I am looking for volunteers to take part in a study of *(enter topic and short description)*.

What is involved:

As a participant in this study, you would be asked to *(describe what participant will be asked to do, eg interview, online questionnaire,. . .)*.

Your participation would involve *(enter number, sessions and time needed for each).*

In appreciation for your time, you will receive *(insert details of any financial or other remuneration if any).*

Who is conducting the research:

(insert your name, under the supervision of, supervisor's name and department)

How to participate:

For more information about this study, or to volunteer for this study, please contact:
*(insert your name)*at 071...... or
email: *(use your university email) or weblink to survey*

FIGURE 7.1 Participant recruitment template

TABLE 7.2 Guidelines for producing a participant information sheet

Structure	*Example*
Title of the research and invitation	You are invited to take part in a research study 'MA TESOL students self-efficacy beliefs'. Before agreeing to take part in the study please read the following information carefully.
Researcher	The study is being conducted by Sarah Lee as part of a MA TESOL degree under the supervision of Lindy Woodrow.
Purpose of the study	The study explores the self-efficacy beliefs of MA TESOL students at the Tyne University and how these beliefs relate to past experience in teaching and their experiences on the MA course.

(*Continued*)

TABLE 7.2 (Continued)

Structure	*Example*
Why participant has been invited to take part	You have been invited to take part because you are currently enrolled on the MA TESOL at the Tyne University.
What participation involves	If you agree to take part in this study, you will be invited to complete a questionnaire sent via email and a face-to-face interview. The questionnaire will take approximately 10 minutes and the interview approximately 20 minutes. The interview will be held in the Department of Language and Linguistics at the Tyne University.
Finding out about the results	A report about the results of the study will be sent to you upon completion of the research.
Possible benefits of the study	The study is of value to future MA TESOL students at the Tyne University because it can inform course designers of students' beliefs and the influence of professional experience on the choice of modules and materials.
Withdrawing from the study	Participation in this study is entirely voluntary. You are under no obligation to participate. You can withdraw from the study at any point without affecting your relationship with the Tyne University. If you do this your data will be erased and your information will not be used in the study.
Assurance of confidentiality	All aspects of the study are confidential, and your identity will be known to only the researchers. If a report about the study is submitted for publication, individual participants will not be identifiable.
	All data will be kept as password protected computer files on the researcher's computer for three years and then erased.
Further information and contact details	If you have any questions or concerns about this study, please contact me via email. sarah.lee@tyne.ac.uk
Ethics approval	This study has been reviewed and approved by the Department of Language and Linguistics at the Tyne University on 9 May 2019.
Signature	Sarah Lee

7.3.1 Textual data

Using purely textual data is quite common on master's degree projects. The term 'textual data' refers to written or spoken texts. These may be printed texts, for example, newspaper articles or course-books. They may be spoken texts, for example, radio interviews or listening comprehension transcripts. Using existing textual data is usually easier than recruiting participants to provide data and can be useful in settings where the ethics approval procedure is complex and time consuming. However, the student must check whether ethics approval is necessary, and the copyright requirements of the text also need to be checked to see whether permission to use the text is required. Using textual data requires expertise in computing

TABLE 7.3 Examples of text-based research projects

Project	*Example*	*Explanation*
Course -book analysis Materials analysis	Vocabulary learning opportunities in a commercial ELT course-book (Matsuoka, 2009)	Examining the vocabulary demands of a popular EFL textbook and comparing this to the activities.
Establishing corpus	The technical vocabulary of newspapers (Zhu, 2017)	Constructed a corpus of 7 million words based on articles in a newspaper.
Analysis of test scripts	Academic vocabulary at the word and formula level: An examination of test taker discourse (Ohlrogge, 2009)	Analyses an entire cohort of scripts produced for formal English tests from the perspective of vocabulary.
Linguistic analysis of texts	Newspaper discourses on Andy Murray's performance at Wimbledon: A contrastive corpus driven investigation of successful and unsuccessful tennis match reports (Dickson, 2015)	Examined match reports from number of newspapers to discern attitude.
Linguistic analysis	Text complexity in graded readers: A systemic functional look (Newnham, 2013)	Uses SFL framework to analyse and compare range of graded readers used in EFL classrooms.
Online analysis	How universities in China introduce themselves in Chinese and English on the Internet: A contrastive genre study (Tu, 2010)	Genre analysis compares information about university details published online in English and Chinese.

and analysis, for example, generating corpora of texts or vocabulary and using the appropriate analytical software. Table 7.3 shows some examples of dissertations that use textual data. Chapter 16 shows an abstract of a study based on existing textual data (Matsuoka, 2009).

7.3.2 Questionnaire data

Collecting data using a questionnaire is one of the most common ways of collecting data. While a questionnaire can be either qualitative, with open ended questions, or quantitative, with closed questions, or a combination of both, as a research tool it is most commonly quantitative. Typically, participants are required to fill in a quantifiable questionnaire. This data is then input into an analytical programme that facilitates analysis, such as SPSS. Questionnaires can be given to groups of participants face-to-face – for example, giving a questionnaire to classes of students – or administered electronically via email. Two examples of questionnaires are a can-do scale, where respondents provide answers based on their belief they are able to complete a given action on a scale of one to ten; and a five-point Likert scale, which provides a series of possible answers to a question.

Many projects use an existing questionnaire. This is a good idea because the study will usually have reliability data, will usually generate the expected data and because questionnaires can be hard to produce. One of the main issues in collecting data using a student designed questionnaire is clarity. The participants must have a comprehensive idea of what is required so, the instructions for answering the questions need to be very clear. These instructions may be in the participant information sheet if this is presented at the same time, but it is a good idea to include directions in the questionnaire itself. Figures 7.2 and 7.3 give examples of the types of questions and instructions from a study into personal factors that influence academic success

Part B: Self-efficacy (Items 5–13)

Directions: Indicate (X) the level of confidence that indicates how sure you are that you can do the study tasks on your English programme.

0% sure I can do	25% sure I can do	50% sure I can do	75% sure I can do	90% sure I can do	100% sure I can do

No.	Your confidence	0%	25%	50%	75%	90%	100%
5.	Pass this programme						
6.	Get a high grade for English						
7.	Get a high grade for my subjects						
8.	Read and understand academic material, such as text books and articles in English						
9.	Write a data commentary academic essay						
10.	Write an argument essay						
11.	Write a long essay						
12.	Present a group project						
13.	Take part in class discussion						

FIGURE 7.2 Example of a can-do scale with directions

Part D: Academic difficulty (Items 25-34)

Directions: Indicate (X) how much difficulty you have with each of these in your current programme of study using the following 1 to 5 scale.

No difficulty	Slight difficulty	Moderate difficulty	Great difficulty	Extreme difficulty
1	2	3	4	5

No.	**Difficulty**	**1**	**2**	**3**	**4**	**5**
25.	Making friends with local (Australian) students					
26.	Making friends with students from other countries					
27.	Making friends with students from your country					
28.	Making yourself understood when speaking English					
29.	Making yourself understood when writing English					
30.	Understanding what you read in texts					
31.	Understanding lectures					
32.	Understanding tutorial discussions					
33.	Participating in tutorial discussions					
34.	Understanding what is required of you in assignments					

FIGURE 7.3 Example of a five-point Likert scale with directions

Source: Phakiti, Woodrow, and Hirsh (2013)

of students on a foundation programme. If the questionnaire is student designed, it should be piloted to ensure all the items work and that the directions are clear. Ideally the questionnaire should be piloted with a group of similar but not the same participants. Realistically this is often not possible. A compromise is to test the questionnaire on fellow students or friends who can report on any obvious errors.

The use of a language other than English in data collection is very common in TESOL and applied linguistics research. It is perfectly acceptable to produce the participant information sheet, consent form and data collection tools in a language other than English. However, the translation of these to be provided and this needs to be validated by an expert, for example, a translator or student of translation in the language area. A lot of students will use their fellow students to do this.

TABLE 7.4 Methods of administering questionnaires

Method	*Advantages*	*Disadvantages*
Mail	Can produce attractive questionnaire with colours May get additional data beyond items Easy to maintain anonymity Clear to read	Expensive: paper, printing and posting Low response rate Needs a lot of time to wait for responses Time consuming to enter data into analytical software
Email	Easy to send via email lists Cheap Quick Possible to access large sample	Poor response rate Need to design form that can be filled electronically Need a system for anonymity
Online software	Easy to use template to design questionnaire Can be sent to large sample Easy to complete Data can be electronically exported to analytical programme	Need to learn how to use survey programme Need to choose most appropriate software Need to take steps for anonymity Survey software template may be inflexible May need to pay for software
Face-to-face	High response rate, especially with intact classes	Need to attend in person Not appropriate for participants who live a long way from the research site

As mentioned, questionnaires can be administered in different ways, for example, via mail, email, online or face-to face. Each method has its advantages and disadvantages. Table 7.4 presents these methods and lists the advantages and disadvantages of each method.

Using online methods of collecting data are very popular; one example of such a tool is Survey Monkey. Students should check with their department to see if they have free access to software of this type. For a list of programmes that can be used to collect data see https://mopinion.com/top-21-best-online-survey-software-and-questionnaire-tools-an-overview/ (accessed 29 April, 2019).

7.3.3 Interviews

Another very common method of collecting data is by conducting interviews. Like questionnaires, interviews can be either quantitative or qualitative, or a combination of both, but tend to be qualitative. Qualitative interviews can offer insights into issues that questionnaires cannot access because of the restrictions of a numerical scale. Interviews may be of three types: structured, unstructured and semi-structured. Structured interviews involve asking the participants the same questions without deviation. They provide data similar to questionnaires and may be analysed quantitatively. Unstructured interviews on the other hand vary between individuals and provide a vast amount of data that needs to be sifted and analysed qualitatively. Semi-structured interviews represent a compromise. These interviews have structure but include general open ended questions that offer the opportunity for deeper probing of specific area of interest.

Like questionnaires, interviews can be conducted in different modes. The most common is the face-to-face interview. However, this is not always possible, particularly in master's projects where time and funding is limited. Video interviews often work well using programmes such as FaceTime or Skype. In some instances, even this type of interview is not possible. Although not ideal, electronic interviews using email or chat software such as 'messenger', 'we chat' or 'what's app' may be used.

The procedure for interviews is similar to other data collection types. First, the participant information sheets need to be distributed and the participants sign the consent form. For interviews, a suitable a venue for needs to be found; ideally, this would be an office or quiet place in the university. The venue needs to be in a neutral space; that is, not in a home environment as this is not usually acceptable in terms of ethics approval. Noisy places such as a café should be avoided, as these can be very distracting for both the interviewer and interviewee. Table 7.5 presents some advice for conducting interviews that can help to get the most information from the interviewee.

TABLE 7.5 Advice for interviewing

Do's	*Don'ts*
Test the interview on a colleague first.	
Find a quiet place for the interview.	Avoid places that are noisy and too public.
Check the recording devices before every interview.	Do not rush the participant.
Have spare batteries or a spare recording device.	Do not draw attention to the equipment by checking it too much during the interview.
Introduce yourself at the beginning of the interview.	Do not talk too much.
Introduce the purpose of the interview.	Do not appear judgemental.
Inform the participant the interview will be recorded.	Do not allow participant to go off topic too much.
Use a pleasant and encouraging facial expression.	Avoid using technical language that participant may not understand.
Put participant at ease with conversational questions at the beginning of the interview.	Be wary about taking notes too enthusiastically based on a given response.
Allow participant to reach end of explanation.	Do not interrupt.
Use open ended questions.	Avoid yes/no questions.
Use strategies to get extended answers such as 'hmmm', 'that's interesting', 'Tell me more'.	

TABLE 7.6 Example of general interview question and prompts

Research question: What factors contribute to NNESTS with prior teaching experience taking the decision to enrol on Initial Teacher training Courses (ITC)?

Initial question to ask	*Potential prompts for clarification, elicitation, details, summary etc*
Could you tell me about why you decided to enrol on the course and how it fitted into your career path?	**Prompts for more reasons:** Any other reasons? **Career related reasons:** Did you anticipate a change in career direction? Did you expect to get an advantage in the job market? At that time, where did you expect to teach after the course? **General learning:** What did you expect to learn from the course? **Methodology:** How important was the methodology? **Comparing reasons:** Which was the most important reason? Why?

Source: Anderson (2016)

Prior to interviews it is usual to draft an interview guide that lists the main interview questions and further probes based on this. It is a sensible idea to trial the interview with a critical friend to ensure that the questions provide the information sought and are comprehensible. Table 7.6 presents an example of a research question, the main interview question and probes based on these.

Most interviews are audio-recorded and then transcribed. The transcription is then analysed qualitatively. It is a good idea to leave the analysis until all the data has been collected and transcribed. Even though the interview is recorded it is wise to take notes during the interview just in case audio data is lost. Soon after the interview, the recording together with the notes should be reviewed and transcribed, if possible, while still fresh in the mind. This makes the thinking though of themes and categories much easier as the researcher becomes immersed in the data. The interview data will need to be gone through several times to find patterns and reach conclusions about the data.

7.4 Unforeseen circumstances

In every research project there are always some unexpected events. As far as possible, researchers should try and predict problems when they are at the design and data collection stages, but of course this is not always possible. Following are some of the more common problems encountered in data collection.

7.4.1 Not getting permission to access participants

TESOL and applied linguistics researchers often use language teaching institutions as research sites. To gain access to these participants it is necessary to get permission from the manager of the institution. Sometimes this is not given, or access is given based on strict conditions, such as not going into classes to recruit participants. If this is the case it may be necessary to relocate the research site or recruit participants independently from the research site, for example, placing recruitment advertisements in the student café.

7.4.2 Participants do not respond

This is probably the most common problem with conducting master's research. The time available for data collection is very limited and novice researchers tend to think everyone is very interested in their project. The best strategies to recruit participants are listed in 7.1. Sometimes participants do not respond or, worse, promise to take part and then do not turn up. The best way to deal with this problem is to recruit more participants than are required. Alternatively, it may be necessary to reschedule sessions or think of other strategies. For example, if a participant cannot make an interview they may be prepared to complete a virtual interview or email interview.

7.4.3 Insufficient or incorrect materials

It is important to over-estimate the amount of materials needed. Sometimes participants take more than one questionnaire; perhaps they take one for their friend, or they may make a mistake and need another. Participants may unintentionally walk off with pens, pencils and erasers. It is always a good idea to locate the nearest photocopier in case additional photocopies are needed.

7.4.4 Research site is inadequate

It may be that the site chosen for data collection is too noisy or busy for the chosen data collection method. The sessions would then have to be relocated or rescheduled. In most cases this can be avoided by visiting the research site prior to data collection; however, some thought should be paid to this, with perhaps an alternative data collection method or research setting in mind.

7.4.5 Participants turn up late

Researchers need to be prepared to be flexible in the scheduling of sessions so that they can maximise the data collected with the minimum of annoyance to the participants.

7.4.6 Recording device fails

Researchers should ensure they have sufficient back up, such as an additional recording device and/or a back-up power supply. They also should have materials to take notes manually should all else fail.

TASK 7.3 Suggest how you could deal with the following problems with data collection the data collection procedure.

1. The Director of Studies of the local language centre will not give you permission to recruit participants for your research project directly.
2. Three out of your intact class group have not given permission to be videoed in class.
3. Your sample of participants is not available until three weeks before your dissertation is due.
4. Too few participants have returned your questionnaire. For example, you need at least 100 for your statistical analysis and you only have 75.
5. You find your questionnaire has been copied with the page numbers in the wrong order.
6. Two out of your five interview participants do not turn up for their interview.

Summary

This chapter has focused on the procedure of data collection. Two major methods of data collection were reviewed: questionnaires and interviews. These were chosen because they are very common in master's level research. Advice is given for this stage of the research project and how to solve possible problems with data collection.

Common mistakes in the procedure of data collection

- Leaving the organisation of the data collection too late (participants may have left school/university)
- Not getting permission to conduct research
- Not getting enough participants
- Having ambiguous questions in data collection resulting in unanalysable data
- Fabricating responses
- Not recording data accurately during session (notes/audio or video recording)

FAQs

1 *Can I collect data before I have my proposal or ethics application approved?*

Although the time for a master's research project may be very tight, researchers must not collect data without getting ethics and proposal approval. Sometimes the student may not be aware of potential problems or threats to the ethical execution of research, so this needs to be scrutinized before any data is collected.

2 *How many participants do I need?*
The number of participants needed for a project depends on the research approach. So in a case study, for example, it may be possible to use only three or four participants, while in a quantitative project more than 100 may be needed. The minimum number of participants for data collection and analysis can be found by consulting the research methods literature. For quantitative research most inferential analyses will include a minimum number in the test assumptions.

3 *I don't have enough participants; can I get my friends to take part to make up the numbers?*
No. The sample needs to be chosen based on common characteristics or pre-determined features. It is unlikely friends would have these characteristics. Using this method would skew the data and lead to unreliable results. If insufficient participants are available, then alternatives need to be found by using different data collection procedures, widening the pool of possible participants or changing the data analysis method.

4 *Can I get another person to collect my data?*
This depends upon department regulations. Many departments are happy for students to get friends or colleagues to collect data on their behalf. This is useful if the data collection occurs off-shore, as it would be very expensive and time-consuming for the student to travel to the research site.

5 *Do I have to get my participants to sign a consent form?*
Yes. Every participant needs to sign a consent form. In the case of participants under 16 parental consent is also needed. The consent forms need to be collected and stored in a safe location, for example, a password protected folder on the student's computer.

6 *Do I submit all my consent forms with the dissertation?*
Usually departments do not require students to submit their consent forms. However, these need to be able to be accessed in case of queries about the research.

Further reading

Blaxter, Hughes, and Tight (2010) have a good chapter on managing a research project (Chapter 5) and have a chapter devoted to collecting data (Chapter 7). Bell and Water's (2018) book has several chapters on the process of collecting data, including using the internet and social media.

References

Anderson, J. (2016). *A qualitative study into the role of initial teacher training courses in the professional development of experienced non-native speaker teacher.* (Master's Dissertation), Kings College, London.

Awder, R. A. (n.d.). *Investigating spelling errors of Kurd EFL learners in the eighth year of basic school.* (Master's Dissertation), Newcastle University.

Bell, J., & Waters, S. (2018). *Doing your research project: Advice for first time researchers* (7th ed.). London: Open University Press.

Blaxter, L., Hughes, C., & Tight, M. (2010). *How to research* (4th ed.). London: Open University Press.

Cardiff, P. (2015). *Perspectives of EAP: Students' perspectives of pre-sessional English courses at Newcastle University English Language Centre.* (Master's Dissertation), Newcastle University.

Dickson, B. (2015). *Newspaper discourses on Andy Murray's performance at Wimbledon: A contrastive corpus driven investigation of successful and unsuccessful tennis match reports.* (Master's dissertation), University of Stirling. Retrieved from https://englishagenda.britishcouncil.org/sites/default/files/attachments/dissertation_for_publication_stirling_university.pdf (Accessed 30 April, 2019)

Jiang, Y. (2017). *Teachers' feedback as a space for learning.* (Master's Dissertation), Newcastle University.

Marsh, D. (2011). *Using critical discourse analysis to raise critical language awareness in Japanese medical students: An exploratory action research project.* (Master's Dissertation), University of Birmingham. Retrieved from http://asian-efl-journal.com/wp-content/uploads/mgm/downloads/64517300.pdf (Accessed 30 April, 2019).

Matsuoka, W. E. (2009). *Vocabulary learning opportunities in a commercial ELT coursebook.* (Master's Dissertation), University of Sydney.

Newnham, S.-A. (2013). *Text complexity in graded readers: A systemic functional look.* (Master's Dissertation), Marshal University. Retrieved from https://mds.marshall.edu/etd/498/ (Accessed 30 April, 2019)

Ohlrogge, A. C. (2009). *Academic vocabulary at the word and formula level: An examination of test-taker discourse.* (Master's Dissertation), Michigan State University.

Phakiti, A., Woodrow, L., & Hirsh, D. (2013). It's not only English: Effects of other individual factors on English language learning and academic learning of ESL International students in Australia. *Journal of Research in International Education, 12*(3), 239–258.

Tu, W. (2010). *How universities in China introduce themselves in Chinese and English on the internet: A contrastive genre study.* (Master's Dissertation), University of Sydney.

Xu, J. (2013). *An investigation of differences in the levels and types of writing anxiety experienced by Chinese postgraduates in the UK and China.* (Master's Dissertation), Newcastle University.

Zhu, J. (2017). *The technical vocabulary of newspapers.* (Master's Dissertation), Western University. Retrieved from https://ir.lib.uwo.ca/etd/4872/ (Accessed 30 April, 2019)

Data Collection software

Survey Monkey www.surveymonkey.com/
Google Forms www.google.co.uk/forms/about/

8

DATA ANALYSIS

This chapter is about the main methods of data analysis used for small scale research projects. It reflects the stages of data analysis from first impressions to final analyses. These include descriptive techniques and univariate statistical analysis for quantitative data and for qualitative data, coding and classifying data.

Most master's in TESOL and applied linguistics include a research methods course prior to designing the research project for the dissertation, so it's a good idea to go through the materials from this course prior to analysing data. However, the decisions about how the data are to be analysed should have been made at the research design phase and explained in the proposal. For an example of this see the sample proposal in Chapter 16.

Quantitative and qualitative analysis are different; quantitative analysis relies on the use of numbers, while qualitative analysis relies on the words and language; however, there can be a crossover between the two. Qualitative data is frequently analysed quantitatively by transforming language into numerical values – an example would be counting the number of times participants refer to a particular view. Similarly, not all questionnaires are quantitative; many include an open ended section eliciting views and comments in an extended form. These approaches are discussed in more detail in the following sections.

8.1 Keeping a research diary

Although the master's dissertation endeavour does not last for a long time, and the projects tend not to be very complex, it is a sensible idea to keep a research diary. A research diary is a day-to-day account of the progress and activities of the research project. It is a private document for the researcher only. It is useful because it keeps thoughts and ideas in one place and can be referred to during the research progress. The research diary should start at the beginning of the dissertation process, but is especially useful during the data collection and analysis stage. In these phases it is very easy to drown in data and become hopelessly muddled. If a daily record of activities is kept, this is much less likely.

In qualitative studies where the role of the researcher is an important part of the study and is discussed in detail in the dissertation, a research diary can facilitate reflexivity. Reflexivity refers to researcher assumptions, goals and thoughts that can influence the research outcome. Reflexivity is very important in action research, which usually seeks to improve pedagogy at a class level. Here is how one master's student referred to the importance of the diary (journal) in his dissertation: "The keeping of this journal enhanced my capacity to reflect upon both the students and my own practice, a crucial aspect of action research which informed the amendments made in future cycles" (Kelly, 2015).

The other big advantage of keeping a research diary is the opportunity for writing. Many students struggle with dissertation writing and leave the 'write-up' until toward the end of the study period; writing then becomes a great challenge. By keeping a diary, the writing process starts at the very beginning of the research process and the writing of the dissertation should be easier.

The research diary should be portable so that it can be added to or referred to on the move. It is also a good idea to do a weekly review of entries, so thoughts, ideas and references do not get lost. Cabraal (2013) writes about the advantages of keeping a research diary and how this can be useful in the different stages of research, from choosing a topic through writing the dissertation. Figure 8.1 presents a list of areas that can be covered in a research diary.

Reports on daily research activities

Progress

Thoughts

Ideas

Reports on activities, eg interviews

References

Questions

Notes from readings or seminars

Views and opinions

Problems you need to solve

FIGURE 8.1 What to include in a research diary

There is not a preferred format for a research diary. Some prefer an electronic blog style of diary, which is searchable, while others prefer a portable notebook. Table 8.1 presents an example of research diary entries during the analysis phase of the research.

TASK 8.1

Prepare a research diary.
What areas do you think are important to include in your study?
How will you record your activities?

TABLE 8.1 Example of a research diary from the analysis phase of research

Date	*Plan*	*Action*	*Comments/thoughts*
12 July	Enter questionnaire data into SSS	Made the codebook for the questionnaire variables (see document x)	This will be useful for my logical thinking!
		Entered data for first five questionnaires	Although only done five it will be easy to pick up tomorrow. Must read section on reliability analysis for questionnaire.
	More statistics reading	Read chapter one on screening data	Entering the data is more involved than I thought!
	Marie's seminar	Went to Marie's seminar Asked some questions	I wonder about the relationship between anxiety and classroom performance. Is this something I need to worry about?
	Check participants for interview	Heard from three more participants who agreed to be interviewed	Achieved my target sample of 7 interview participants. Feeling happy!
13 July	Screen data Look for missing values Use Pallant Chapter 2 as I code Arrange interviews, email participants, book room		

8.2 Preparing the data for analysis

Research can be messy, and it is easy to have vast amounts of data and get quite muddled. This leads to the need for time consuming repetition of data analysis tasks. The best way to avoid this is by being very organised as the data comes in. The research diary will help with this. As well as this, it is essential to be organised in terms of recording and labelling data. Figure 8.2 presents some organisational strategies that help can avoid problems with data.

In the following sections the preparation and analysis of quantitative and qualitative data are discussed.

8.3 Quantitative data

Usually quantitative analysis is facilitated by computer software. It is very unusual for analyses to be conducted by hand. There are many software packages that are available, for example, statistical package for the social sciences (SPSS). A list of these is presented at the end of this chapter.

Some statistics programmes are free – for example, R – but it is common for universities to provide students free access to software programmes for statistical analysis. The two most common programmes used to analyse data in TESOL and applied linguistics are Microsoft Office Excel and SPSS. Excel is a much simpler method of analysis to execute but much less sophisticated than SPSS. The decision of which software should depend upon the complexity of the intended analysis, the preference of academic department, the availability of software and supervisors' advice.

SPSS is a tailored statistical programme for the social sciences and is the most widely used in TESOL and applied linguistics quantitative research. In addition, there are many 'how to do it' books available for this programme, for example, Pallant (2016) and Field (2017).

In corpus analysis there are many types of software that can perform different functions. For a list see http://linguistlist.org/sp/SearchWRListing-action.cfm?subclassid=7223&SearchType=LF&WRTypeID=2 (accessed 8 May, 2019).

A good starting point for vocabulary analysis is Lawrence Anthony's home page, which provides a good introduction to analysis and links to software www.laurenceanthony.net (accessed 8 May, 2019). Again, as with quantitative analysis

Number and arrange questionnaires in a sequential pile.

Transcribe transcripts accurately.

Number and allocate participant labels/codes.

Label audio files labelled; make copies and store in multiple locations.

Colour-code files.

FIGURE 8.2 Strategies for organising data

mentioned previously, it is best to go with the software recommended and/or provided by the academic department.

8.3.1 Preparing the codebook

When using a quantitative analysis programme such as SPSS it is a very good idea to set out a codebook. Due to the restrictions of the analytical database systems it is not possible to enter a large amount of textual information about the variables and responses, so variables and responses need to be assigned numerical codes in order to analyse the data. These need to be recorded and explained in a codebook. The codebook is useful throughout the analytical process and can be referred to when analysing and interpreting data. In particular, it is useful to see what analysis has been conducted on which data set. During the analysis it is likely the original data set will be modified several times through the screening process and the removal of outliers.

Figure 8.3 shows an example of a questionnaire used to measure English speaking anxiety in classroom settings and in out-of-class settings. Table 8.2 presents an example of a codebook based on this questionnaire.

In the column **anxiety** fill in the circles according to how anxious you feel when you ***speak English*** in the following situations.

1	2	3	4	5
Not at all anxious	**Slightly anxious**	**Moderately anxious**	**Very anxious**	**Extremely anxious**

Situation	**Anxiety**				
1. The teacher asks me a question in English in class.	O 1	O 2	O 3	O 4	O 5
2. Speaking informally to my English teacher out of class.	O 1	O 2	O 3	O 4	O 5
3. Taking part in a group discussion in class.	O 1	O 2	O 3	O 4	O 5
4. Taking part in a role-play or dialogue in front of my class.	O 1	O 2	O 3	O 4	O 5
5. Giving an oral presentation to the rest of the class.	O 1	O 2	O 3	O 4	O 5
6. When asked to contribute to a formal discussion in class.	O 1	O 2	O 3	O 4	O 5
7. Talking to administrative staff of my language school in English.	O 1	O 2	O 3	O 4	O 5
8. Taking part in a conversation out of class with more than one ***native speaker*** of English.	O 1	O 2	O 3	O 4	O 5
9. Starting a conversation out of class with a friend or colleague who is a ***native speaker*** of English.	O 1	O 2	O 3	O 4	O 5
10. A lecturer/supervisor in my intended university faculty of study asks me a question in English.	O 1	O 2	O 3	O 4	O 5
11. Asking for advice in English from a lecturer/supervisor in my intended university faculty of study.	O 1	O 2	O 3	O 4	O 5
12 A ***native speaker*** I do not know asks me questions.	O 1	O 2	O 3	O 4	O 5

FIGURE 8.3 Example of a five-point Likert scale used to measure in-class and out-of-class anxiety

TABLE 8.2 Example of a codebook for an anxiety study based on the questionnaire in Figure 8.3

Variable name	*SPSS label*	*Coding instruction*
Identification number	ID	Identification number
Sex	Sex	1 = female 2 = male
Nationality	Level	1 = Chinese 2 = Japanese 3 = Thai 4 = Indonesian 5 = Vietnamese
Class	Class	1 = elem 2 = int1 3 = int2 4 = int3 5 = adv
Q1 Answer teacher question	ANX1	Fill in: 1 = Not at all anxious 2 = Slightly anxious 3 = Moderately anxious 4 = Very anxious 5 = Extremely anxious
Q2 Speaking teacher informal	ANX2	
Q3 Group discussion	ANX3	
Q4 Role play class	ANX4	
Q5 Oral presentation	ANX5	
Q6 Formal discussion	ANX6	
Q7 Admin staff	ANX7	
Q8 Native speaker conversation	ANX8	
Q9 Start conversation native speaker	ANX9	
Q10 Answer question supervisor	ANX10	
Q11 Get advice supervisor	ANX11	
Q12 Unknown native speaker	ANX12	

A codebook can be done by hand or on the computer; it can also be created within the SPSS programme itself. For further guidance on creating a codebook within SPSS see https://libguides.library.kent.edu/SPSS/Codebooks (accessed 8 May, 2019).

TASK 8.2

Generate a codebook for your quantitative data analysis based on Table 8.2.

8.3.2 Screening the data

After drawing up a codebook the data needs to be entered into the data base, for example, SPSS. Inevitably, mistakes happen when entering numerical data, so the first step before any analysis is to screen the data for errors. An example of an error is scores that are outside the possible range; for example, if the data for sex is 1= males and 2 = females there should be no values exceeding 2. For a five-point Likert scale there should be no values that exceed five. Errors can be found and corrected manually by sorting the file or by using the maximum/minimum facility available within the descriptive tab in SPSS. The data should also be examined for missing data. If a variable has a large number of missing values – that is, questions that have not been answered – the researcher needs to explain this. It may be that the question was inappropriate, or it may be an entry problem. This needs to be accounted for and explained.

8.3.3 Describing the data

After inputting the data and screening for errors and outliers, the next step is the analysis. Usually this begins with describing the data by producing what are referred to as 'descriptives'. These results can give the researcher deep insights into the data, and it is a necessary step in all quantitative analysis. Some studies, particularly those that combine qualitative and quantitative methods, may not go beyond a descriptive analysis. Descriptives are calculated by counting the responses and examining the frequency of answers, referred to as 'frequencies'. The usual descriptive information presented in a study are the mean, standard deviation, percentages and numbers. Tables 8.3, 8.4, 8.5 and 8.6 show some examples of the most common descriptive statistics.

TABLE 8.3 Descriptive statistics in a quantitative study

Descriptive	*Explanation*
Frequencies	Number of responses
Range	Range of scores for different options
Percentages and numbers	Percentages of whole group number of participants
Mean	The average of the scores
Median	The middle score
Mode	The most commonly occurring score
Standard deviation	The difference of the scores from the mean

TABLE 8.4 Example of descriptive statistics reporting number and percentage

Reported stressor	*N*	*%*
Giving an oral presentation	20	44
Speaking in English to native speakers	18	42.7

TABLE 8.5 Example of descriptive statistics using range

Item	*Min*	*Max*	*Mean*	*SD*
Self-efficacy in academic achievements	25.00	100.00	77.99	14.44
Self-efficacy in reading and writing	18.75	100.00	76.61	14.84
Self-efficacy in oral discussion	16.67	100.00	83.92	13.16

TABLE 8.6 Example of mean (M) and standard deviation (SD)

In-class anxiety	*M*	*SD*
Giving an oral presentation	2.93	1.09
Role-play in front of class	2.73	1.09

8.3.4 Further analysis

After the data has been screened, missing values dealt with and descriptive statistics generated, the main analysis can begin. Figure 8.4 outlines the typical steps in a quantitative study. The choice of analysis depends upon the research questions and the nature of the data. Table 8.7 shows the major statistical analyses used in master's research projects. When using inferential statistics it is important that the assumptions of the test are considered. This is particularly important when the sample is not random and non-parametric tests may need to be used instead. Another assumption that is common is that the data are normally distributed. If this is not the case then a non-parametric equivalent should be chosen. Table 8.8 shows the major parametric tests and their non-parametric equivalents. Some statistical tests have quite detailed assumptions, so these should be checked. Pallant (2016) includes these assumptions for most of the tests master's students are likely to use.

Assign codes to variables

Enter data into database

Screen data for errors, missing values and outliers

Conduct descriptive analysis

Generate graphics if required

Address assumptions of parametric tests–for example, normal distribution of scores

If assumptions violated choose non-parametric equivalent

Conduct inferential analysis

FIGURE 8.4 Stages in quantitative analysis

TABLE 8.7 Typical statistical analyses in master's research studies

Analysis	*Use*	*Example research question*
t-test – independent samples	Identifies differences between two groups	Is there a difference between class A and class B in terms of English test performance?
t-test – repeated measures	Identifies differences between time one and time two of the same group	Have the English test scores of class A improved from time one to time two?
ANOVA – independent measures	Used to identify difference between more than two groups	Is there a difference between class A, class B and class C in terms of English test performance?
ANOVA – repeated measures	Compares scores of one group on different occasions	Have the scores of class A improved from time one, time two and time three?
Regression Multiple regression = multiple variables	Predicting one or more variables on one or more other variables	

(*Continued*)

TABLE 8.7 (Continued)

Analysis	*Use*	*Example research question*
Linear regression	Two variables	Do IELTS scores predict L2 postgraduate MA university students' academic performance?
Multiple regression	More than two variables	Do specialist vocabulary knowledge and content knowledge predict academic performance?
Correlation	Identifies a relationship between two variables	Is there a relationship between English test writing and speaking scores?
Chi-square	Identifies a relationship between two categorical variables	Do international and local student differ in their choice of academic modules on MA TESOL?
Factor analysis	Examines underlying structure of related variables, reduces large number of variables or items to a smaller group	Is there evidence for the hypothesised model of language learning strategies

TABLE 8.8 Non-parametric equivalents to parametric tests

Parametric test	*Non- parametric equivalent*
Independent samples t-test	Mann-Whitney
Repeated measures t-test	Wilcoxon signed-ranks test
One-way independent measures ANOVA	Kruskal-Wallis
One-way repeated measures ANOVA	Friedman's ANOVA
Pearson correlation coefficient	Spearman's rho

TASK 8.3

Which descriptive statistics will you generate for your study?
What statistical analysis will you conduct in your study?
What are the assumptions of the analyses?

8.4 Qualitative data

8.4.1 Interviews and documents

The data used in qualitative analysis is usually in document form. This may be text or a transcription of an interview, a class observation or may include visuals. Interviewing is a widely used method of collecting data in master's research projects in

TESOL and applied linguistics. Usually the researcher records the interview and then transcribes the recording. The analysis is then conducted on the written text. It should be remembered that transcribing can take a very long time; it can take three hours for one hour of an interview. Group interviews, focus groups and class observation are particularly difficult to transcribe, as interlocutors tend to talk over the top of each other.

The first step in transcribing is to decide the level of detail required in the transcription. If the study focuses on discourse analysis, the transcription framework is likely to be quite detailed reflecting pauses, overlaps and hesitations. The analysis hopes to uncover information that is not immediately evident in a transcript of an oral interaction. However, the focus in many interviews is on the information contained in the answers, for example, "How do you motivate your students?" In this case a simple verbatim transcription is all that is required. It is recommended that all the interviews are transcribed before starting the analysis to maintain consistency in the analysis.

Like quantitative analysis, the procedure goes through stages. These stages are shown in Figure 8.5.

Transcribe audio file/collect documents.

Label and catalogue files/documents.

Annotate transcription/documents using field notes and initial thoughts.

Identify major themes in data.

Identify codes.

Devise analytical framework of codes to be used.

Code data.

Display coding.

Interpret the data.

FIGURE 8.5 Stages in analysis in a qualitative study

With interview data it is important to keep multiple copies of the original recording and transcription. Losing data can be catastrophic for a research project, and, as with quantitative analysis, it is very easy to get into a muddle with multiple copies of transcriptions and analyses at different stages of the analysis, so these need to be carefully labelled and stored.

8.4.2 Approaches to qualitative analysis

Denscombe (2017) refers to five common approaches to the qualitative analysis of talk and text. These are content analysis, grounded theory, discourse analysis, conversation analysis and narrative analysis.

Content analysis is a very common method of data analysis in master's dissertations. It refers to the analysis of data based on the words and phrases in the data that concern facts and opinions. This analysis is done using an analytical framework of categories that emerge from the data. Content analysis often involves the counting of responses; for example, "15 participants referred to a shortage of materials as an issue in language teaching".

Grounded theory aims to develop theory emerging from the data and focuses on the implications within the data set. The analysis is very detailed and should not be based on any preconceived notions or codes thus emphasising the meaning and interpretation of the data. The data is coded based on emerging themes in the data, which tend to be numerous so that subtleties are not lost.

Discourse analysis examines the words, sentences and linguistic features of text and context. There are a range of types of discourse analysis from the very detailed conversation analysis that analyses a fragment of discourse to genre analysis that focuses on features of entire texts.

Narrative analysis focuses on the social implications of text. The analysis is based on whole stories or texts that are deciphered to examine the symbolic significance of the story.

8.5 Getting help with research process

Getting help with the analysis of data is common in research projects, particularly large-scale funded projects; however, when a dissertation for assessment is involved the situation is more complicated. Students should always check with their supervisor that external help can be used. Institutions vary in the extent to which they will allow external help. It should be remembered that all external help should be referred to in the dissertation in the acknowledgements section.

It is not unusual, particularly with international students, to enlist the help of research assistants to collect data. For international students investigating issues in their home country it can be too time consuming and expensive to travel home to collect data. There may also be visa complications for these students upon their return. Using colleagues to distribute and supervise the completion of questionnaire is usually acceptable. However, conducting interviews, which requires more

TABLE 8.9 Acceptability of getting help with collecting and analysing data

Skill	*No*	*Maybe*	*Yes*
Developing questionnaire, using someone else's questionnaire			✓
Distributing questionnaires			✓
Videoing classrooms			✓
Conducting and recording structured interviews			✓
Conducting semi-structured or unstructured interviews	✓		
Transcribing interviews		✓	
Analysing transcripts	✓		
Entering data into database			✓
Conducting statistical analysis		✓	
Interpreting data	✓		

research skill, would usually not be allowed. Some students get help with statistical analysis; while this may be acceptable, it is certainly important that students understand the conceptual aspect of the statistical analysis even if they do not do the data entry and computer-based analysis. Table 8.9 presents the acceptability of getting help with the data collection and analysis process.

If possible, it is a good idea for the student to collect and analyse the data without help, as this promotes a deeper connection with the data. For example, transcribing interview data may be viewed as the first step in analysis.

TASK 8.4

What is your university's policy on getting help with master's research projects? Consider the areas listed in Table 8.9.

Summary

This chapter has discussed the analysis phase of master's research. The choice of analytical methods should have been finalised at the proposal stage, and information about these can be found in Chapters 4 and 5. This chapter stressed the importance of keeping a research diary and provided a template for this purpose. Both quantitative and qualitative analyses were outlined with examples. Finally, areas where external help may be sought were suggested.

Common mistakes in data analysis

- Not leaving enough time to conduct analysis thoroughly
- Getting data files mixed up through lack of labelling

- Presenting raw data without analysis
- Not mastering the analytical techniques
- Not taking into account the assumptions of statistical tests
- Not having a sound analytical framework for qualitative analysis

FAQs

1 *Do I have to learn SPSS for my quantitative data analysis?*
This depends upon the type of analyses needed. If the analyses are purely descriptive, then it is better to use Excel, as this programme is easier to learn. If the study involves inferential tests such as correlations or t-tests, then it is better to use SPSS, as it is more powerful.

2 *Can I pay someone to do my data transcription and my data analysis?*
It is better to do this yourself, as it helps with the understanding of the data. In qualitative studies it is possible to pay someone to transcribe data, but the coding and the analysis of this should be done by you. In quantitative studies it may be acceptable to have the statistical analysis done by someone else (see Table 8.9).

3 *Will my supervisor help me with the analysis?*
Usually no. Data analysis is very time consuming, so it is unlikely your supervisor will be able to go through all of the analysis with you.

4 *My analysis does not produce the results I expected. What should I do?*
The first thing to do is to check the input of data and the screening process to check whether there are any mistakes. Then repeat the analysis. Mistakes in data entry can completely reverse the results of a study. If the results are the same, then go back to the literature to find a possible explanation.

5 *How long will it take to transcribe my interviews?*
This very much depends upon the depth of transcription. A simple verbatim transcription can take as little as twice the length of the interview, but a detailed transcription can take many hours. It is best to have a trial run with a friend before collecting the final data. It may then be necessary to reduce the number or length of the interviews in order to complete the transcription in the allocated time.

Further reading

An excellent book for quantitative analysis is Pallant's (2016) SPSS survival guide. This book takes the researcher step by step through the basics of SPSS entry and analysis in a very accessible way. Field (2017) has a comprehensive volume pitched at different levels of expertise on how to enter data and addresses both the concepts and the execution of a range of statistical tests. Another useful book for quantitative analysis is Larson-Hall's (2015) book, which focuses on research in second language research. Rose, Spinks, and Conhoto (2015) have a chapter freely available online on using Excel for data analysis.

For qualitative analysis, Richards (2003) is a very useful and accessible book addressing qualitative research skills and analysis in TESOL. Silverman (2017) has an excellent volume on qualitative research geared toward novices addressing the development of a qualitative research project, to analysing data to writing. Although this volume is written for PhD students it is also useful for master's students. For an in-depth treatment of qualitative approaches and analysis, Denzin and Lincoln's (2018) edited volume, now in its 5th edition, is the key work. Menhdi Riazi's encyclopedia (2016) covers quantitative, qualitative and mixed methods research in applied linguistics and is certainly useful.

References

Cabraal, A. (2013). Keep a research journal: It's important. Retrieved from https://anuja-cabraal.wordpress.com/2013/07/03/keep-a-research-journal-it-is-important/ (Accessed 20 May, 2019)

Denscombe, M. (2017). *The good research guide: For small-scale social research projects* (6th ed.). Maidenhead: Open University Press.

Denzin, N. K., & Lincoln, Y. S. (Eds.). (2018). *The Sage handbook of qualitative research* (5th ed.). Thousand Oaks, CA: Sage Publications.

Field, A. (2017). *Discovering statistics using IBM SPSS statistics* (5th ed.). London: Sage Publications.

Kelly, R. (2015). *An exploration of Instagram to develop ESL learners' writing proficiency*. (Master's Dissertation), Ulster University. Retrieved from https://englishagenda.britishcouncil.org/sites/default/files/attachments/dissertation_for_publication_ulster_university.pdf (Accessed 20 May, 2019)

Larson-Hall, J. (2015). *A guide to doing statistics in second language research using SPSS* (2nd ed.). Abingdon: Routledge.

Mehdi Riazi, A. (2016). *The Routledge encyclopedia of research methods in applied linguistics: Quantitative, qualitative and mixed methods research*. Oxford: Routledge.

Pallant, J. (2016). *SPSS survival manual* (6th ed.). Maidenhead: Open University Press.

Richards, K. (2003). *Qualitative inquiry in TESOL*. Basingstoke: Macmillan.

Rose, S., Spinks, N., & Conhoto, A. I. (2015). *Management research: Applying the principles*. Oxford: Taylor & Francis. Retrieved from http://documents.routledge-interactive.s3.amazonaws.com/9780415628129/Chapter%2013%20-%20Using%20Excel%20for%20Quantitative%20Data%20Analysis%20final_edited.pdf (Accessed 20 May, 2019)

Silverman, D. (2017). *Doing qualitative research* (5th ed.). London: Sage Publications.

Links to statistical analysis programmes

SPSS www.ibm.com/products/spss-statistics
Stata www.stata.com/
SAS www.sas.com/en_gb/learn/academic-programs.html
R. www.r-project.org/

PART III

Writing the dissertation

9

GENERAL WRITING GUIDELINES

This chapter addresses the overall approach to writing a dissertation. It starts with when to start writing the dissertation and how the dissertation should be organised. This is followed by a section on academic style including vocabulary; grammar and punctuation are then discussed.

9.1 When to start writing

One of the most inaccurate phrases associated with dissertation writing is 'writing up'. This implies that the writing of the dissertation is the final activity in the project; taking this view can have disastrous results in terms of passing the dissertation component of the degree. If a student leaves writing until the end of the study period, it is unlikely that a good piece of writing will be the product. Writing is an integral part of researching and learning, so it is a good idea to become very familiar with academic writing at the beginning of the project; in this way the writing of a large 15,000-word document is not so daunting. One of the biggest problems writers have when writing is procrastination – putting off activities, particularly writing, to another day. Table 9.1 shows some common excuses used to avoid writing and some strategies to overcome procrastination.

Writing is an integral part of the research process. There are many types of writing required during the dissertation, for example, taking notes, reflective and personal writing and writing an argument. One way to highlight the importance of writing is to keep a writing diary. In this way it is very clear how much writing and what type of writing has been completed each day. Table 9.2 shows an example of a writing diary.

TABLE 9.1 Avoiding procrastination in writing

Excuses	*What should happen*
I'll transcribe the data when I have finished all of the interviews.	Transcribing is very time consuming and can be tedious, so an early start is best. Also, it is easier to transcribe while the interview is still fresh in the mind.
I'll start writing my dissertation when I have finished all my other assignments.	This will be too late! The more dissertation writing completed at an early stage, the better the final product.
I'll write my dissertation in one go.	Dissertation writing should start in week one of the course. It is always easier to revise a draft than start from scratch.
I'll start at the beginning and write the dissertation in order.	Writing is cyclical, drafting and redrafting. It is also necessary to write more than one chapter at one time. So, for example, drafting the methodology and the literature can be done at the same time.
I'll finish the writing on the due date.	It is essential to leave enough time for editing and proof-reading the text.
The writing is not very important, it's the results that count.	The significance of the project is communicated or obscured by the writing. With poor writing the content is not clear. Also, writing is assessed. There is usually one category of assessment criteria that refer to the presentation and writing of the dissertation.

TABLE 9.2 Example of a writing diary

Date	*Goal*	*Action*	*Number of words*		*Comments*
3 Sept	Write summaries of anxiety readings.	Completed four summaries. Put into End Note.	1000	✓	Need to work more quickly. Use better reading strategies.
3 Sept	Work on supervisor's feedback on literature review.	Got through all comments. Drafted changes.	650	✓	Chapter looking a bit better now.
4 Sept	Draft literature chapter structure.	Not finished yet.	250	✗	Have another go tomorrow.
4 Sep	Draft contents page based on examples.	Used correct layout.	145	✓	Very satisfying!

TASK 9.1

Make a writing dairy and list all the writing you do over a week.
Does this help with your writing productivity?

9.2 Organisation of a dissertation

This book has focused on the traditional structure of a dissertation: introduction, literature, methodology, results and discussion. This is the most common way of organising dissertations but not the only way. Paltridge and Starfield (2019) present alternative structures for PhD theses, from traditional, to complex traditional that includes extra elements based on the traditional structure, to topic based with each chapter focusing on one element, for example, a case or geographical area. Such text organisation also occurs in master's dissertations. Perhaps the most common deviation from the traditional format is combining the results and discussion chapters. This is particularly common in qualitative studies, where the overlap between the results and implications may be less distinct. The decision as to which type of dissertation to do should be informed by the department guidelines. Figures 9.1–9.3 show some examples of typical dissertation organisation. Figure 9.3 is taken from an action research project.

Title page

Abstract

Acknowledgements

List of terms

Introduction

Literature review

Research methodology

Analysis and results

Discussion

Conclusions

References

Appendices

FIGURE 9.1 Dissertation organisation, example 1

Declaration

Acknowledgements

Table of contents

Introduction

Methodology

Results and discussion

Conclusion

References

Appendices

FIGURE 9.2 Dissertation organisation, example 2

Table of contents

Introduction

The issue

The goal

Action plan

Results and next steps

References

Appendices

FIGURE 9.3 Dissertation organisation, example 3

TASK 9.2

What are your department guidelines on the organisation of the dissertation?
Look at some previous dissertations. Do they all have the same structure?
What type of organisation will you have for your dissertation?

9.3 General requirements of a dissertation

The specific requirements of the individual chapters will be discussed in the following chapters; however, it is useful to bear in mind the general requirements of a dissertation when writing so the overall criteria are met. Figure 9.4 presents the overall requirements of the dissertation. Chapter 16 presents a detailed checklist that can be used for editing the final dissertation.

Clear and unambiguous research questions

Questions supported by literature: research and theory

Has an appropriate research design

Shows understanding of research methods

Reflects an overarching argument

Has an element of originality

Results related to current thinking and research

Research questions clearly answered

Well organised

Believable

Appropriate writing style

FIGURE 9.4 General requirements of a dissertation

9.4 Academic writing

The academic style of a dissertation is like that of other master's level academic assignments. However, there is a need for dissertations to include a much deeper level of critique and evaluation supported by evidence. It is important, as with any form of writing, to consider the audience, purpose and expectations of the dissertation (Paltridge & Starfield, 2019).

9.4.1 Audience

The audience of the dissertation may differ between contexts. The most important readers are the examiners because they will assign the grade. In Australia these examiners may be internal staff members but often not the supervisor. In this case the student may not know who the examiners are. In UK universities it is usual for the dissertation to be examined by the supervisor and one other department staff member.

9.4.2 Purpose

It is useful to consider the purpose of the dissertation. Students have differing purposes in writing the dissertation. The dissertation is often a mandatory part of a master's course, but in some programmes it is an elective that serves as a pathway to further study or career development. Some students view the dissertation as a pathway to a higher research degree, while others view the dissertation as a difficult but necessary assignment.

9.4.3 Expectations

Expectations and norms of the dissertation are not universal, universities and academic departments have differing expectations of the dissertation. Usually departments have guidelines for student to follow; these guidelines would include the assessment criteria, the layout of the dissertation and style guide. These guidelines should be followed to the letter. The assessment criteria offer valuable information about the features of different grades of dissertation from a high distinction through to a fail. It is an excellent idea to read through these at the very beginning of the dissertation module.

9.5 Features of academic style

The first place to start to ensure that the style of the dissertation is appropriate is the department handbook and any university style guides that are available. There are many guides to generic academic writing available; for example, Purdue university has a good online writing lab that has links to exercises. See https://owl.purdue.edu (accessed 8 May, 2019). Chapter 16 provides further links to academic writing sites.

9.5.1 Vocabulary

Academic vocabulary is formal in style and uses the appropriate terminology in the field, eg communicative language teaching (CLT). The simplest and most direct choice of vocabulary should be used rather than using complex obscure constructions in the belief that it will read more 'learned'. Such writing is very hard for any reader to follow. Vocabulary should be formal, with no short forms or slang or words used. Table 9.3 lists expressions with examples to avoid in academic writing.

9.5.2 Grammar

There are four main areas that academic writers need to beware of: run on sentences, sentence fragments, verb–subject agreement and using the correct tense. Sentences should not be very long and difficult to follow. Each sentence should have a verb and subject and contain only one idea. Table 9.4 illustrates some common errors and the corrections.

TABLE 9.3 Academic style: vocabulary

Avoid	*Example*
Imprecise expressions	Really, stuff, lots of, actually, thing
Overly formal	Endeavour (try) Peruse (read)
Value judgments	Unfortunately, fantastic
Shortened forms	Isn't, can't
Wordiness	Due to the fact that (because)
Slang	Baby boomers, OMG
Clichés	Tongue in cheek
Run on expressions	Etc, so on
Personal pronouns*	I, we, you

*In some qualitative studies the use of 'I' is quite acceptable. The rule of thumb is to use 'I' if the role of the researcher is relevant to the overall study.

TABLE 9.4 Academic grammar

Avoid	*Example*
Run on sentences	👎 The results show students like teacher feedback they know better than peers. 👍 The results show that students like teacher feedback because they think teachers know better than peers.
Long sentences	👎 This study demonstrated that the respondents showed a strong preference for teacher feedback in contrast to peer feedback for the reason that it is perceived as useful and constructive in order to assist with the writing of dissertations and may be related to higher assessment grades in the examination of the texts.

(*Continued*)

TABLE 9.4 (Continued)

Avoid	*Example*
	👍 This study demonstrated that the respondents preferred teacher feedback to peer feedback. They reported that such feedback can help with dissertation writing. They also believed the feedback could be related to assessment grades.
Inaccurate verb subject agreement	👎 The variable of anxiety were found to be related to language mistakes when speaking. 👍 The variable of anxiety was found to be related to language mistakes in speaking.
Incorrect tense	👎 The study will use a correlational analysis to investigate the relationship between anxiety and speaking performance. (in a dissertation) 👍 The study used a correlational analysis to investigate the relationship between anxiety and speaking performance. (in a dissertation)

9.5.3 Punctuation

It is important that the writing in a dissertation is appropriately punctuated with the correct use of capitals, full stops, commas and punctuation marks. Table 9.5 summarises the use of the major forms of punctuation in academic writing. It is important that the style guide that is recommended by the department or university is consulted because some of these rules may differ. For example, in some style guides, single quotation marks rather than double quotation marks are used in quoting. Many writers are not familiar with the rules of punctuation; however, there are many online punctuation guides that can be consulted. For example, the University of Bristol has a very good site for grammar and punctuation in academic writing: www.bristol.ac.uk/arts/exercises/grammar/grammar_tutorial/page_01.htm (accessed 14 July, 2019).

TABLE 9.5 Common types of punctuation

Punctuation		*Use*	*Example*
Full stop	.	At the end of a sentence	The findings of the research suggest Chinese students indicate teacher feedback to peer feedback.
Comma	,	To separate clauses, used in lists	Participant A3 arrived late, but was able to participate in the second phase of the research. Twenty participants completed a background questionnaire, a self-efficacy can-do scale and participated in a semi-structured interview.

(*Continued*)

TABLE 9.5 (Continued)

Punctuation		*Use*	*Example*
Colon	:	To introduce lists To separate clauses, eg dissertation titles	There are three main reasons students experience anxiety: inadequate command of the language, fear of making mistakes and fear of failure. Newspaper discourses on Andy Murray's performance at Wimbledon: A contrastive corpus-driven investigation of successful and unsuccessful tennis match reports.
Semi-colon	;	Lists that are too large to be separated by a comma Citation of multiple authors	The intervention was very successful: many students reported no anxiety; over half reported higher self-efficacy and two thirds score higher on the language test. Anxiety is related to low self-efficacy (Smith, 2018; Jones, 2017; Brown, 2016).
Apostrophe	'	Missing letter Possession	It's a difficult project. The participants' scores reflected a high level of anxiety.
Quotation marks	" " ' '	For a quotation For a single item or term within a quotation	According to Horwitz, Horwitz, and Cope (1986) "foreign language anxiety (FLA) refers to a distinct complex of self-perceptions, beliefs, feelings and behaviours related to classroom learning." An important element of speaking according to Woodrow is that of 'perseverance', which refers to not giving up while speaking.

9.6 Use the marking scheme while writing

Dissertations are marked according to the department's marking scheme. Usually there is a list of criteria at each level according to specific aspects of the dissertation. Some departments provide a very detailed marksheet and assessment criteria. It is a very good idea to use the marking scheme while writing so that the writer can ensure the criteria are met. Some of the criteria are very easy to fulfil at a high level, for example, using correct referencing, layout and presentation. Others are more difficult, for example, showing a high level of critical engagement with the literature. Before submitting, it is a good idea to 'mark' the dissertation using the marking scheme.

TASK 9.3

Download the style guide from your department or from the library. What are the requirements in terms of the following:Presentation
Layout
Headings
Spacing
Font
Grammar
Vocabulary
Citations
Referencing style

TASK 9.4

Print off the marking scheme and/or marking criteria for your dissertation. Use this while writing.
With a partner mark sections of the dissertation using the criteria.

9.7 Process of writing

As mentioned earlier, writing is not a linear process; drafting and redrafting are very important. Writing drafts enables writers to get feedback from supervisors and peers. As there may be limited opportunities for supervision session, a peer network group is very effective as a means of getting feedback. Setting up a writing group is one way that writers can get feedback from others and see how others write. Chapter 16 includes a section on how and why to set up a writing group. Figure 9.5 illustrates the process of writing. Pre-writing refers to writing activities prior to drafting a text, for example, taking notes from relevant sources.

Summary

This chapter has discussed the general writing requirements of a master's dissertation. It has addressed problems with writing and the organisation of dissertations. The role of grammar, vocabulary and punctuation have also been discussed. In the next three chapters the focus is on the writing individual sections of the dissertation.

Common mistakes in writing

- Leaving dissertation writing too late
- Procrastination
- Not writing drafts
- Using informal language
- Not adhering to the department style guide
- Incorrect grammar
- The dissertation is not proof-read

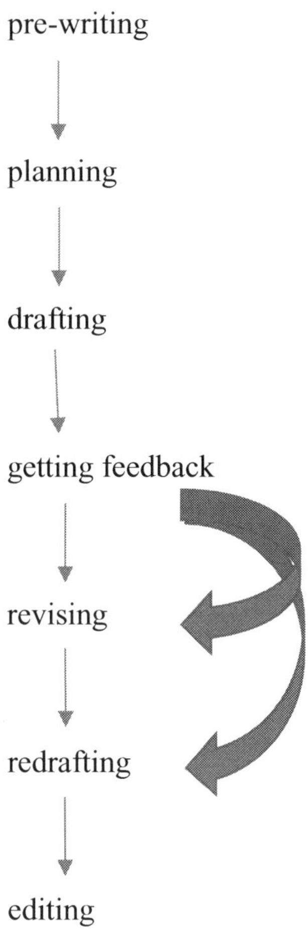

FIGURE 9.5 Process of writing

FAQs

1 *I am a non-native English speaker. Does my writing have to be grammatically flawless?*
In TESOL and applied linguistics, examiners tend reasonable tolerant to minor language errors; however, this can vary between departments and between individual markers. The most important thing is that the error does not cloud the meaning.

2 *What percentage of the overall grade is based on the quality of the writing?*
This will vary between departments, but writing is certainly an important factor in assessment.

3 *When should I start writing my dissertation?*
Day one! All writing counts toward the final product and will make the final draft easier.

Further reading

The best place to start reading is the department style guide. It should be remembered that universities differ in the expectations and norms of academic style. For help with academic expression and vocabulary, the Manchester Phrasebank is an excellent resource. It addresses a range of academic writing areas (www.phrasebank.manchester.ac.uk). While not specifically targeting dissertation writing, the site is categorised based on the sections of a dissertation: introducing work, referring to sources, describing methods, reporting results, discussing findings and writing conclusions. The resource is also available for purchase in PDF form. Purdue University has an online writing lab (OWL) that is publicly available (https://owl.purdue.edu/writinglab/the_writing_lab_at_purdue). The site includes information and exercises in a range of areas of academic writing such as organisation, developing arguments and grammar. Bristol University has an excellent accessible site that provides explanations and exercises for grammar in academic writing (www.bristol.ac.uk/arts/exercises/grammar/grammar_tutorial/page_41.htm).

References

Crofton, B. (2011). *The usefulness of decision-forcing case studies in helping to prepare new and experienced English language teachers.* (Master's Dissertation), Concordia University, Portland.

Horwitz, E., Horwitz, M., & Cope, J. (1986). Foreign language classroom anxiety. *Modern Language Journal, 70*, 125–132.

Paltridge, B., & Starfield, S. (2019). *Thesis and dissertation writing in a second language: A handbook for students and supervisors* (2nd ed.). Abingdon: Routledge.

Purdue University. (n.d.). *Purdue Online Writing Lab (OWL).* Retrieved from https://owl.purdue.edu/writinglab/the_writing_lab_at_purdue.html (Accessed 8 May, 2019)

University of Bristol (n.d.). Faculty of Arts. *Improve your writing.* Retrieved from www.bristol.ac.uk/arts/exercises/grammar/grammar_tutorial/page_41.htm (Accessed 8 May, 2019)

University of Manchester. *Academic phrasebank.* Retrieved from www.phrasebank.manchester.ac.uk/ (Accessed May 8, 2019)

10

WRITING THE LITERATURE REVIEW

The literature review chapter provides the theoretical and research-based underpinnings of the research project. The process of reviewing the literature is presented in Chapter 3; this chapter focuses on the nuts and bolts of writing the review. The two processes are very closely linked and by adopting sound practices when reviewing the literature, the writing will be much easier.

The literature review is discussed from the perspective of purpose, content, structure and language. The discussion is supported by examples from authentic master's dissertations. The starting point for writing the literature review is the dissertation proposal upon which the dissertation chapter can build on.

10.1 The purpose of the literature review

The literature review in a master's dissertation has several purposes. It is used to inform the research design and research questions; it is used to establish a gap in knowledge which the current study will fill; it is also used to demonstrate higher order thinking skills, such as critical evaluation, to the examiner. These three main purposes should be remembered while writing the review.

The literature review section of the dissertation is assessed according to specific criteria that the student should bear in mind when writing the review. Table 10.1 lists the typical characteristics of high and low scoring literature review chapters.

TASK 10.1

Find the assessment criteria used to assess the literature chapter of master's dissertations in your department. What are the characteristics of a high scoring chapter?

TABLE 10.1 Characteristics of the dissertation literature review chapter

High scoring literature review	*Low scoring literature review*
Selection of sources supports research aims.	Selection of sources is vaguely related to topic. Uses obscure sources by unknown authors.
Chapter is well structured.	Text does not include any signalling.
Shows a deep level of critical evaluation.	Literature dealt with in a descriptive way. Reads like a list of sources.
Chapter is concise and focused.	Chapter is long winded and too long.
Has a high level of synthesis.	Sources and arguments are not synthesized.
There is a clear progression of argument.	There is no a clear argument running through the literature review.
Review includes key seminal works.	Review is missing key works. Theoretical framework may be absent.
Includes recent research.	Based on old sources.
Indicates a gap in knowledge.	No research gap indicated.
Sources are cited appropriately.	Has too many direct quotes.
	Citations do not match style guide.

10.2 Organisation of the literature review

One of the characteristics of a good dissertation is that it is easy to read and well organised. There are two main ways of doing this: first, by headings and sub-headings, and second, using meta-text – that is, the explicit ordering of text using language. Using headings and sub-headings helps map out the chapter, it also highlights the progression of argument that ultimately leads to the gap in knowledge that the study intends to fill. Figures 10.1 and 10.2 show two examples of how literature chapter can be organised in a dissertation using this method.

TASK 10.2

Map your literature chapter into headings and sub-headings, as it will appear in your Table of Contents. It is better not to use more than three levels of organisation.

Meta-text refers to non-content expressions that serve to organise the chapter and inform the reader of what will be, or has been, addressed in the chapter. This is achieved by using introductions and conclusions for each chapter. The use of this type of language helps the reader follow the text, which is essential for the reader when reading a long document like a dissertation. Figures 10.3–10.5 show some examples of how this is done in the first paragraph of literature chapters. The introductions are followed by an explanation of the generic structure of the paragraph sentence by sentence.

Instagram to develop writing

2. Literature Review

Introduction

2.1 Second Language Acquisition

2.2 Theoretical Framework

2.3 Definitions

2.4 Social Media Applications and L2 Education

2.5 Social Network Sites and L2 Education

2.5.1 Social Network Sites and L2 Education: Challenges

2.5.2 Social Network Sites and L2 Education: Learner Attitudes

2.6 Key Issues

Conclusion

FIGURE 10.1 Organisation of the literature chapter using headings, example 1

Source: Kelly (2015)

Culturally sensitive alternatives for FCE

Chapter 2: Key Concepts & Literature Review:

2.1 Cambridge Language Testing & the FCE

2.2 Culture & Cultural Validity

2.2.1 Whose Culture? Whose English?

2.3 Cambridge's Commitment to Fairness

2.3.1 Overview of FCE Claims

2.4 Proposed Solutions

2.4.1 Learner Authentication

2.4.2 Multi-Dimensional Mental Representation

2.4.2.1 Experiential Learning

2.4.2.2 Neurological & Psychological Background

2.4.2.3 MDMR & the 'Multi-Dimensional Approach'

FIGURE 10.2 Organisation of the literature chapter using headings, example 2

Source: O'Donovan (2015)

In this chapter I shall start by reviewing the role of pronunciation in language teaching methodology over the last century.[1] I shall then look at how the shifting role of pronunciation has affected pronunciation goals in teaching.[2] Following this, I shall turn to 'perceptions', exploring and critiquing the research into students' and teachers' views on pronunciation.[3]

1. Broad topic - historical perspective
2. Second broad topic – shifting roles
3. Third broad topic.– perceptions and critique

FIGURE 10.3 The structure of literature chapter introductions, example 1

Source: Crofton-Martin (2015)

The key aim of this dissertation is to offer empirical evidence that addresses the question of whether motivational strategies as proposed by Dörnyei (2001) are effective.[1] Chapter 1 has provided an overview of this dissertation and outlined the rationale and methodology of this dissertation.[2] This chapter discusses the literature on L2 motivation.[3] It will provide an overview of the important theories and previous research on L2 motivation in order to identify a relevant conceptual framework for this research.[4] It will also offer a critical assessment of the field of L2 motivation research and identify the important gaps and needs that this dissertation will address.[5] Ultimately, it will provide the background, reasons, and justification for the research questions being addressed in this dissertation.[6]

1. Aim of dissertation
2. Summary of previous chapter
3. Summary of this chapter
4. First broad topic - theories and research
5. Second broad topic - critical assessment and gap
6. Summary and reference to research questions

FIGURE 10.4 The structure of literature chapter introductions, example 2

Source: Wilson (2013)

This chapter, first, discusses the definition of beliefs and the approach to them within this study for the exploration of identity formation.[1] Next, a sociocultural approach as theoretical lens is considered along with its key notions such as mediation, transition and context.[2] The third section, as important theoretical background, explores the NS construct with reference to current discussions around it and its implications for NNESTs.[3] Finally, I discuss how the NS construct has been tied to NNSETs' identities through previous research and present the influential identity theories with the key features of NNSETs' identity on which this study is based.[4]

1. Broad topic – definitions
2. Broad topic 2 – theoretical perspective
3. Broad topic 2 – theoretical perspective
4. Synthesis of topics

FIGURE 10.5 The structure of literature chapter introductions, example 3

Source: Kong (2014)

TASK 10.3

Which of the literature review introductions do you prefer?
Which would be most appropriate for your literature review chapter?
Draft the introduction to your literature review chapter.

10.3 Sources to include in the review

The review chapter should be viewed as a coherent argument supporting the research study. As such, writers need to use sources to support the argument rather than list everything read. This is particularly important in a master's dissertation because the space is limited. Typically, the literature review in a 15,000-word dissertation would be between 3000–4500 words, so it is inevitable that many sources read will not make it into the review chapter.

10.4 Critical reading and writing

When writing the literature review it is very important to demonstrate critical reading and writing skills. The word 'critical' is often mistaken to mean to criticise or to adopt a contrary position. In academic writing being critical means being evaluative, this can be achieved by asking questions of the text and looking for evidence for claims made in the text. Chapter 3 has addressed critical reading and presents some strategies in Table 3.6.

Writing critically refers to providing evidence for views and claims. This evidence comes from logical argument and/or published authoritative sources. At the writing stage it is a good idea to map out the argument structure of the literature review and then assign sources that support and provide evidence for this argument.

Figure 10.6 presents an example of critical writing. The writer compares evidence from different sources to support her argument; she also compares contrasting views which leads to a claim for further research.

> Weigle (2004) also acknowledges that writing on an isolated topic is not authentic as students are unlikely to encounter this in their real academic life. Furthermore, she goes on explaining that academic discourse is generally written to respond to previously written discourse. In line with this argument, Keck (2006) also states that students are often required to reference readings in writing assignments and exams. All of these arguments support the notion that integrating reading and/or listening into the testing of writing will enhance test task authenticity.[1]
>
> However, experts are not unanimous in their views about the positive consequences of increased authenticity in testing. Weigle and Parker (2012),[2] for example, raise the issue that task authenticity may be a threat to test validity because the possibility of test-takers' over-reliance on the source texts in integrated writing tests may interfere with the measurement of their true writing ability. This issue, thus, has led to the need for more research into test-takers' source text borrowing practices in integrated writing tests.[3]
>
> [1]Synthesising sources to support own view
>
> [2]Comparing contrasting viewpoints
>
> [3]Making a claim based on evidence – need for research

FIGURE 10.6 Example of critical writing: combining views in literature review

Source: Lestari (2014)

10.5 Referring to the gap in knowledge

One of the purposes of the literature review is to convince the reader of the importance of the study by identifying a need for research. This is usually achieved by finding the gap in knowledge based on published sources. Figures 10.7–10.9 and show examples of writing about the gap. Finding a gap can be quite difficult for a small master's course-work dissertations. One way of doing this is by narrowing the context of investigation, for example, in primary schools in Tyneside or Chinese English teachers at Fudan University.

> Despite the considerable number of studies and frameworks presented on this concept, their findings fail to specify the "critical age" after which native-like accent is unachievable. The cause of age effects is still not explained convincingly. In addition, critics have emerged concerning the use of inexperienced judges, which entails subjective pronunciation assessment in such research (Thompson, 1991). The lack of long-term study to evaluate the development of acquisition is also emphasised (Ioup, 2008). Nevertheless, age of acquisition is still agreed to be "the most important predictor of degree of foreign accent" (Ioup, 2008, p. 46).

FIGURE 10.7 Establishing a gap in knowledge, example 1

Source: Le (2017)

> As we have seen, relatively few studies have been conducted into teacher WCF using corpus analysis. To the best of my knowledge there have been no studies that have focused on teachers' word choice in WCF*, and this research contributes to the current literature by analysing teachers' word choice patterns for positive and negative comments.
>
> *WCF = Written Corrective Feedback

FIGURE 10.8 Establishing a gap in knowledge, example 2

Source: Philip (2017)

The current study addresses a limitation of the intelligibility and comprehensibility studies reviewed here: the vast majority of studies consider all segmentals together, so it is impossible to identify which hinder intelligibility. Jenkins (2000) attempts this with the LFC, but on an apparently ad hoc basis. Thus more robust studies of the intelligibility and comprehensibility of specific segmentals are required in distinct contexts. In a Korean context a list of likely problematic features is compiled from several Korean/ English contrastive analyses, and this forms the basis of this study. The current study thus addresses the following research questions all in the context of L1 Korean speakers and L1 Mandarin raters.

FIGURE 10.9 Establishing a gap in knowledge, example 3

Source: Barrass (2017)

10.6 Citing

There are two main ways of using citations in a text: paraphrasing and quoting. In a dissertation there is an expectation that there will be few direct quotes and that paraphrasing should reflect a deep understanding of the issue addressed rather than merely rephrasing a direct quote. In writing a literature review the issue of authorial voice is very important. This refers to the extent that the writer portrays an authority. If a writer relies on the views of others, uses too many quotes or too much close paraphrasing, then the author's view is obscured. Authorial voice is achieved by constructing an argument and leading the reader through this argument using sources as evidence to support the argument. Synthesising a number of authors' views is a useful technique that shows the writer has read widely and has synthesised views. An example of this is shown in Figure 10.10.

There are two methods of citing: placing the reference at the beginning of the claim using citing verbs, which highlights the author as being prominent, and placing the reference at the end of the claim, which highlights the research as being prominent. Figure 10.11 shows an example of an author prominent and a research prominent citation.

There are a wide range of verbs that can be used when citing research. When using citing verbs, a common mistake is to think it is necessary to use a large range of verbs; however, this is not necessary and can lead the writer into inappropriate usage. Using the most appropriate verb is far more important. Verbs should be formal and not reflect emotion, for example, "Brown (2018) *thinks* that . . ." is too informal. Table 10.2 lists some examples of appropriate and inappropriate reporting verbs. The Manchester Phrasebank has an excellent section on the language used in referring to sources; see www.phrasebank.manchester.ac.uk/referring-to-sources/.

A number of studies that have adopted NCSSFL-ACTFL can-do statements have been empirically validated in the study abroad context and have been shown to effectively help learners to evaluate their abilities accurately (Brown et al., 2014; Dewey, Belnap, & Hillstorm, 2013; Dewey et al., 2012).

FIGURE 10.10 Synthesising studies

Source: Xie (2017)

Author prominent citation

Mann (2005) argues that reflection develops in teachers an awareness of their practice, and that this forms a basis for sustainable professional development, creating opportunities for self-evaluation and experimentation.

Research prominent citation

Reflection and research can be seen as opposite ends on a spectrum of approaches to professional development (Mann, 2005).

FIGURE 10.11 Author and research prominent citations

TABLE 10.2 Verbs for referring to the literature

Inappropriate verbs	*Appropriate verbs*
says	claims
tells	asserts
feels	suggests
likes	maintains
supposes	concludes
guesses	states
thinks	indicates
reckons	proposes
comes up with	confirms
	shows
	argues
	demonstrates
	points out

Summary

This chapter has addressed issues in the writing of the literature review chapter. It has focused on the purpose and organisation of the chapter. The literature review should provide a theoretical and research framework for the study. Reading and writing critically is an essential skill to produce a good chapter.

Common mistakes in writing the literature review

- Structuring the literature review as a list of authors
- Being too descriptive in the literature review
- Not providing a strong authorial voice
- Relying too much on direct quotes and near paraphrases
- Using informal language
- Cutting and pasting literature review
- Making the literature review chapter too long

FAQs

1 *How long should my literature review be?*
There is no definitive answer to this question. The best way to find out is to ask your supervisor. As a general rule of thumb, in a 15,000-word dissertation the literature review would be between 2500 and 4500 words. Some projects require a lot of support from the literature, and some projects do not need quite so much. In some projects the literature may be very limited.

2 *How many references should I have in my literature review?*
Again, there is no right answer to this, more is not necessarily better. What is important is the quality of the references and how they are used to support arguments.

3 *How can I be critical when I am not an expert? How can I question the experts?*
It is very common for new researchers to experience a lack of confidence in this area. The easiest way to develop critical ability is to practice asking questions about a text such as the following:

- What is the main argument of the article?
- What is the evidence for this argument?
- Is it convincing?
- Could there be an alternative view?
- Would it apply to the situation you are researching?

4 *What happens if I accidentally have the same idea as an author I have not read? This is plagiarism, right?*
It is virtually impossible to accidentally plagiarise in this way. The way to avoid plagiarism is to keep meticulous records of reading and citations and report these in the appropriate way in the dissertation based on the department referencing guide.

5 *How do I know whether I need to reference or not?*
Text and ideas that belong to someone else need to be referenced. This means there needs to be a citation in the main body of the writing and the full reference should appear in the reference list.

6 *If I want to use a quote taken from a textbook from someone else – for example, Brown (2017) referring to Smith (1985) – how do I reference this?*
This is known as a secondary citation. This should be referenced as (Smith 1985, cited in Brown, 2017, p. 33). In the reference list, only Brown should be included, as this is the text that has been read. As a rule of thumb, a dissertation should include few secondary citations, as it is expected that the writer should read the original source.

Further reading

Boote and Beile (2005) published a seminal work on the importance of the literature review that, although targeting doctoral students, is well worth a read. Hart's book *Doing a literature review* is now in its second edition (2018) and is a very useful publication covering the nuts and bolts of both the process of reviewing the literature and writing the literature. In addition to these sources, the best further reading that can be done to assist with writing the literature review is to look at past dissertations from the department. It is important to look at a number of these to get a clear idea of the norms of this type of writing. The Manchester Phrasebank is a useful tool for writing the literature review and gives a lot of examples of how to refer to the literature.

References

Barrass, J. (2017). *The intelligibility of Korean English pronunciation from a Lingua Franca perspective.* (Master's Dissertation), University of Oxford. Retrieved from https://englishagenda.britishcouncil.org/sites/default/files/attachments/justin_barrass_university_of_oxford_dissertation.pdf (Accessed 1 March, 2019)

Boote, D. N., & Beile, P. (2005). Scholars before researchers: On the centrality of the dissertation literature review in research preparation. *Educational Researcher, 34*(6), 3–15. Retrieved from http://eprints.rclis.org/16929/1/diss_lit_review.pdf (Accessed 1 March, 2019)

Crofton-Martin, I. (2015). *Perceptions of pronunciation in the EFL classroom.* (Master's Dissertation), Canterbury Christchurch University. Retrieved from https://englishagenda.britishcouncil.org/sites/default/files/attachments/cantenbury_christ_church_university_isabel_crofton-martin_dissertation.pdf (Accessed 1 March, 2019)

Ellman, M. (2017). *"You're more likely to pick up on stuff": Evaluating the impact of video evidence on English language teachers' post-observation reflections.* (Master's Dissertation), University of Birmingham. Retrieved from https://englishagenda.britishcouncil.org/sites/default/files/attachments/matthew_ellman_university_of_birmingham_dissertation.pdf (Accessed 1 March, 2019)

Hart, C. (2018). *Doing a literature review: Releasing the research imagination* (2nd ed.). London: Sage Publications.

Kelly, R. (2015). *An exploration of Instagram to develop ESL learners' writing proficiency*. (Master's Dissertation), Ulster University. Retrieved from https://englishagenda.britishcouncil.org/sites/default/files/attachments/dissertation_for_publication_ulster_university.pdf (Accessed 21 May, 2019)

Kong, Y. (2014). *The discovery if future selves as TESOL professionals: Exploring the identity formation of in-service teachers*. (Master's Dissertation), University of Edinburgh. Retrieved from http://asian-efl-journal.com/wp-content/uploads/mgm/downloads/56770800.pdf (Accessed 1 March, 2019)

Le, Q. K. (2017). *English final consonant clusters in the interlanguage of Northern Vietnamese young adult learners*. (Master's Dissertation), Newcastle University.

Lestari, S. B. (2014). *Paraphrasing in high-scoring and low-scoring L2 integrated writing test task responses*. (Master's Dissertation), University of Warwick. Retrieved from https://englishagenda.britishcouncil.org/sites/default/files/filefield_paths/paraphrasing_in_high_scoring_and_low_scoring_l2_integrated_writing_v2.pdf (Accessed 1 March, 2019)

O'Donovan, E. (2015). *Exploring culturally sensitive alternatives for the first certificate in English*. (Master's Dissertation), University of Liverpool. Retrieved from https://englishagenda.britishcouncil.org/sites/default/files/attachments/dissertation_for_publication_2016_liverpool_university.pdf (Accessed 3 May, 2019)

Philip, C. (2017). *Positive and negative written corrective feedback: A mixed-method investigation of EAP teachers' word choices*. (Master's Dissertation), University of Stirling. Retrieved from https://englishagenda.britishcouncil.org/sites/default/files/attachments/claire_philip_university_of_stirling_dissertation.pdf (Accessed 1 March, 2019)

University of Manchester. (n.d.). *Academic phrasebank, referring to sources*. Retrieved from www.phrasebank.manchester.ac.uk/referring-to-sources/ (Accessed 1 March, 2019)

Wilson, O. (2013). *Teachers' motivational strategies and students' motivated behaviour in the tertiary Australian ESL context*. (Master's Dissertation), University of Sydney.

Xie, Y. (2017). *Who do you hang out with? A mixed-methods study on how Chinese students' social networks relate to their oral proficiency gains during study abroad*. (Master's Dissertation), University of Cambridge. Retrieved from https://englishagenda.britishcouncil.org/sites/default/files/attachments/yushan_xie_university_of_cambridge_dissertation.pdf (Accessed 1 March, 2019)

11

WRITING THE METHODOLOGY CHAPTER

Research design, the choice of methodological approach and data collection methods are addressed in Chapter 4. This section addresses the purpose, organisation and writing of the methodology chapter.

11.1 The purpose of the methodology chapter

The methodology chapter provides a framework and justification for the chosen research design. It shows the reader the most appropriate methods have been chosen. The chapter should guide the reader through the research process explaining the who, what, where and why of the research project; it should address the methodological approach, the methods of data collection, the procedure of the research and the data analysis. These areas should be supported by reference to the literature concerned with the area. Table 11.1 lists the characteristics of high and low scoring methodology chapters taken from a range of university assessment criteria for master's dissertations.

TASK 11.1

Find the assessment criteria used to assess the methodology section of master's dissertations in your department.

What are the characteristics of a high scoring chapter?

TABLE 11.1 Characteristics of a dissertation methodology chapter

High scoring methodology chapter	*Low scoring methodology chapter*
The study shows appropriate research design.	The study shows poor research design.

(Continued)

TABLE 11.1 Continued

High scoring methodology chapter	*Low scoring methodology chapter*
The chosen methodology is justified and discussed using good literature sources.	The methodological approach not addressed.
Research methods are justified with reference to literature.	Justification for research methods not evident.
The strengths and weaknesses of methods addressed.	The method chapter relies on introductory research methods books.
Good quality data.	Data and sources not fitting for research design.
Clear description of the research procedure.	Research procedure is hard to follow.
The study shows appropriate data analysis.	No data analysis included.
The data analysis is clearly explained and justified.	There is no explanation of analysis.
Reliability and validity addressed.	No discussion of reliability and validity.
There is clear evidence of ethical research.	Data collected without informed consent.

11.2 Organisation of the methodology chapter

As with the literature review, organisation is crucial to a good methodology chapter. The chapter should have a clear introduction and include sub-headings. Figures 11.1–11.3 show some examples of how the methodology chapter can be organised in a dissertation, focusing on sub-headings.

The methodology chapter typically has sections on participants, procedure and methods of data collection and analysis. These sections are discussed here with examples taken from master's dissertations.

11.2.1 Research questions

Most departments have a preferred position of the research questions in a dissertation; some feature in the introduction, some in the literature review, but mostly research questions will be outlined and repeated in the methodology chapter. At the same time how the data was collected and analysed to answer these questions is addressed in this chapter. While research questions are usually settled on at the proposal stage, it is possible to tweak the wording of these right up until submission.

TASK 11.2

Where do the research questions typically occur in dissertations from your department? Do they appear in more than one chapter of the dissertation?

11.2.2 Methodological approach

The methodological approach refers to whether the study is quantitative, qualitative or mixed methods. A good quality dissertation will address this and provide justification

3. METHODOLOGY

3.1 Type of research

3.2 Research design

3.3 Method and instrumentation

 3.3.1 Online questionnaire survey

 3.3.2 Interviews

3.4 Participants

 3.4.1 Setting

3.5 Data analysis

 3.5.1 Data analysis plan

 3.5.2 Interpretation of entire analysis

3.6 Ethical issues

3.7 Limitations

FIGURE 11.1 Organisation of the methodology chapter, example 1

Source: Su (2107)

for the approach taken with evidence from research methodology literature. An example of how this approach can be referred to in the chapter is shown in Figure 11.4.

11.2.3 The role of the researcher

In qualitative research the researcher plays an important role in collecting and interpreting the data, especially in ethnographic research. This role should be discussed in the methodology chapter.

11.2.4 The research context

If the research project includes collecting data from participants as contrasted with textual sources, it is usual to include a description of the research setting,

Chapter 3: Methodology

3.1 Outline

3.2 Research Questions

3.3 Participants

3.4 Approach

3.5 Conversation Analysis

3.5.1 Theoretical Underpinnings of CA

3.5.2 Epistemology

3.5.3 Details of Conversation Analysis

3.6 Methodological Procedures

3.6.1 Methods of Data Collection

3.6.2 Methods of Data Analysis

3.7 Validity and Reliability

3.8 Ethics

FIGURE 11.2 Organisation of the methodology chapter, example 2

Source: Spencer (2018)

for example, the university where the data was collected. When naming an institution, ethical issues should be considered. It is very important that participants cannot be recognised from the context. So, for example, if the vice chancellor of Tyne University is interviewed for the study it would be very easy to identify this person without naming the person, therefore the data could not be classed as confidential. In this instance the university should not be named in the text.

11.2.5 Participants

If the data collected comes from people, then information about the participants should be included. This is usually addressed in a separate section. The amount of information included in the methodology chapter may be rather general, with

CHAPTER 3: METHODOLOGY

3.1 Research questions

3.2 Context of the study

3.3 Participants

3.4 Instruments

3.4.1 Quantitative instrument: Questionnaire

3.4.2 Qualitative instrument: Interviews

3.5 Procedure

3.6 Data analysis

3.6.1 Quantitative data analysis

3.6.2 Qualitative data analysis

3.7 Ethical considerations

FIGURE 11.3 Organisation of the methodology chapter, example 3

Source: Alghamdy (2016)

Thus, considering the complexity of the data, and exploratory nature of this study, a mono-method, qualitative approach was deemed to be most appropriate approach. This is supported by Dornyei's (2007) belief that a qualitative approach is suitable for areas of research in which very little is known, and his assertion that qualitative research is especially useful "for making sense of highly complex situations" (ibid: p.39). It was hoped that this would allow the reader the best opportunity to make sense of the data and realise the significance of any results.

FIGURE 11.4 Referring to methodological approach in a dissertation

Source: Spencer (2018)

specific details presented in the following results chapter. Usually the methodology chapter discusses and justifies how the participants were selected, for example, was the group selected using random or purposeful sampling. Figures 11.5 and 11.6 present two examples of referring to participants in the methodology chapter.

3.1 Selection of participants

Before the study was conducted, all participants were fully informed of the research aims and procedures. The participant information sheet and the consent form were provided in the participants' first language and sent to them to sign (see Appendix 1).

The participants in this study were 36 adult Vietnamese learners of English (see Table 1). They were approached through the head teachers at their respective schools located in Hanoi, Vietnam. The study implemented a quasi-experiment research design, which means the participants were not randomly assigned to any treatment groups. 18 participants were recruited from the English centre which used the code-mixed reading texts to teach new words to form the experimental group. The control group, with an equal number of 18 participants, was recruited from a nearby English centre using the standard instruction method, where word list was the main way to introduce vocabulary. With the intention of creating a natural research setting, it was hoped that the participants' reactions to the treatment could be more genuine as they were already familiar with the vocabulary learning method in their schools. In advance of the course at these centres, the participants took a placement test and were expected to be at elementary level. They were then placed into classes aimed towards helping them achieve the B1 level in English after completion of the course. Participants' personal information was collected through a survey using SurveyMonkey and kept in a password protected file.

FIGURE 11.5 Describing and selecting participants, example 1

Source: Mai (2018)

The participants were 50 EFL students studying at a U.K. language college. As the students had been rigorously level tested by the college where the study took place, it can be assumed that their L2 level is fairly uniform. The nationalities of the participants were diverse, with representation from Europe, the Middle East and the Far East. Ages ranged from mid-twenties to mid-thirties, and of the 50 participants 26 were female and 24 male. The participants were more or less evenly distributed across the C (with captions) and NC (without captions) groups, providing a fairly balanced composition. The study took place over the duration of a month and each session lasted for approximately 70 minutes.

FIGURE 11.6 Describing and selecting participants, example 2

Source: Hicking (2015)

11.2.6 Methods of data collection

In this section of the methodology chapter, the variables of the study should be identified and the research instrumentation described and justified. Instrumentation refers to the data collection methods, for example, a questionnaire or an interview protocol; these should be included in the appendix. It is usual to provide evidence from the literature to support the choice of approach and methods. When using the literature to support claims regarding the methods used it is recommended that the writer goes beyond introductory textbooks and consults authoritative sources in the specific research method area. Paltridge and Phakiti (2015) have an edited volume that covers a number of popular approaches and methods in TESOL and applied linguistics.

11.2.7 Methods of data analysis

How the data was analysed needs to be described and justified in this chapter. If the study uses statistical tests, then the assumptions for these should be addressed. For both quantitative and qualitative approaches, the process from data collection to interpretation needs to be explained. Figure 11.7 shows an excerpt from the methodology chapter that refers to the analysis in a qualitative project (Anderson, 2016).

3.7 Data analysis

As soon as possible after face-to-face interviews, I listened again and typed up detailed interview notes (as advised by Rubin & Rubin 2005: 203) using a pro forma that followed the order of the interview schedule (see Appendix 8). With each comment, I also included relevant extracts, with time references for easy access during data analysis (see Appendix 8). After the first interview, I initially transcribed the data in full using basic transcription (see Appendix 7) and attempted to use this transcription to identify key themes (see 3.7.1 below). However, I found it easier to work with my typed-up interview notes than the transcription for two reasons:

1. Length of the interview (8400 words) made it difficult to find specific comments, given that relevant comments were interspersed with less relevant tangents and details.
2. The interviewee (as did others after her) sometimes addressed one research question during our discussion of another, or made a comment relevant to two research questions. In my interview notes, I was able to organise these comments according to research questions as recommended by Cohen et al. (2011: 552).

FIGURE 11.7 Writing about analysis

Source: Anderson (2016)

This excerpt provides references to the research methods literature and to the analytical framework presented in the appendix. It is interesting to see that this excerpt also explained a deviation from the intended procedure and a justification for this.

11.2.8 Reliability and validity

Usually there will be a section on the reliability and validity of the study in the methodology chapter. Reliability refers to replicability – that is, how likely similar results would be achieved if the study was repeated. Validity refers to whether the study measures what it purports to measure. In quantitative studies reliability is usually achieved using statistical analysis, as is shown in Figure 11.8. In qualitative studies other means are used, as is shown in Figure 11.9.

Research Question 2 **– What are students' perceptions of pre-*writing strategies before and after pre-writing strategy intervention?***

Data analysis was performed using the following instruments: (1) Pre-Intervention Questionnaire, (2) Immediate Post-Intervention Questionnaire, and (3) Delayed Post-Intervention Questionnaire. A Cronbach's alpha (α) estimate ensured instrument reliability. According to Dornyei (2007, as cited in Phakiti, 2014, p. 235), a reliability coefficient of 0.70 or above is acceptable. Reliability analysis is necessary with each use of the instrument as reliability is a property of the data collected when using the instrument rather than a property of the instrument itself (Woodrow, 2014, p. 26). Cronbach's alpha reliability estimate was calculated for each group for the Pre-Intervention Questionnaire revealing the following: Outlining Group ($\alpha = 0.79$) Concept Mapping Group ($\alpha = 0.82$), and Groups combined ($\alpha = 0.81$), as shown in Table 3.1. Given that all estimates exceed 0.70, it can be said that the pre-intervention questionnaire items were reliable.

Regarding the reliability estimates of Immediate Post-Intervention Questionnaire, the results - in order of essay section from introduction to conclusion, ending with all sections combined - in Tables 3.2 and 3.3, reveal slightly higher values for the Outlining Group ($\alpha = 0.85$, $\alpha = 0.88$, $\alpha = 0.86$, $\alpha = 0.94$) compared to the Concept Mapping Group ($\alpha = 0.74$, $\alpha = 0.80$, $\alpha = 0.72$, $\alpha = 0.88$). Similar comparative findings were found for Delayed Post-Intervention Questionnaire, as shown in Tables 3.4 and 3.5: Outlining Group ($\alpha = 0.84$, $\alpha = 0.87$, $\alpha = 0.88$, $\alpha = 0.95$) and Concept Mapping Group ($\alpha = 0.80$, $\alpha = 0.73$, $\alpha = 0.83$, $\alpha = 0.90$). This indicates that Immediate and Delayed Post-Intervention Questionnaires used by the participants in the Outlining Group were seen to be more reliable than those used by the participants in the Concept Mapping Group; however, all estimates are still considered acceptable.

FIGURE 11.8 Writing about reliability in a quantitative study

Source: Steinhoff (2018)

6.2 Validity and Reliability

According to Watling (2000, cited in Golafshani,2003), reliability and validity are both essential tools for positivism, which is essential for the quality of research. An excellent qualitative study should be able to make sense to every reader and generate understanding in its research topic. As Johnson (1997) claims, the validity of research refers to its 'trustworthiness,' that is, how the research can be credible. This research uses good quality classroom recordings videos, which offer compelling evidence. To ensure transcript accuracy, the three teachers were invited to double check the transcripts to see that they showed the classroom interactions completely and objectively. Then, to ensure that the participants' completed assessment forms truly revealed their thinking, interviews were conducted to allow them to elaborate on their answers in detail. Additionally, as previously mentioned, SETT is international and so is a reliable framework that can fit various classroom situations.

Stenbacka (2001) suggests that the generalisability of results in a field can determine a researcher's validity. However, because this research has only three participants, it would be wrong to assume that the problems of feedback shown in this case study can be extrapolated to all the English teachers in China, especially because there is a huge variety of educational levels in China. Despite this, these problems may be similar to other teachers in similar levels, so this research is useful.

In terms of reliability: reliability is the demonstration that research will achieve consistent results if it is reproduced in a similar way (Golafshani, 2013; Joppe, 2000). For this case study, due to the uniqueness of three participants, if other researchers use similar ways to conduct research among them, the results could be similar. But, if the participants change, their different results could be obtained. At least this research is repeatable, so it could be followed in the future and serve as a sample for teachers to self-evaluate their teacher feedback. That is the value of this research.

FIGURE 11.9 Writing about reliability and validity in a qualitative study

Source: Lin (2018)

Ethics

The researcher sought approval for the study to be conducted involving an EAP student cohort in a university setting (Appendix 29). Upon approval, tailored participant information statements - to avoid participants from either group learning of the other groups' intervention - were prepared for potential students in the Outlining (Appendices 1-5) and Concept Mapping Groups (Appendices 6-10). Additionally, teachers of classes A4.1-A4.11 and A4.12-A4.22 received participant information statements specific to outlining (Appendices 11-15) and concept mapping (Appendices 16-20), respectively.

To ensure voluntary participation, student participant consent forms tailored to outlining (Appendices 21-22) and concept mapping (Appendices 23-24) and teacher participant consent forms [Outlining Group (Appendices 25-26), Concept Mapping Group (Appendices 27-28)] were provided. Class sets of completed participant consent forms were compiled by individual class teachers and returned to the researcher.

FIGURE 11.10 Example of referring to ethics approval

Source: Steinhoff (2018)

TASK 11.3

How will you address reliability and validity in your dissertation?
What methods did you use to make your claims?

11.2.9 Ethics

It is important that the study is conducted in an ethical manner. How this is achieved needs to presented in the methodology chapter, as is shown in Figure 11.10. This refers to how participants were selected, how informed consent was given and how anonymity of participants was achieved. It is usual to include the ethics approval letter in the appendix of the dissertation.

11.3 Language in the methodology chapter

The important aspect of language use in the methodology chapter study is that as the study is complete, the main tense for describing the study is in the past tense – 'the

> The main source of data was classroom observations recorded using a video camera. Richards (2003) points out the attention in video cameras is usually given to picture quality, over sound quality, therefore an audio recording device was also used as a back-up.

FIGURE 11.11 Tense in the methodology chapter

Source: Cooper (2016)

data was collected'– unlike the proposal, which uses the future tense – 'the data will be collected'. However, the present tense is used when referring to the research methods literature in the same way as the literature review. Figure 11.11 shows an example of this tense usage.

TASK 11.4

Look at some sample dissertations from your department, library or the British Council site at https://englishagenda.britishcouncil.org/research-publications/elt-masters-dissertations.

Comment on the following:

Area	*Comments*
The organisation of the methodology chapter	
Types of sources used	
Use of quotes	
Use of paraphrasing	
Critique	
The use of language	
How context, sampling and participants is described	
How methods are reported	
How the data collection procedure is referred to	
Reference to validity and reliability	
Reference to ethical considerations	

Summary

This chapter has focused on writing the methodology chapter in a dissertation. The typical sections of the chapter are discussed and include describing the participants, method and procedure; examples of how these chapters can be organised were presented. Task 11.4 brings these considerations together and bases the activity on relevant dissertations.

Common mistakes in writing the methodology chapter

- Missing important information in the methodology chapter such as who, what, where, how
- Not showing an understanding of research methods
- Cutting and pasting methodology section from proposal
- Using an inappropriate method for the research design
- Referring to introductory research method books only

FAQs

1 *Do I have to use references in the methodology chapter?*
Yes. In this chapter you need to demonstrate that you have a good understanding of research methods in general and expertise in your chosen methods. This means referring to sources other than one general introductory research method book.

2 *What's the difference between methodology and methods?*
Methodology refers to the approach taken to research. This can be quantitative, qualitative or mixed methods. These three approaches are informed by different views of knowledge (epistemology) and truth (ontology). Methods are the techniques used to collect data, for example, interviews and questionnaires. Chapter 4 addresses these issues.

3 *Why do I need to show I have ethics approval?*
Most university research needs to have ethics approval. By providing the approval letter, the participant information sheet and the consent form, you will demonstrate that you have abided by these requirements.

4 *Is it necessary to include a discussion about reliability and validity?*
It is a good idea to address these issues in the methodology chapter, and all high scoring dissertations will have this feature. You should check the assessment criteria to see if validity and reliability are assessed; if they are, then omitting discussion about these two aspects could result in a penalty in marks.

5 *My methodology is the same as my proposal, can I cut and paste this?*
It's not a good idea to cut and paste from the proposal. At the very least there will be a need for language changes, so that the references to the future change to past tense – 'the questionnaire will be distributed' becomes 'the questionnaires were distributed'. However, it is highly likely that there will be other changes that need to be made based on a second reading at the later stage of writing.

Further reading

Some sources for further reading about methodology have been listed in Chapter 4. As well as these sources the best further reading that can be done to assist with writing the methodology is to look at past dissertations from your department. It is important to look at a number of these to get a clear idea of the norms of this type of writing. Chapter 16 includes some sources that can help with the general writing and academic style of the dissertation.

References

Alghamdy, S. (2016). *Motivational strategies in an EFL classroom: Students' Perceptions vs. Teachers' Practices*. (Master's Dissertation), Newcastle University.

Anderson, J. (2016). *A qualitative study into the role of initial teacher training courses in the professional development of experienced non-native speaker teachers of English*. (Master's Dissertation), Kings College, London. Retrieved from https://englishagenda.britishcouncil.org/sites/default/files/attachments/mda2017_winner_jason_anderson_king_s_college_london.pdf (Accessed 13 May, 2019)

Cooper, C. (2016). *Scaffolding during the initial reading of picture books in Japanese elementary school EFL classrooms:A qualitative study investigating how teachers and learners co-construct meaning during whole class picture book reading*. (Master's Dissertation), Sheffield Hallam University. Retrieved from www.asian-efl-journal.com/10422/thesis/scaffolding-during-the-initial-reading-of-picture-books-in-japanese-elementary-school-efl-classrooms-a-qualitative-study-investigating-how-teachers-and-learners-co-construct-meaning-during-whole-clas/ (Accessed 13 May, 2019)

Hicking, R. (2015). *Subtitles in authentic video listening: An exploration of the benefits of captions in relation to sensory preference types*. (Master's Dissertation), University College, London. https://englishagenda.britishcouncil.org/sites/default/files/attachments/dissertation_for_publication_ucl.pdf (Accessed 13 May, 2019)

Lin, Q. (2018). *Assessing teacher verbal feedback using the SETT framework: A case study on three English classes in a high school in China*. (Master's Dissertation), Newcastle University.

Mai, N. (2018). *Investigating the effects of code-mixed reading texts on vocabulary learning of Vietnamese adult learners*. (Master's Dissertation), Newcastle University.

Paltridge, B., & Phakiti, A. (Eds.). (2015). *Research methods in applied linguistics*. London: Bloomsbury.

Spencer, M. (2018). *Synchronous online learning via Zoom Videoconferencing: A multimodal conversation analytic study of teacher-student interaction*. (Master's Dissertation), Newcastle University.

Steinhoff, A. (2018). *The influence of pre-writing strategies on the quality of essay structure and topic sentences in ESL academic writing*. (Master's Dissertation), University of Sydney.

Su, L. (2107). *Identifying dyslexia in children learning English as an additional language: Primary school teachers' perceptions of the main challenges: A Somerset study*. (Master's Dissertation), Bath Spa University. Retrieved from https://englishagenda.britishcouncil.org/sites/default/files/attachments/laura_su_bath_spa_university_dissertation.pdf (Accessed 13 May, 2019)

12

WRITING THE RESULTS AND DISCUSSION CHAPTERS

This chapter addresses the main components of the dissertation, namely the research findings and the discussion. It is in these sections that new knowledge can emerge. In some dissertations the results and discussion sections are combined in one chapter, in some dissertations there are multiple chapters for the results section, typically based on the methodological approach(es), for example, a quantitative chapter and a qualitative chapter. Here the focus will be on the traditional ordering within a dissertation of separate results and discussion chapters, but it is worthwhile to look at several dissertations from the department to see what the usual practice is. This chapter addresses the purpose and structure of results and discussion chapters and considers the typical use of language.

TASK 12.1

Look at several dissertations from your department.
How are the results and discussion organised?
How many chapters are devoted to the results and discussion?
How are these organised?
Is there a tendency for particular types of organisation in qualitative and quantitative dissertations?
What about mixed methods?

The results section focuses on the selection and ordering of the presentation of the findings of the research and often uses of graphics to promote understanding. The discussion section focuses on relating these findings to the literature and making claims about the significance of the research.

12.1 The results chapter

This section focuses on the most important aspects of writing about the results. Both quantitative and qualitative results are discussed, as these tend to differ in how the results are reported.

12.1.1 The purpose of the results chapter

The results chapter is the most important chapter in the dissertation, as it is here new knowledge is presented. This is then expanded on in the discussion chapter. The results chapter should do more than describe the findings of the research; it should guide the reader to a clear understanding of what the study has found out, but without much discussion, as this is presented in the following chapter. It can be difficult to separate the findings and the discussion, particularly in qualitative studies. It is for this reason that some dissertation writers combine these two chapters. The important features of a results chapter is the order of the presentation of the results, highlighting the most important findings and very briefly evaluating these. The results presented in the chapter should not be the raw data, nor should there be references to the literature unless the results and discussion chapters are combined.

One challenge that dissertation writers face is what to include in the results section and justification for this. It is usual for a research project to generate a huge amount of data, and some data will be discarded. Obviously, some of the data is more interesting than other data. A good starting point is to focus on the research questions and then to exclude any data that is not relevant to these. This can be done by examining the analysis output or texts and highlighting the relevant information in relation to the research questions. However, there may be other reasons for including specific results, for example, the data may be used to triangulate findings from another method used in the study. Figure 12.1 shows some of the criteria that can be used when deciding whether to include results.

A useful task to decide on what to include and on the ordering of the results chapter is to start by asking 'What is the most important finding of this study?' and work from there.

Relevant to research questions

Frequently referred to in dissertation

Concurs or refutes previous research findings

Is pedagogically important

Subjective reason – finding is interesting

Triangulation needs

FIGURE 12.1 Criteria for selecting results

TASK 12.2

What are the most important results from your study?
Summarise your findings into one paragraph.
Have you answered your research questions?
Were there any unexpected results in your study?

12.1.2 Organisation of results chapter

There are several ways that the results can be organised within the chapter. Results can be ordered according to importance of the findings, themes that emerged from the data, the phases of the research or by research questions. Organising the results based on research questions is perhaps the most common method. If this method is used it is important not to refer to research questions solely by number but to include a description, as is shown in Figure 12.2. This will help the reader access the most important information without having to flip through the dissertation. Figure 12.3 shows how the results can be ordered in a case study in a results and discussion chapter.

Chapter 4 Results

4.1 Research Question 1: Linguistic Complexity of the Collected CEAL-PSs

4.1.1 Analysis of Lexical Diversity

4.1.2 Analysis of Readability

4.2 Research Question 2: Content Focus of the Collected CEAL-PSs

4.2.1 Analysis of Lexical Frequency

4.2.2 Analysis of Collocates

4.2.3 Analysis of Concordance Lines

4.3 Research Question 3: Functional Moves of the Collected CEAL-PSs

4.3.1 Analysis of Move Frequency

FIGURE 12.2 Examples of organisation of the results by research question

Source: Chen (2011)

CHAPTER 4 FINDINGS AND DISCUSSION

4.1 Educational Beliefs of the FLA Participants

4.1.1 Archie - Educational Beliefs

4.1.2 Nanette - Educational Beliefs

4.1.3 Matilda - Educational Beliefs

4.2 Function of the F-move in Discourse Analysis

4.2.1 Archie - Teaching Strategy

4.2.2 Nanette - Teaching Strategy

4.2.3 Matilda - Teaching Strategy

FIGURE 12.3 Organisation of results chapter by cases

Source: Jones (2011)

This chapter reports the results of the data analysis that has been described in Chapter 3. The results are reported in two parts: the communicative skills in writing of the participants and their attitudes towards using collaborative blogging. In the first part, the results are classified and discussed under the writing codes, namely, creativity, critical thinking, voice and comments and contributions. The second part discusses the participants' attitudes and experiences before and after the collaborative blogging project.

FIGURE 12.4 Example of introduction to results by describing what will follow

Source: Iyer (2013)

As with every other chapter in a dissertation, the results chapter needs to have an introduction. The introduction to the results chapter may be an announcement of what is to follow, as is shown in Figure 12.4, or it may contain an overview of the major results, as is shown in Figure 12.5.

The findings presented here support the claim that co-construction of professional knowledge is only possible through some form of collaborative dialogic reflective practices (CDRP). Reflection gives EFL teachers the space to evaluate areas of their practicum, and "notice" (Schmidt, 1990) possible areas for professional development. The analysis examined here focuses on dialogic interactions between EFL teachers who are employing CDRP to both reflect-on-action and reflect-for-action. The interaction creates a heuristic professional development space where interactants can use CDRP to aid the externalisation and internalisation of professional knowledge. Thus, the data suggest that CDRP both supports the co-construction and appropriation of professional knowledge and aids teacher learning, as it is evident at different stages in the interactions within this data set. As a result, four central themes have been identified:

1. Opening the floor to CDRP;
2. CDRP and the co-construction of professional knowledge;
3. CDRP and the appropriation of professional knowledge;
4. CDRP and EFL teacher learning in the staffroom.

FIGURE 12.5 Example of introduction to results chapter using summary of findings

Source: Forde (2018)

12.1.3 Reporting quantitative results

In a quantitative dissertation it is usual to go into detail about the analysis. The types of tests and the results need to be presented. It is usual to move from descriptive analyses through to inferential analyses. The descriptive analysis may be placed at the beginning of the results chapter, or may have a dedicated section on analysis in the methodology chapter.

12.1.4 Using tables and graphics

It most dissertations students will present some of their results in a graphic form. Quantitative studies will usually present more graphics than qualitative studies. The types of graphic presentation include tables, graphs and charts. In a quantitative dissertation the presentation of information in tables should abide by the style guide for the department. Often this is the *Publication Manual of the American Psychological Association (APA), 6th edition*. Some writers choose to put the majority of tables and graphs in the appendix because this is not usually included in the word count; however, it is important that the flow of reading is not interrupted by this. It is very difficult to read a text that frequently requires the reader to look in another section of the dissertation. On the other hand, it is important that the reader is not overloaded with graphics, for example, by including graphs for responses to all the questions in a Likert scale of 20 items.

The rule for the inclusion of graphics is that it helps with the understanding of the text. Information in graphics should always be referred to in the text, but the information presented in the graphic should not be described in detail, as this would be repetition. Each graphic should have a meaningful title that is referred to in the text, and the graphic should be placed close to the corresponding text.

Using tables is one of the most common ways of presenting quantitative data. It is usual to include a table that summarises the number of participants, the percentage and the actual number. Table 12.1 shows an example of this.

Tables are also a common method of reporting results of statistical tests. The data analysis software usually provides printable output in the form of tables, but these are very detailed and usually present a lot of information that is not relevant. The writer should decide which of the results are relevant and draft a table to display this rather than cutting and pasting from the data analysis programme. Figure 12.6 shows an example of a section in a results chapter from a quantitative study using correlation analysis and reference to this in the text.

Using graphs and charts is another common way of expressing quantities. Typical graphs are bar charts, line graphs and pie charts.

If the dissertation includes a number of graphics then it is usual to include a list of tables and figures at the beginning of the dissertation after the contents page. Figure 12.7 shows an example of a list of tables and figures in a dissertation.

12.1.5 Reporting qualitative results

In a qualitative dissertation results are less likely to be presented in a tabular and numerical format and more likely to be presented in a text form. The usual way to report results is to make a claim based on the analysis and then present excerpts from the data to support the claim. Figures 12.8 and 12.9 show some examples of how this may be done in a dissertation.

TABLE 12.1 Example of a table showing descriptive statistics in a quantitative study

Types of errors	*N*	%
Type 1: Omission of the definite article (*the*) and the indefinite article (*a/an*)	135	38.57%
Type 2: The indefinite article (*a/an*) used instead of the definite article (*the*)	51	14.57%

Source: Zhou (2017)

Table 5.5 Correlations between foundation exit measures and academic performance during first year at University

	IELTS	English	FGPA	UGPA
IELTS	1			
Foundation English test	.35**	1		
Foundation GPA	.22**	.61**	1	
University GPA	.41**	.58**	.66**	1

The analysis showed a positive relationship between the Foundation Studies programme GPA exit scores and academic performance at University semesters ($r = 0.66$, $R^2 = 0.44$). This means that 44% of the variance in academic performance at University can be accounted for by the foundation college exit test performance. There was a positive correlation between the English exit scores and academic performance during the first year ($r = 0.58$, $R^2 = 0.33$). This means that 33% of the variance in academic performance can be accounted for by English as measured by the Foundation Studies programme assessment. IELTS entry scores were also predictive of academic achievement although at a lower level ($r = 0.41$, $R^2 = 0.17$).

FIGURE 12.6 Example of table and text reference in a quantitative study using correlations
Source: Woodrow, Phakiti, and Hirsh (2011)

List of tables

Table 4.1 Summary of affective variables
Table 4.2 Anxiety and motivation variables
Table 4.3 Self efficacy and motivation variables

List of figures

Figure 4.1 Hypothesised model of adaptive model
Figure 4.2 Revised model of adaptive model
Figure 4.3 Final model of adaptive learning

FIGURE 12.7 List of tables and figures

However, PC points out two main difficulties for using SETT to assess teacher feedback in China: one is that teachers have limited time, the other is teachers' personal habits. These are explained below:

> R(The Researcher): So did you encounter some difficulties when you used this framework to assess?
>
> PC (Participant C): Um.. If we use this way to assess every class, I think we need some time to get familiar with it. We need to be aware of this and develop a habit about this. At the beginning, it was impossible. Because every teacher has his/her personal habits for using teacher language, and the teacher input is highly relevant to their experience, so I think it took too much time to correct their teacher feedback and get used to it.

FIGURE 12.8 Reporting interview results, example 1

Source: Lin (2018)

Staff members opinions on EAL mainstream education were also gauged through the interview process. Initially, participants were asked if EAL students should be educated within the mainstream school. A number of staff members wholeheartedly agreed that EAL students belonged in the mainstream.

Extract 4.3

Researcher: Should EAL students be educated in mainstream schools?

INT: Yes - Bryony TA

INT: yeah without a doubt - Kirsty Assistant Head

INT: yeah yes there's no reason why they shouldn't once the support is in place – Chris Physics Teacher

INT: yes always any child should never be segregated whatever the ability or disability - Gina Language Support

INT: yes 100% - Aisling TA

FIGURE 12.9 Reporting interview results, example 2

Source: Dry (2017)

The important points to remember when reporting qualitative results in this way are:

- Participant quotes are distinguished from claims and interviewer questions.
- Quotes are reported verbatim even if grammatically incorrect.
- Each quote has an identifying name or code.
- Pseudonyms are used to ensure confidentiality.

TASK 12.3

How will you present your results?
How will the results be ordered?
Will you use graphics?
    What type? (charts, graphs, tables)
    Why did you choose this type of graphic?
    How will the graphic help communicate your message in the results chapter?

12.2 The discussion chapter

This section focuses on what needs to be included in the discussion chapter of a dissertation. It addresses the significance of the research related to existing knowledge.

The discussion chapter is often the longest chapter in dissertation, and assessment of the whole dissertation is often heavily weighted on this chapter. This is because it is in this chapter that the value of the research can be found and reflects the ability of the student to engage in critical thinking. However, this chapter often receives the least attention by students. It is usually the last chapter to be written, and if the student is running out of time the chapter may be prepared too hastily.

12.2.1 The purpose of the discussion chapter

The primary purpose of the discussion chapter is to explicitly answer the research questions and to evaluate the significance of the research. As with the other chapters in the dissertation the writer is advised to consider the assessment criteria in detail before writing. Figure 12.10 shows three examples of the descriptors used to assess the results and discussion in a dissertation. These criteria reflect a distinction grade.

The discussion chapter takes the results and synthesises them with each other and with existing knowledge, the most important results are discussed and related to previous theory and research. The chapter compares the findings of the research to the findings of others and attempts to explain the similarities or differences. Figure 12.11 provides an example of relating findings to published research.

1. Comprehensive links with theory, complete justification with appropriate evidence, very good critical analysis of the implications of the findings, and reflection on the strengths and weaknesses of the research or development.

University of Southampton <http://www.sbsaob.soton.ac.uk/wp-content/uploads/sites/140/2016/10/Masters-Dissertation-assessment-criteria.pdf>

2. Explain the answers which their data suggest for their research questions
   - explore the implications of their results
   - identify strengths and weaknesses in the research they have carried out.

Newcastle University <https://www.ncl.ac.uk/postgraduate/modules/ALC8098/>

3. The author systematically evaluates and discusses his/her main findings, compares them to previous studies and analyses the possible differences. The discussion clearly indicates how the findings answer the research questions, and the author discusses the significance of the findings for practical applications or theory building. The author concludes the discussion with conclusions.

University of Tampere <http://www.uta.fi/hes/tiedostot/Pro%20gradu-kriteerit_2013_EN.pdf>

FIGURE 12.10 Some examples of descriptors at a distinction level used in the assessment of discussion sections

The results of this study can be compared with previous research. With regard to research question (1), the findings contradict those of Montero Perez, et al. (2014), but support earlier research (e.g., Chung, 1999; Markham, 2001; Winke, et al., 2010), which had found that the use of captions provided support to the participants in terms of aiding listening comprehension.

FIGURE 12.11 Referring to previous research in the discussion chapter

Source: Hicking (2015)

TABLE 12.2 Template for relating results to literature

Result	*Similar to*	*Different from*	*Comment*
Low level students do not feel anxious in speaking activities	Smith (2012)		Because participants are beginners so not expected to have good English.
High level students more likely to feel anxious in speaking activities		Jones (2011)	Expectations higher for class 1 students – more years of English. My sample culturally different from Jones's.

One of the main features of the discussion chapter is comparing the results with those of similar studies and explaining similarities and differences. This can be quite daunting, so in the early stages of dissertation writing it is a good idea to draw up a table of results with columns for similarities and differences in relation to literature sources. An example of this is shown in Table 12.2.

TASK 12.4

Using the template in Table 12.2, link the results of your study to the literature.

A summary of the purposes of the discussion chapter is presented in Figure 12.12.

Answer the research questions

Link results with theory

Compare results with previous research

Evaluate the results

Discuss the strengths of the study

Discuss the weaknesses of the study

Present the limitations of the study

Discuss the significance of the study

Implications for theory*

Present implications for practice*

Present implications for research*

*Some dissertations include a separate chapter for implications

FIGURE 12.12 The purposes of the discussion chapter

12.2.2 Organisation of the discussion chapter

The basis of a good discussion chapter is to make a detailed plan before writing. The organisation should comprise meaningful sub-headings, often based on the research questions. One way to start is to make a list of the most important findings of the study and produce one paragraph describing these. Another way to start the plan is with the research questions. It is essential that the research questions are explicitly answered in the dissertation, and the discussion chapter is the usual place for this. The research questions should be written out in full rather than referring to RQ1, RQ2 to help the examiner's uninterrupted reading. Once these organisational strategies have been chosen, then the evidence from the results needs to be identified and then the claim compared to theory and previous research.

Like the other chapters in the dissertation, the discussion chapter should have an introduction and a conclusion. Both of these serve to summarise the findings of the study. Figure 12.13 presents an example from an introduction, and Figure 12.14 shows an example from a conclusion chapter summary.

The results of this study have shown an overall negative view of the mainstreaming process at St John's High. The narrative reports various examples of missed learning opportunities for EAL student's due to the lack of staff training, undifferentiated lessons and classroom resources. Additionally, staff interviews also revealed an unfavourable opinion of mainstreaming, citing a number of practical issues which they experienced on a daily basis whilst attempting to mainstream EAL students. Five findings of specific importance and interest emerged from this study:

1. EAL students should be educated in the mainstream however the process requires significant improvement.
2. Subject specific lexis is the biggest challenge when mainstreaming EAL students.
3. EAL students in low incidence mainstream schools struggle to create and maintain friendships.
4. Mainstream staff members are not trained to deal with EAL needs and demand more professional development in this area.
5. St John's current EAL provisions are not successful in providing learning opportunities for their EAL students.

Each finding is discussed below and linked to the relevant literature in order to explain and understand the results from this study.

FIGURE 12.13 Introduction to the discussion chapter

Source: Dry (2017)

5.1.3 Summary

Using code-mixed reading texts to introduce vocabulary, as compared with the traditional method of using word list, had more significant effect on learners' productive knowledge than their receptive knowledge. The bigger change for the experimental group on the productive tasks implies that a more strategic use of translation employed in the code-mixing method is pedagogically useful for bilinguals' vocabulary development. Main strengths of the method were choosing lexical chunks as target phrases to code-mix in a context and making use of the learning conditions by creating meaningful productive retrievals and varied repetitions.

FIGURE 12.14 Conclusion to the discussion chapter

Source: Mai (2018)

The chapter should clearly answer the research questions and clearly outline the significance of the study. If the discussion chapter does not explicitly answer the research questions, then it would be unable to get a good grade. Based on the purposes of the discussion chapter outlined in Figure 12.12, a suggested structure for the discussion chapter is presented in Figure 12.15.

TASK 12.5

Identify the structure of some discussion chapters from dissertations in your department.
Are there differences between the dissertations?
Which structure would fit your dissertation?

12.2.3 Limitations of the study

The discussion chapter may also include a section on the limitations of the research. In a course-work master's, time and resources are very limited; these constraints can affect the breadth and scope of research, such as sample size, methods used, research design and generalisability. In the limitations section, these perceived shortcomings are addressed, often with reference to the need to address these in future research. This may be useful if the student wishes to progress to a higher research degree. While it is important for the student to demonstrate an awareness of the shortcomings of their study, it is not a good idea to refer to too many limitations, as the examiner may question why these had not been addressed in the research design. Figure 12.16 shows an example of a limitations section taken from a discussion chapter.

Background/purpose/overall research finding

Identification of major point 1/RQ1

  Commentary

  Comparison to previous research/theory

Identification of major point 2 /RQ2

  Commentary

  Comparison to previous research/theory

Limitations

Summary of results

Significance of study

FIGURE 12.15 Suggested structure of the discussion chapter

The researcher acknowledges that, in spite of the use of rigorous methodology like Conversation Analysis, there are still limitations to this study. For example, the data collected were only from the perspective of the teacher – gathering screen recordings from both the teacher and the student could have led to more detailed analyses of the interactions. Finally, the amount of data collected only totalled about four hours. This was caused by participants deciding against participating at a very late stage, leaving little time to find replacements. In spite of these limitations, the data collected were somewhat unique and it is hoped that their addition to the limited body of research in this context.

FIGURE 12.16 Example of the limitations section

Source: Spencer (2018)

12.2.4 Implications of the study

The implications of the study may be included in the discussion chapter or may feature in the conclusion. It is usual to discuss the implications for theory, knowledge and practice. There may also be implications for methodology if a new approach has been used. Relating the research to practice is particularly important in the field of TESOL and applied linguistics, as the focus of the research is often professional. Within this section of the dissertation, recommendations are made for practice and further research. The recommendations section can establish a research area that could be investigated further by a larger scale study such as a PhD project.

12.3 Language of results and discussion

When writing about the results of the data analysis in a dissertation the past tense is usually used, for example, 'students who participated in the intervention scored 15% higher on average in the test than the control group'. When making claims about the findings the present tense is used: 'The results indicate a relationship between explicit vocabulary study and test performance'. Writing about results is largely descriptive, whereas writing the discussion requires making claims about the findings. Making claims needs to be supported by evidence, either from research, theory or from logical and critical argument. The language used in making claims reflects the level of authority and certainty of the conclusions. Typical strategies used to do this are hedges, which modify claims and make them less certain; being assertive, which represents the middle ground and using boosters, which strengthen the claim. It is important that these are used appropriately. This means not using a booster where a hedge should be used. Figure 12.17 shows some of examples of these and includes some boosters that should not be used in academic writing.

TASK 12.6

Look at several dissertations in your department. What sort of language is used to make claims?

Hedges

Assertive language

Boosters

Summary

This chapter has discussed the writing norms of the results and the discussion chapter. In writing about results, a distinction was made between quantitative and qualitative studies. The chapter examined the purpose, structure and language of typical results and discussion chapters in master's dissertations.

Hedges

This might be the reason for the lack of engagement of the students.

The data suggests explicit vocabulary study may enhance exam performance.

It seems the connectedness of the teacher plays a substantial role in learning.

This would seem to suggest a positive relationship between anxiety and a lack of strategy use.

Being assertive

The results indicate a clear relationship between teacher motivation and learner engagement.

This demonstrates translanguaging is a valuable classroom learning activity for these students.

This shows how well students can adapt to exclusive use of L2 in the classroom.

Using boosters

The results clearly indicate the importance of lowering anxiety in the classroom.

Clearly this indicates the need for an improvement in teaching methods at X institution.

Obviously anxiety should not be perceived as a wholly negative emotion.

Indeed, this can be construed as further evidence to support Brown's claim of subjectivity.

Boosters that should not be used

This proves that anxiety causes language failure.

Actually, anxiety can be facilitating.

In fact, this anxiety is not debilitating.

FIGURE 12.17 Language used in making claims

Common mistakes in writing about results

- Not identifying major findings
- Chapter is too long winded
- Presenting too many results

- Not ordering results
- Describing results without any interpretation
- Cutting and pasting tables from SPSS with too many statistics
- Including too many tables and graphs
- Not adhering to department style in using tables and figures
- Putting too much information in the appendix so that it interferes with the flow of the chapter

Common mistakes in writing the discussion chapter

- Not answering research questions
- Not having a clear argument progressing through the chapter
- Not leaving enough time to write a thorough discussion
- Not relating results to theory and research
- Being too descriptive and not critical
- Inflating significance of the results

FAQs

1. *Should I omit to report results that don't come out as I expected or results that do not support my thesis?*
   No. It is essential that results are reported accurately and thought through. If the results do not support your expectations, there will be a reason for this that needs to be uncovered. There may be a very interesting finding in the result that can make a new contribution to the field, or it may be that there is an error in the analysis.
2. *Should I report the answers for every item in my questionnaire using a graph or table in the dissertation?*
   It is not usual to report all answers for every participant. It is usual to synthesise the answers to provide an overall view. In some departments it is necessary to provide the full data set, interview transcripts and questionnaire answers in electronic form. This is provided in case the examiners wish to check the data.
3. *Can I combine the results and discussion chapter?*
   It is wise to check with the norms of the department but usually it is acceptable to have one chapter for the results and discussion. This is particularly true for qualitative research, which is less easy to categorise.
4. *What type of tables and graphs should I use?*
   The golden rule of using graphics is that they help understanding, that they are easy to understand and that they abide by the prescribed style. Using simple graphics with easy-to-identify labels can greatly help understanding. It should be possible for the reader to identify the message at a glance. It is not advisable to use specialised graphic techniques that require expert knowledge to interpret. The graphics should abide by the department style. The most common format in TESOL and applied linguistics is APA 6th edition or Harvard.

5 *Can I cut and paste sections of my literature review for the discussion chapter?* This is not advisable and would certainly put the examiner offside. While many of the same references will be referred to in the discussion chapter, the structure of the argument will be different. The results of the study need to be positioned within the discussion of the literature.

Further reading

Swales and Feak (2012) have a chapter on data commentary and the chapter provides practice in making claims. This includes a section on qualification and strength of claims. Paltridge and Starfield (2019) have a chapter on writing discussions and conclusions. This includes the possible structure for the chapter and a section on language. Bitchener (2010) presents a useful analysis of a quantitative dissertation and includes a chapter about the discussion of results. Woodrow (2014) focuses on writing about quantitative studies in applied linguistics.

References

Bitchener, J. (2010). *Writing an applied linguistics thesis or dissertation: A guide to presenting empirical research*. Basingstoke: Palgrave Macmillan.

Chen, S. (2011). *Genre features of personal statements by Chinese English-as-an-additional language writers: A corpus driven study*. (Master's Dissertation), University of Victoria.

Dry, R. (2017). *EAL in the mainstream: A Northumberland case study*. (Master's Dissertation), Newcastle University.

Forde, R. (2018). *How can I teach this? Examining collaborative dialogic reflection and its impact on teacher learning*. (Master's Dissertation), Newcastle University.

Hicking, R. (2015). *Subtitles in authentic video listening: An exploration of the benefits of captions in relation to sensory preference types*. (Master's Dissertation), University College, London. Retrieved from https://englishagenda.britishcouncil.org/sites/default/files/attachments/dissertation_for_publication_ucl.pdf (Accessed 30 April, 2019)

Iyer, P. (2013). *The effect of collaborative blogging on communicative skills in the writing of Thai EFL students*. (Master's Dissertation), University of Birmingham. Retrieved from http://asian-efl-journal.com/wp-content/uploads/2014/thesis/Purnima_Iyer_M_%20Dissertation.pdf (Accessed 23 April, 2019)

Jones, S. (2011). *Investigating the F-move in teacher talk: A South Korean study on teachers' beliefs and classroom practices*. (Master's Dissertation), University of Birmingham. Retrieved from www.birmingham.ac.uk/Documents/college-artslaw/cels/essays/matefltesldissertations/Jonesdiss.pdf (Accessed 23 April, 2019)

Lin, Q. (2018). *Assessing teacher verbal feedback using the SETT framework: A case study on three English classes in a high school in China*. (Master's Dissertation), Newcastle University.

Mai, N. (2018). *Investigating the effects of code-mixed reading texts on vocabulary learning of Vietnamese adult learners*. (Master's Dissertation), Newcastle University.

Paltridge, B., & Starfield, S. (2019). *Thesis and dissertation writing in a second language: A handbook for students and their supervisors* (2nd ed.). Abingdon: Routledge.

Spencer, M. (2018). *Synchronous online learning via Zoom Videoconferencing: A multimodal conversation analytic study of teacher-student interaction*. (Master's Dissertation), Newcastle University.

Swales, J., & Feake, C. (2012). *Academic writing for graduate students: Essential tasks and skills* (3rd ed.). Ann Arbor, MI: University of Michigan Press.

Woodrow, L. (2014). *Writing about quantitative research in applied linguistics*. Basingstoke: Palgrave Macmillan.

Woodrow, L., Phakiti, A., & Hirsh, D. (2011). *Academic performance of ESL graduates from USFP*. (Unpublished research report), University of Sydney.

Zhou, H. (2017). *An analysis of the misuse of English articles by Chinese University-level EFL students and its relationship to pedagogy*. (Master's Dissertation), University of Newcastle.

13

BEGINNING AND ENDING THE DISSERTATION

While the introduction and conclusion chapters of a master's dissertation are short and do not have individual specific assessment criteria, both are very important. The introduction provides the reader with an overview of the study, while the conclusion identifies the important findings and the contribution the study has made to knowledge. This chapter examines the purpose and structure of these chapters. It also discusses the references section, which comes after the conclusion.

13.1 The introduction

The introduction to a dissertation is typically a very short chapter, sometimes less than 1000 words, as is the case with the example shown in Table 13.1. Its purpose is to situate the study and to highlight the significance of the study. It is important because after the abstract, which may have been written before the submission of the dissertation, it is the first section the reader will read. This chapter can greatly influence a reader's attitude to the text. If it is hard to follow and badly written, then the reader may assume rest of the study is of a similar calibre.

Some departments have suggestions for the structure of this chapter that should be followed. Most introduction chapters start with a broad description of the area of study and provide some background information; this then leads to the statement of the problem and the purpose of the research. The typical structure resembles a funnel, moving from the broad to the specific. Sometimes a writer may include the research questions in this chapter. The introduction usually concludes with an outline to the dissertation. Figure 13.1 shows a typical structure of an introduction.

TABLE 13.1 Example of a master's dissertation introduction

Section	*Function*
The vast majority of English language teachers worldwide are non-native speakers of English (Crystal, 2003; Canagarajah, 2005; Braine, 2012). Most of these teachers work in primary, secondary and tertiary institutions in countries where English is either a second or foreign language, what Holliday calls the TESEP contexts (tertiary, secondary and primary education, 1994b). Their backgrounds, needs and teaching contexts are likely to be significantly different to those of the predominantly native speaker English teachers (NESTs) working in what Holliday calls BANA (Britain, Australasia and North America) contexts (Holliday, 1994b; see also Canagarajah, 1999; Braine, 2005).	General statement, context, background to study
While such non-native speaker English teachers (NNESTs) constitute the majority of English teachers worldwide, it is notable that comparatively little research was conducted into NNESTs until the 1990s (Moussa & Llurda, 2008), either regarding their teaching contexts (Holliday, 1994a; Medgyes, 1994; Canagarajah, 1999) or their needs on teacher education programs, due partly to the Anglophone-centric bias of much research in ELT (Braine, 2005), and partly to the general perception that it is from the Centre1 itself that teacher education research must disseminate (Phillipson, 1992; Canagarajah, 1999; Holliday, 2005). Indeed, nearly all such research conducted on NNESTs in teacher education focuses on their experiences on the programme itself (most commonly in Centre countries), especially their "additional or different training" needs (Moussu & Llurda, 2008, p. 319), challenges and self-image, often described in contrast to native speakers, and often failing to situate their experiences in their own professional and personal development that should incorporate their past experiences, current needs and future teaching contexts (Polio & Wilson-Duffy, 1998; Braine, 1999; Liu, 1998; Canagarajah, 2005). As a native-speaking English teacher and teacher trainer with extensive experience working on initial teacher-training courses (ITCs), than answers with regard to my underlying aim, to understand the role such courses play in the careers of NNESTs. I concluded my article by suggesting that "... further research is needed to identify more specific recommendations to ensure that such courses are better able to cater for the needs of all participants in the future" (Anderson, 2015, p. 11).	More detail to background, commentary, gap in knowledge
have benefited greatly from working with, and learning from, non-native speaker teachers and teacher trainers as colleagues and students. However, I have become concerned over recent years that ITCs themselves have adapted little to the increasing numbers of NNSs, especially NNESTs enrolling on such courses. This concern prompted me, for a prior assignment, to conduct some initial, mainly quantitative research into differences in backgrounds, needs and future teaching contexts between native-speaker (NS) and non-native speaker (NNS) participants on ITCs such as the Cambridge CELTA and the Trinity CertTESOL, a context I know well, having trained teachers extensively on I both courses. The significant	

differences found warranted publication (Anderson, 2015) and included the discovery that, unlike NS participants, the vast majority of NNS participants (89%) were experienced English teachers, not pre-service trainees, often taking these qualifications mid-career. However, given that the questionnaire-based research was submitted anonymously, and included little qualitative data, it left me with more questions than answers with regard to my underlying aim, to understand the role such courses play in the careers of NNESTs. I concluded my article by suggesting that ". . . further research is needed to identify more specific recommendations to ensure that such courses are better able to cater for the needs of all participants in the future" (Anderson, 2015, p. 11).	Rationale of the study, problem statement
In order to understand the issues in question fully, I decided for this dissertation to conduct a qualitative study attempting to situate ITC courses within the individual careers of a variety of NNESTs from different backgrounds.	Purpose statement
I developed four research questions as follows: 1. What factors contribute to NNESTs with prior teaching experience taking the decision to enrol on ITCs? 2. How useful and productive do experienced NNESTs find ITCs (considering suitability to needs and envisaged future teaching contexts, and challenges faced on courses)? 3. What impact do ITCs have on experienced NNESTs, including impact on own teaching practice, and on career development? 4. With the benefit of hindsight, what suggestions/feedback do respondents have for other NNESTs and also for course providers and validators to ensure that ITCs are as useful for NNESTs as for other participants? I chose to conduct detailed, semi-structured interviews with a small number of experienced NNESTs who had completed ITCs at least six months previously, supported by a larger number of email interviews with NNESTs to enable me to answer these questions both from individual and shared perspectives, drawing on as wide a range of teaching contexts as possible.	Research questions, research methodology
After initial clarification of important terminology, this study begins with a literature review including background to the study, discussion of the very limited literature on NNS participants on ITCs, and wider discussion of the four research questions, considering both mine (Anderson, 2015) and other studies on NNS participants on TESOL programs. This is followed by a description of the methodology used in this study, presentation of findings and discussion of these findings. The conclusion offers a number of practical recommendations for ITC validators and course providers.	Outline of the dissertation

Source: Anderson (2016)

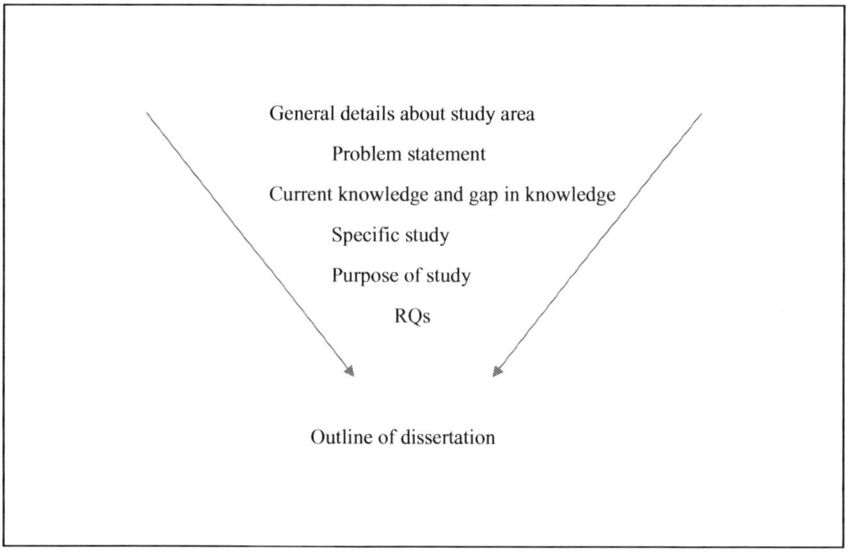

FIGURE 13.1 Structure of a master's dissertation introduction

It is important to include the purpose of the research at the beginning. This acts as the introduction to the introduction and is often written as a purpose statement. Figure 13.2 shows some sample purpose statements.

Table 13.1 shows an example of a dissertation introduction and its structure. This introduction is quite short and clear and includes a background, rationale, purpose and an outline of the dissertation.

TASK 13.1

Look at a range of dissertations from your department.

1. What is the typical structure of the introduction?
2. Identify purpose statement.
3. Write out a purpose statement for your dissertation beginning "the aim of the current study is . . ."
4. Plan the generic structure of the introduction to your dissertation.

13.2 The conclusion

Conclusions vary across dissertations in terms of length and content. Some dissertations include a lengthy discussion about the contribution to knowledge, limitations and implications for practice and research. Other dissertations include these details in the discussion chapter and the conclusion serves to bring the dissertation to a close by highlighting the findings and areas for future research.

Usually the conclusion will start with an overview of the research, the significance of the research, a brief mention of the limitations, the contribution to practice if relevant and areas for further research.

Example 1

The current study attempts to contribute to the body of literature exploring students' beliefs and perceptions on the use of translanguaging. In particular, it focuses on how the university students who were enrolled in the General English classroom perceive this translanguaging strategy performed by the course instructor.
(Fitriani, 2018).

Example 2

The aims of this research are: firstly, to raise teachers' awareness of feedback; secondly, to assess the quality of teacher feedback; thirdly, to provide strategies to improve teacher feedback; fourthly, to have a sample of teachers, using SETT, self-evaluate their feedback to see whether these strategies can be used in the future.
(Lin 2018).

Example 3

This paper aims to provide more insights into the effect of code-mixing on vocabulary learning and to discuss its principled use as a method of teaching and learning vocabulary. To be specific, the goal of the study is to assess the effectiveness of code-mixed reading texts on learners' receptive and productive vocabulary knowledge, as well as their memory recall.
(Mai, 2018).

Example 4

The aim of the current study was to gain evidence that suggests whether or not ALT reading picture books to the whole class promotes opportunities for scaffolding.
(Cooper, 2016).

FIGURE 13.2 Examples of purpose statements

Table 13.2 shows an example of a conclusion chapter, and Table 13.3 shows an example of a short concluding paragraph. Each of these have the sections and functions identified.

TABLE 13.2 Example of a master's dissertation conclusion chapter

Section	*Function*
This study sought to use CA to provide a detailed analysis of the pedagogical affordances of Zoom Videoconferencing in one-on-one, teacher-student contexts, and to identify how interlocutors utilise multiple modes while teaching/learning on this platform. Unique, video-based data in the form of screen recordings were collected and transcribed in detail, which gave a participant-centred, micro-analysis of online interaction on Zoom.	General statement about study
This conclusion will start with a summary of the literature and where this study fits into it. After this, there will be a summary of the findings and their significance to the field. Finally, it will end with some recommendations for future studies.	Organisation of chapter
The study focussed on the interactional practices which interlocutors adopt in this context. A review of the literature demonstrated the value of CA as a methodology for the analysis of multimodal interaction, and also demonstrated a lack of CA studies in DVC contexts. The previous research in this area has either been quantitative, which removed context from findings, had sought to compare DVC with other mediums, or have used a wide variety of data analysis procedures. This, therefore, provided a clear need for conducting a solely CA study, which puts the interactions as the main focus of analysis.	Need for research, reference to literature review
However, there was previous research that provided important introductions to different types of turn-design and how they understood, as well as different forms of gesture and how they are deployed in interaction. The results of this study build on this literature by demonstrating how these aspects of interaction are utilised on in a synchronous DVC context on Zoom. The findings here go some way towards filling a large gap in CA DVC studies, which will be reviewed in the following paragraph.	Contribution to knowledge
The findings in the present study highlight the value of Zoom Videoconferencing as a medium for online pedagogy. The study revealed instances in which interlocutors had the ability to dynamically adjust their strategy to achieve an interactional goal if their previous attempt(s) were unsuccessful. While also highlighting that some of the strategies failed or succeeded multiple times, thus providing important information for teachers and learners alike. The combination of the textual and aural mode was found to help teachers and students overcome technical problems during lessons. The study also revealed how teachers and learners have the ability to deploy a variety of paralinguistic features to maintain interactional order. Interlocutors are able to deploy regulator gestures to control turn-taking, iconic gestures in support of lexical explanations, and self-regulators to show feelings of nervousness as a means to encourage the initiation of repair. These features are made possible by the visual mode afforded by webcam image, which highlights the importance of the framing choice used by participants. A framing choice which creates a gesture space is necessary to ensure interlocutors have access to as many nonverbal features.	Summary of findings

The findings in this study contribute a small amount of research to a very under-researched area in online pedagogical interaction, however, there is still a lot more research needed to fully understand how these interactions are organised. Future research may seek to build on this study to add depth to its findings, by finding further instances in which interlocutors make use of varies embodied actions as a means of maintaining interactional order. However, these studies will need to ensure they adopt an emic approach to data collection and analysis to ensure that the interlocutors are the main foci of any future study.	Limitations and future research

Source: Spencer, 2018)

TABLE 13.3 Example of a master's dissertation concluding paragraph

Section	*Function*
Teacher verbal feedback is undoubtedly influencing students' learning of foreign languages. Good teacher feedback may stimulate students' motivations in studying and create more learning opportunities for them. Hence, the consideration of assessing teacher feedback and improving the quality of feedback are both essential.	General statement based on research findings
Though there were some difficulties when applying SETT into a Chinese context, the three participants all acknowledged the usefulness of SETT of highlighting their issues with their feedback.	Limitation
If teachers are able to use this for their self-reflections of feedback in the future, hopefully more good-quality feedback will be provided in Chinese English Language Teaching classrooms.	Implication

Source: Lin, (2018)

TASK 13.2

Look at a range of dissertations from your department.

1. Does your department favour short or long conclusions?
2. Summarise in one or two sentences the contribution to knowledge your dissertation has made.
3. Summarise in one or two sentences the implications of your study.
4. Summarise in one or two sentences the limitations of your study.

13.3 The reference list

The reference list comes immediately after the conclusion. This is a list of all the works referred to in the dissertation; it is not a list of all the works consulted. So, the citations and reference list should match. If there is a citation in the text, this should appear in the reference list, and if there is a reference in the reference list, it should appear as a citation in the text. The sources in the reference list should be those that have been consulted and should not include secondary citations unless these are specifically referred to. For example, with the secondary citation (Brown, 2012 cited in Smith, 2018, p. 18), only Smith should appear in the list as this is the source consulted. If there are multiple works by the same author in the same year, it is usual to use letters to distinguish between the works. In the text numbers are used: eg (Brown, 2018b). An example of how the reference list would look for this type of citation is shown in Table 13.4. With multiple works it is important to note that the citation is based on works actually consulted and not the classification of others.

The correct reference style should be used both for citations and for the reference list, and the style should be accurately used. The correctness of the reference list and citations is usually assessed in the examination of the dissertation, and it is an easy if somewhat tedious task. The appropriate referencing style is usually available in the department handbook. Common styles in TESOL and applied linguistics are the American Psychological Association (APA) 6th edition and Harvard, which is very similar. Table 13.4 shows some examples of different types of references in APA 6th edition. The following web tool is very useful to check the correct way to reference in different styles: www.cite.auckland.ac.nz/2.html.

TABLE 13.4 Example of an excerpt from a reference list in APA 6th edition

Example reference	*Type*
Bitchener, J. (2010). *Writing an applied linguistics thesis or dissertation: A guide to presenting empirical research.* Basingstoke: Palgrave Macmillan.	Book, single author, 1st edition
Denzin, N. K., & Lincoln, Y. S. (Eds.). (2018). *The Sage handbook of qualitative research* (5th ed.). Thousand Oaks, CA: Sage.	Edited book, 5th edition
Kennedy, S., & Trofimovich, P. (2016). Research timeline: Second language communication strategies. *Language Teaching, 49*(4), 494–512. doi:0.1017/S026144481600015X	Journal article with DOI
Mai, N. (2018). *Investigating the effects of code-mixed reading texts on vocabulary learning of Vietnamese adult learners* (Unpublished master's dissertation). Newcastle University.	Unpublished dissertation
Paltridge, B., & Woodrow, L. (2012). Dissertation writing: Moving beyond the text. In R. Tang (Ed.), *Academic writing in a Second or Foreign Language: Issues and challenges facing ESL/EFL academic writers in higher education contexts* (pp. 88–104). London: Continuum.	Book section from edited book
University of Manchester. (n.d.). Academic phrasebank. Retrieved from www.phrasebank.manchester.ac.uk/	Webpage
Woodrow, L. (2006a). Academic success of international post-graduate education students and the role of English proficiency. *University of Sydney Papers in TESOL, 1*, 51–71.	References by same author in same year
Woodrow, L. (2006b). Anxiety and speaking English as a second language. *RELC Journal, 37*, 301–328.	
Woodrow, L. (2006c). A model of adaptive second language learning. *Modern Language Journal, 90*(3), 297–319.	

- Academic writing, presentation accuracy of quotations, referencing
- Reference list and references set out in appropriate format
- In-text citations set out appropriately
- Academic style adheres to APA 6th edition

FIGURE 13.3 Examples of assessment criteria for a reference list

There will often be a category in the assessment criteria that refers directly to referencing. This is usually within the style and presentation category. Some examples of these criteria are presented in Figure 13.3. So, it is important that the reference list is accurately written with no mistakes in punctuation, authors' names and page numbers. This can be tedious, but it can be alleviated with the use of referencing software, which automatically generates a reference list based on the sources cited in the text. This is discussed further in section 13.1.2.

13.3.1 Digital object identifiers (DOIs)

A DOI is a unique alpha-numeric code assigned to a published document. This does not change over time. Increasingly, publications are requesting that authors include DOIs in their reference lists, although at present it is unusual for this to be a requirement at a master's level dissertation. If required, the DOI can be found at www.crossref.org/guestquery.

13.3.2 Referencing software

Many students choose to use referencing software. This helps store and keep track of sources used in the dissertation. The software is extremely useful when writing the reference list, as most programmes generate a list in the correct style automatically. This saves a lot of work and helps avoid mistakes. However, some care is needed when including this in the dissertation. The reference list should be in the same format as the rest of the dissertation. This can be quite fiddly. For example, EndNote generates a single-spaced list, and the dissertation may be written with double spacing. To change the spacing the EndNote programme should be closed and the spacing of the list reformatted. However, if the programme is opened again, the formatting reverts to single spacing. Some examples of referencing programmes are listed in the references list at the end of this chapter. RefMe, Zotero and Mendeley are free programmes, while EndNote is often available as a site licence through the university.

TASK 13.3 Generate a reference list for your dissertation and complete the following:

Check the style is appropriate
Check author's name is correct, do not mix up family name and given name
Check use of initial of given name
Check year of publication is correct
Check punctuation is correct
Check use of capital letters
Check style appropriate to type of publication, eg journal, book
Check page numbers are included if required

Summary

This chapter has looked at the beginning and end of the dissertation. It has presented some examples of introductions and conclusions and how they can be structured. The chapter provides advice on the reference list, which comes after the conclusion.

Common mistakes in writing the introduction, conclusion and references

- The introduction is badly written with grammatical errors and spelling mistakes.
- The introduction is not very clearly linked to the study.
- The introduction is too long/too short.
- The conclusion makes inflated claims about the significance or the contribution of the study.
- The conclusion identifies too many shortcomings in the research.
- The reference list contains works not consulted.
- The reference list includes poor sources, eg obscure web materials.
- There is no obvious reference style in the reference list.
- The reference list includes many styles. This is usually because references have been copied from different sources that do not reflect the required style.
- The reference list has many spelling and punctuation errors.

FAQs

1 *When should I write the introduction?*
It is usual to write the introduction late in the dissertation writing process as it needs to reflect the content of the dissertation accurately. The introduction can be written just before submission.

2 *Why have a section about conclusions and a conclusion?*
Different departments have different practices in terms of labelling the sections of a dissertation. Basically, 'conclusions' refer to findings, whereas the 'conclusion' refers to the section at the end of the dissertation. You should always check the practices for your department.

3 *What style of referencing should I use?*

You should always use the style recommended by your department. Be careful not to copy styles from publications, as this will probably be different from the department style. It is also important not to mix referencing styles within the reference list.

4 *Do I need to use DOIs?*
It is unusual for departments to require DOIs in a master's dissertation, but it is a good idea to include these in your reference database. Some academic journals require DOIs, and this may become more common in the future. So, if you plan to publish your research at some stage, having the DOIs available will be useful.

5 *Why do markers make such a fuss about referencing style?*
Adhering to the department referencing style is a way of belonging and identifying as a member of your academic community. Correct referencing can also provide evidence for the sources used and shows there has been no plagiarism.

Further reading

Feak and Swales (2011) have published a book devoted to writing introductions in different types of academic texts. The book takes a genre-based approach and examines the moves in introductions in a range of discipline. Paltridge and Starfield (2007) (Chapter 10) have a good section on the language of conclusions. Bitchener (2018) examines feedback from supervisors on dissertation chapters in Chapter 4. This includes introductions and conclusions. This book is written from supervisor perspective, which can be quite informative for the student. The section includes examples taken from student theses and dissertations and provides some examples of tasks that can facilitate the writing of these sections.

References

Anderson, J. (2016). *A qualitative study into the role of initial teacher training courses in the professional development of experienced non-native speaker teachers of English.* (Master's Dissertation), Kings College, London. Retrieved from https://englishagenda.britishcouncil.org/sites/default/files/attachments/mda2017_winner_jason_anderson_king_s_college_london.pdf (Accessed 13 May, 2109)

Bitchener, J. (2018). *A guide to supervising non-native English writers of theses and dissertations focusing on the writing process.* London: Routledge.

Cooper, C. (2016). *Scaffolding during the initial reading of picture books in Japanese elementary school EFL classrooms: A qualitative study investigating how teachers and learners co-construct meaning during whole class picture book reading.* (Master's Dissertation), Sheffield Hallam University.

Feake, C., & Swales, J. (2011). *Creating contexts: Writing introductions across genres.* Ann Arbor, MI: Michigan University Press.

Fitriani, R. (2018). *EFL students' perceptions on translanguaging in the general English classroom at an Indonesian university.* (Master's Dissertation), University of Sydney.

Lin, Q. (2018). *Assessing teacher verbal feedback using the SETT framework: A case study on three English classes in a high school in China.* (Master's Dissertation), Newcastle University.

Mai, N. (2018). *Investigating the effects of code-mixed reading texts on vocabulary learning of Vietnamese adult learners*. (Master's Dissertation), Newcastle University.

Paltridge, B., & Starfield, S. (2007). *Thesis and dissertation writing in a second language: A handbook for supervisors*. Abingdon: Routledge.

Spencer, M. (2018). *Synchronous online learning via Zoom Videoconferencing: A multimodal conversation analytic study of teacher-student interaction*. (Master's Dissertation), Newcastle University.

Referencing software programmes

RefMe www.citethisforme.com/uk

Zotero www.zotero.org/

Mendeley www.mendeley.com/?interaction_required=true

PART IV

Dissertation submission

14

THE FINISHING TOUCHES

The final sections of the dissertation to write before submission are the abstract, table of contents, acknowledgements and appendices. This chapter discusses these sections with examples and then provides some advice for final editing and proof-reading.

14.1 Title page

Usually the academic department will provide a dissertation template for the dissertation title page. Typically, this includes the name of the student, the title of the dissertation and the name of the supervisor. It may also include a word count. An example of a title page is shown in Figure 14.1.

14.2 The dissertation abstract

Dissertation abstracts are very important because the reader reads the abstract first and thus forms an impression of the whole text. In some departments abstracts are submitted independently a few weeks before the formal submission date. This process may be used to select the most appropriate examiner for the dissertation. The abstract is also important because it should include descriptors that make the work searchable in text and online. Like thesis and dissertation introductions, there has been a lot of research into the structure and language of these (Swales & Feak, 2009). Abstracts are found in a range of texts such as journal articles, conference papers and book sections. In master's dissertations the typical length of an abstract is 200–300 words, however, it is important to follow the department guidelines and not go over the word limit.

The dissertation abstract should capture the essence of the dissertation and should reflect the contents of the dissertation: background, aim, results, discussion

Tyne University

School of Applied Linguistics

MA TESOL

Teachers' and students' anxiety reactions to CEFR assessments

Rita Lee

SID 156789

NAME OF SUPERVISOR: Lindy Woodrow

10 August, 2019

WORD COUNT 14,999

FIGURE 14.1 Sample title page

and implications in a few words. Figure 14.2 presents the typical generic structure of a master's dissertation abstract. Tables 14.1 and 14.2 demonstrate this in sample abstracts. In Table 14.2 the research questions are included in the research purpose section.

In some abstracts it is a requirement to include descriptors. Descriptors or keywords are words that are central to the dissertation. They are important because these words are searchable in databases and online, so they can contribute to the dissemination of the dissertation, which is very important for the writer's academic profile. So, possible descriptors for the abstract in Table 14.1 could be 'EFL, Chinese learners, English articles, grammar instruction'.

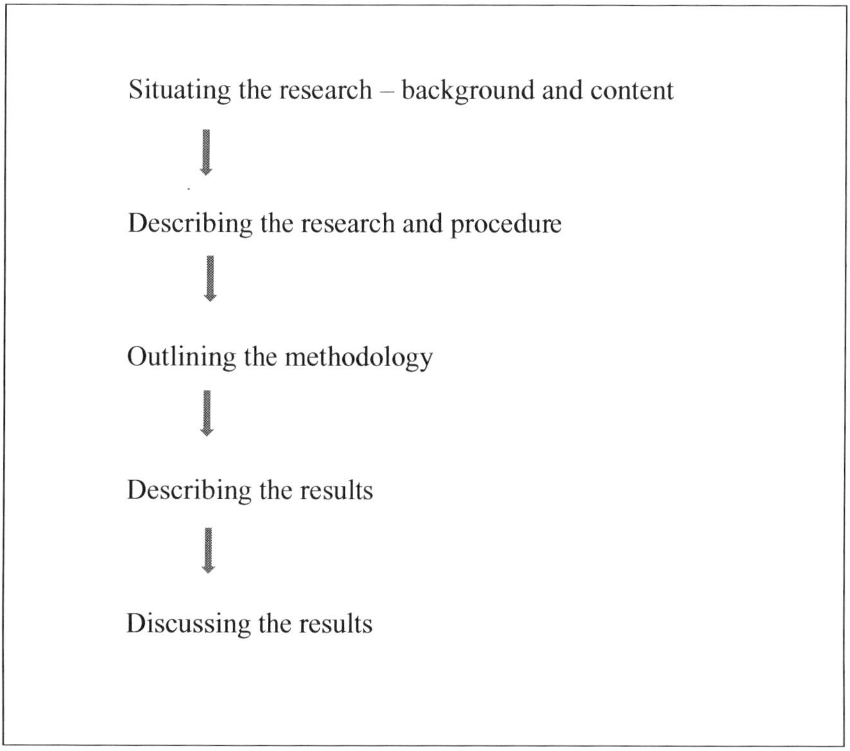

FIGURE 14.2 Typical structure of dissertation abstracts

TABLE 14.1 Dissertation abstract, example 1

Abstract section	*Structure*
The English article system (definite article *the*, indefinite article *a/an* and zero article Ø) is a widely acknowledged issue for Mandarin Chinese learners whose first languages lack articles, despite the high frequency and early input of English articles (Lu, 2001).	Background, introduction to situation
One of the purposes of this study is to explore English article errors Chinese learners make in order to find the frequent types of errors. More importantly, some researchers (e.g., Butler, 2002) claim that learners tend to be influenced by textbooks (instruction materials) during the acquisition of the English article system. Thus, this study mainly focuses on grammar instruction and aims to reveal the possible relationship between the information in the textbook and article errors.	Research purpose and importance

(*Continued*)

TABLE 14.1 (Continued)

Abstract section	*Structure*
A total of 20 Chinese university-level EFL (English as a Foreign Language) students participated in this study. They were required to fill in a borrowed cloze test from Master (1994) and copies were taken of the English article system section from their grammar textbook.	Research procedure and methods
The results show that the most frequent type of error is overuse of articles, then article omission, and the least frequent is article substitution.	Results
The quantitative and qualitative analyses reveal that the information in the textbook has some influence on the article errors participants make. It also suggests that the instruction material should balance the "rules" of article usage, although learners can benefit from this instruction material and explicit grammar instruction in teaching the English article system.	Discussion, implications

Source: Zhou (2017)

TABLE 14.2 Dissertation abstract, example 2

Abstract section	*Structure*
According to Vongpumivitch, Huang, and Chang (2008) and Shawn (1991) the use of academic vocabulary is one of the main difficulties encountered by English as a foreign language students when reading and writing academic English.	Background, introduction to situation
Therefore, the aim of this study is to explore the use of academic vocabulary in a corpus of Brazilian students in order to propose pedagogical implications for the teaching of EAP in Brazil. The research questions are: a) what is the vocabulary profile of assignments written by Brazilian students?; b) how does it compare to the vocabulary profile of other academic corpora presented in the literature review?; c) what words in the AWL do Brazilian students use?; and d) how does the use of academic words differ between Brazilian students and students represented in the BAWE corpus?	Research purpose and importance
In order to answer these questions a corpus of assignments written by Brazilian students was compiled and analysed using Range and Sketch Engine.	Research procedure and methods

Abstract section	*Structure*
The results show that the corpus of Brazilian students present the same coverage of AWL words as other academic corpora. However, the word forms selected are different, some of the reasons for this are the underuse of lexical bundles and derivations processes.	Results
These findings provide insights on topics that could be addressed in classes of EAP for Brazilian students.	Discussion, implications

Source: Da Silva (2016)

TASK 14.1 Use the following template to produce an abstract for your dissertation.

Abstract section	*Structure*
	Background, introduction to situation
	Research purpose and importance
	Research procedure and methods
	Results
	Discussion, implications

Write out six keywords from your dissertation.

Chapter 16 includes examples of abstracts from different types of master's research projects.

14.3 Acknowledgements

It is usual in a dissertation to acknowledge all who have provided assistance in the study. It is essential that the funding body and those who provided direct help be acknowledged. This includes the supervisor, statistics advisor, research assistants and editor or proof-reader. Many students also choose to acknowledge participants and significant others, such as partners and family. Figure 14.3 shows an example of the acknowledgements section from a master's dissertation and Figure 14.4 presents a template that can be used to write the acknowledgements.

TASK 14.2

Who will you acknowledge in your dissertation?
Draft an acknowledgements section using the template in Figure 14.2.

14.4 The table of contents

It is usual to include a table of contents at the front of the dissertation. Unlike the dissertation abstract, which is written after the dissertation is completed, producing

I am deeply grateful to my supervisor, Elaine Lopez, whose generous encouragements, strict requirements and enthusiasm have helped me much during the process of my dissertation writing. I would like to express my sincere gratitude to her. What she said in our meetings has encouraged and helped me a lot and provided inexhaustible guidance in my academic performance. Without her patience and guidance, my work would not have been finished in due course. In addition, I would like to thank the participants and the module leader and the module leader of English major in the Xianda college of Economics and Humanities Shanghai International Studies University in China, for taking time away from their busy schedules to participate in my study. Meanwhile, I extremely appreciate the support and encouragement from my parents all the times.

FIGURE 14.3 Example of an acknowledgements section

Source: Zhou (2017)

I would like to thank my supervisor (*title and name*) for her unfailing support and guidance during this study.

Thanks go to the (*funding body*) for the postgraduate scholarship that funded this research.

I'd also like to thank the participants in the study (*institution*) for devoting time and effort to help my study.

Thanks also go to (*name*) for proof-reading my final dissertation.

Finally, heartfelt thanks go to (*my family, partner, friend*) for their unfailing support during the past few months.

FIGURE 14.4 Template for acknowledgements

a contents page can be a useful activity at the beginning of the writing stage, as it helps clarify thinking about the structure of the dissertation. The contents page would then be revised just before submission so that the page numbers match.

The contents page is placed in the front section of the dissertation, which is numbered using Roman numerals. The contents page should reflect the sections and sub-sections of the thesis and students often choose to use hyperlinks to facilitate reader access of the different sections of the dissertation. When using sections and sub-sections it is usual not to go beyond three levels – for example, 3.4.2 – otherwise it can be quite difficult for the reader to follow. If the dissertation includes a number of tables and figures, separate entries should be made for a list of tables and a list of figures. Figure 14.5 shows the typical ordering of sections in a dissertation.

Title page

Declaration

Acknowledgements

Abstract

Table of contents

List of tables/figures

List of abbreviations or key terms

Chapter 1 Introduction

Chapter 2 Literature review

Chapter 3 Methodology

Chapter 4 Results

Chapter 5 Discussion

Chapter 6 Conclusion

Reference list

Appendices

FIGURE 14.5 Typical sections and ordering of a dissertation in the table of contents

TASK 14.3 Complete the sections and sub-sections for your dissertation based on the following table of contents.

Section	Sub-sections
Title page	
Declaration	
Acknowledgements	

(Continued)

TASK 14.3

Abstract
Table of contents
List of tables/figures
List of abbreviations or key terms
Chapter 1 Introduction
Chapter 2 Literature review
Chapter 3 Methodology
Chapter 4 Results
Chapter 5 Discussion
Chapter 6 Conclusion
Reference list
Appendices

14.5 Declaration

Most departments require that a declaration page be included in the dissertation. This is usually in line with the university's plagiarism policy and is a page that states that the dissertation is the work of the student him- or herself. Some institutions have quite complex declarations that include a reference to ethics approval and a claim about not exceeding the word length as well as originality statements. The department should provide a template or regulations for this document. Figure 14.6 provides an example of a declaration page.

14.6 List of terms and abbreviations

Many dissertations include a list of the important terms used and any acronyms used. This is not usually an essential component of the dissertation and should not replace explanations within the text, as it is inconvenient for readers to keep flipping to the front of the dissertation to see what a particular acronym stands for. The list usually provides the term in full and the acronym used in the dissertation. An example of this is provided in Figure 14.7.

14.7 Appendices

The purpose of the appendices is to include additional material and information that is not essential for the study. Departments may have regulations for what is included in the appendices, for example, the appendices may include an example of how the raw data was analysed, such as a sample interview transcript with analysis. Some departments ask for the whole data set, which may be copied onto a USB and included with submission.

DECLARATION

I confirm that this dissertation is all my own work. I certify that all the material in this dissertation that is not my own work has been identified and that no material is included that has been submitted for any other award or qualification.

Rita Lee

Date: 10 February, 2019

Signature: R. L. Lee

FIGURE 14.6 Example of a declaration page

List of Abbreviations

BE (teachers): Bilingual (non-native) English (teachers)

CLT: Communicative Language Teaching

ELT: English Language Teaching

FDH: Fundamental Difference Hypothesis

ICC: Intercultural Communicative Competence

L1: First (native) Language

L2: Second (non-native) Language

NES (teachers): Native English Speakers/Speaking (teachers)

NNES (teachers): Non-Native English Speakers/Speaking (teachers)

SLA: Second Language Acquisition

TESOL: Teaching English to Speakers of Other Languages

FIGURE 14.7 Example of a list of abbreviations

Source: Asada (2013)

The text in the appendices is not usually included in the word count, so some writers are tempted to include too much information in the appendices as a way of keeping within the word limit. This is a mistake, and examiners will see through this. It is essential that the material included in the appendices does not interfere with the flow of the dissertation.

Figure 14.8 shows some type of information that may be included in the appendix, and Figure 14.9 shows an example of the appendices taken from a table of contents. Appendices should be given a number or a letter and a title, as is illustrated in the example in Figure 14.9.

TASK 14.4

What material will you include in your appendices?

Schedules

Descriptions of research sites

Ethics approval

Consent form

Participant information sheet

Letters of permission

Detailed participant profiles

Questionnaire

Tests

Assessment criteria for test

Detailed analytical framework

Interview protocol

Large tables of data

Transcriptions

FIGURE 14.8 Examples of material that may be included in the appendix

Appendices 73

Appendix A: Ethics approval 73

Appendix B: Participant information sheet 75

Appendix C: Participant consent form 80

Appendix D: Paper questionnaire 82

Appendix E: Interview questions 85

Appendix F: Sample of the interview transcript 86

FIGURE 14.9 Example of appendices

Source: Fitriani (2018)

14.8 Editing and proof-reading

The final stage in the dissertation is the editing and proof- reading stage. Editing should have been happening throughout the writing of the dissertation, but proof-reading happens at the end. The dissertation writer often finds it very difficult to spot mistakes because of being so close to the text, so it is a good idea, if possible, to get someone else to read the final draft. Some students decide to get a professional editor to go through the final version; however, universities vary in their attitudes to this. Some universities encourage this practice, but some universities actively discourage such practices, believing the dissertation should be entirely the student's own work. A compromise is to get a friend to read through the final draft. Whichever method used it is necessary to thank the proof-reader/editor in acknowledgements.

If the writer plans on self-editing, then an editing checklist will be useful. Editing and proof-reading need to be focused because it is unrealistic to expect all errors to be obvious in a single reading. Table 14.3 is a general checklist for editing the organisation of the dissertation. Table 14.4 is a general checklist for language editing. A more detailed dissertation editing checklist can be found in Chapter 16. It is a good idea for the writer to develop his/her own checklist that reflects his/her particular weaknesses and common errors, for example, Singaporean users of English typically have a problem with verb–subject concord. When doing a final proof-read, most readers find reading is easier on a hard copy of the text rather than on a computer screen.

TABLE 14.3 General editing checklist for organisation of the dissertation

Areas of focus	✓
Dissertation within word limit.	
Written in correct font – eg Times New Roman 12.	
Correct line spacing – eg double spaced.	
Each chapter is on a new page.	
Dissertation has correct chapters, eg Introduction, Literature, Methods, Results and Discussion.	
Each chapter has an introduction.	
Each chapter has a conclusion.	
The dissertation has page numbers.	
Page numbers and contents page agree.	
Every table and figure has a title and a number.	
All tables and figures are referred to in the text.	

TABLE 14.4 General editing checklist for language in the dissertation

Areas of focus	✓
No informal language, eg lots of, fantastic.	
No imprecise language eg etc, and so on.	
No run on sentences – check conjunctions.	
Correct tense is used – eg past for results, present for implications.	
Paragraphs have a topic sentence.	
All verbs and subjects agree.	
Each paragraph deals with one idea.	
Each sentence has a capital letter and a full stop.	
Good use of cohesive markers to link text – eg however, despite.	
Personal grammatical weakness:	
Spelling is correct	
Punctuation is correct	

One way of highlighting errors is to read the text aloud. Another strategy is to leave the final draft of the dissertation for a couple of days before doing the final proof-read. This gives the writer's mind a chance to distance itself from the text.

Summary

This chapter has considered the final stage of dissertation. This includes the sections at the beginning of the dissertation: the contents page, abstract and acknowledgements.

The chapter addressed editing and proof-reading, including general guidelines for this. A more detailed chapter-by-chapter checklist is presented in Chapter 16.

Common mistakes in completing the dissertation

- Not completing on time
- Not leaving enough time for editing and proof-reading
- Using an inaccurate abstract
- Not including all the material required in the appendices (eg transcripts, ethics approval)
- Including too much material in the appendix so that it detracts from the flow of the dissertation
- Going over the word limit
- Not achieving the word limit
- Using incorrect grammar and spelling

FAQs

1 *Can I get an extension on my dissertation if I cannot finish on time?*
Usually not for this reason. In most departments extensions are only granted for a sound reason, such as illness. Part of the dissertation task is to be able to work independently, and this involves time management. One of the problems with getting an extension for the dissertation for whatever reason is the complication with completion in terms of the academic year and the examinations board of the university. It can be very complex if examiners need to be recruited out of session, and it may be up to a year before the board of examiners can ratify the results.

2 *Can I use a professional dissertation writing service to edit my dissertation?*
No. Professional proof-readers are usually acceptable, but they should not alter the structure or content of the text. Web-based essay writing and editing services should be avoided, as the assistance provided may be classed as academic dishonesty. Some universities do not allow any external assistance with the dissertation, including proof- readers.

3 *Are the examiners really concerned about word length?*
While it is unlikely that examiners will conduct a word count unless they feel there is a problem with the length of the dissertation, it is unwise to go significantly over or below the word limit. Many departments demand the number of words be listed at the beginning or end of the dissertation. Often there will be a category of the assessment criteria that reflects whether the dissertation is within the required word range.

4 *What is included in the word length?*
It is best to check with the department, as there can be differences between departments, but generally the bibliography or reference list, appendices, acknowledgements, the table of contents and the title page are excluded from the word count. Citations and headings are included in the word count.

5 *If I have too many words can I put a lot of material in the appendix?*

The appendices are for material that is related but not central to the study. An examiner should be able to read the dissertation without the flow being interrupted by referring to the appendices.

Further reading

Swales and Feak (2009) published a book focusing exclusively on writing abstracts in a range of texts including theses. Purdue University has an excellent site for academic writing. They have a section on proof-reading from language perspective. Denscombe (2017) has a good chapter on writing research reports that focuses on style and presentation.

References

Asada, A. (2013). *An investigation of the impact of bilingualism on the identity of a sample of bilingual English teachers*. (Master's Dissertation), Canterbury Christ Church University. Retrieved from www.asian-efl-journal.com/8681/thesis/an-investigation-of-the-impact-of-bilingualism-on-the-identity-of-a-sample-of-bilingual-english-teachers/ (Accessed 21 March, 2019)

Da Silva, L. (2016). *Academic vocabulary: A corpus linguistic study on how Brazilian students write academic English*. (Master's Dissertation), University of Warwick. Retrieved from https://englishagenda.britishcouncil.org/sites/default/files/attachments/mda2017_special_commendation_larissa_goulart_da_silva_university_of_warwick.pdf (Accessed 24 May, 2019)

Denscombe, M. (2017). *The good research guide for small scale social research projects* (6th ed.). London: Open University Press.

Fitriani, R. (2018). *EFL students' perceptions on translanguaging in the general English classroom at an Indonesian university*. (Master's Dissertation), University of Sydney.

Purdue Online Writing Lab. (n.d.). Purdue University. West Lafayette, Indiana. Retrieved from https://owl.purdue.edu/owl/general_writing/the_writing_process/proofreading/proofreading_for_errors.html (Accessed 21 March, 2019)

Swales, J., & Feak, C. (2009). *Abstracts and the writing of abstracts*. Ann Arbor, MI: Michigan University Press.

Zhou, H. (2017). *An analysis of the misuse of English articles by Chinese University-level EFL students and its relationship to pedagogy*. (Master's Dissertation), Newcastle University.

15

THE EXAMINATION AND BEYOND

This chapter focuses on the examination process by considering dissertation assessment criteria. The chapter then moves on to discuss what follows submission and examination. This includes oral presentation, resubmission, PhD pathways and publication. Each department has its own procedure for submitting the dissertation. In the UK this is usually done electronically through Turnitin. Turnitin is a text-matching software used to detect plagiarism. In some universities it is necessary to submit an intention to submit before submitting the final dissertation. This gives the department time to find appropriate examiners for the dissertation.

15.1 Examination of the dissertation

15.1.1 Who marks the dissertation?

The examination process for the dissertation varies among institutions. For example, in some Australian universities the dissertation is marked by examiners other than the supervisor, while in the UK the supervisor is the first marker, and a member of the TESOL/applied linguistics team is the second marker. It is usual to have two examiners for a master's dissertation. These examiners mark the work independently, then agree on a final mark. Unlike a higher research degree, such as an MPhil or PhD, it is unusual for the student to have any input concerning the selection of examiners. However, if there is an opportunity to do this, then the examiner should be selected based on expertise in the field and having a similar theoretical perspective to that of the dissertation. Another factor in the decision of examiner is whether the examiner could be called upon to provide a reference for future study or employment. Examiners should not be chosen because they are perceived as being 'easy markers' or because they have some sort of personal relationship with the student or supervisor.

Sometimes it is necessary for the dissertation to be marked by a third examiner if the first two differ greatly in their proposed mark. In addition, in most cases the grading of dissertations will be ratified by an external examiner or a member of the university's board of examiners.

TASK 15.1

How is the dissertation examined on your programme?
How many examiners are there?
Is your supervisor an examiner of your dissertation?
Are the examiners internal or external?

15.1.2 Dissertation assessment criteria

Assessment criteria have been discussed in previous chapters of this book, however it is worth considering these again at this stage. The assessment criteria are the guidelines examiners use to award a grade to the dissertation. The examiner will read the criteria as they mark the dissertation. The bottom line is that if the dissertation adheres to the criteria, then it will be successful, so it is vitally important that the writer accesses the assessment criteria.

It is usual for the dissertation assessment criteria to be presented in the student guide or at least available online. Different universities vary in the level of detail available for students. It is a good idea to look at previous dissertations and the feedback provided, as the links among the dissertation, the assessment criteria and the outcome can be seen. It is also useful to ask questions of supervisors, staff and previous students about the assessment procedure.

Table 15.1 presents the basic broad criteria that refer to the assessment of the dissertation as whole.

TASK 15.2

Make a list of questions you have about the assessment procedure of the dissertation.
Make a list of questions you have about the assessment criteria of the dissertation.
Where can you find the answers to these?
Who can you consult to answer these questions?

TABLE 15.1 Broad assessment criteria for a master's dissertation

Area in dissertation	*Assessment criteria*
Topic	Based on theory and practice, worth researching
Literature	Shows good knowledge of relevant literature, is evaluative
Research design	Sound research questions, clear research goal, appropriate approach and methods for research problem
Analysis	Sound and accurate analytical procedures
Results	Good quality data, presentation and interpretation
Discussion	Findings linked to theory, previous research and practice
Presentation	Well organised, adheres to department style

15.1.3 Feedback on the dissertation

Typically, the marking criteria are presented as a set of descriptors for each area according to grade: high distinction, distinction, merit (credit), pass and fail. Table 15.2 presents a list of criteria based on the sections of a dissertation. These criteria are based on a range of assessment grids used by universities in the UK, US and Australia.

TABLE 15.2 Breakdown of assessment criteria by dissertation section

Section	*Grade*	*Descriptor*	*Area*
Literature	High distinction Distinction Merit/Credit Pass Fail	Excellent Very good Good Average Inadequate	Choice of sources, relevant and up to date; theoretical framework; knowledge of field; argument evident throughout; analysis of sources; synthesis of sources
Research design and methods	High distinction Distinction Merit/Credit Pass Fail	Excellent Very good Good Average Inadequate	Understanding of methodological approach; research purpose; research questions; evidence of significance of research; methods appropriate to research; originality; expertise in research methods and analysis; contribution to knowledge
Analysis	High distinction Distinction Merit/Credit Pass Fail	Excellent Very good Good Average Inadequate	Accurate analysis; level of understanding of analysis; excellent potential for research
Results	High distinction Distinction Merit/Credit Pass Fail	Excellent Very good Good Average Inadequate	Quality of data; analysis of data; interpretation of results; presentation of results; interpretation of data; justification of findings
Discussion and conclusions	High distinction Distinction Merit/Credit Pass Fail	Excellent Very good Good Average Inadequate	Reflections on strengths and weaknesses of research; link to previous research; discussion of contribution to knowledge; link to theory; link to practice
Presentation	High distinction Distinction Merit/Credit Pass Fail	Excellent Very good Good Average Inadequate	Flow of argument; use of language; spelling; organisation using headings and sub-headings; use of graphics, tables and charts; referencing

Different departments have different examination norms; some departments use detailed grids of descriptors, or request examiner comments, or both. These reports are usually given to the student when the marking is complete. Usually, students will get two examination reports, which highlight the strengths and weaknesses of the dissertation. Figure 15.1 shows an example of a dissertation feedback form. Figure 15.2 shows an example of an examiner's report about a study that investigated the perceived usefulness of a pre-sessional EAP course. With the use of text matching software such as Turnitin, it is becoming common for marking and comments to be done exclusively online.

MA TESOL

MARKING SCHEME

Student name

1st marker **Agreed mark:**

2nd marker

Area	**%**	
1. Aims and objectives	10	_____
2. Literature review	20	_____
3. Research methodology	15	_____
4. Results and discussion	20	_____
5. Conclusions and recommendations	15	_____
7. Referencing	10	_____
8. Presentation	10	_____

Comments:

FIGURE 15.1 Example of a dissertation feedback form

This is a very good dissertation that investigates the important area of pre-sessional EAP. The research is well designed and executed. The theoretical perspective adopted is relevant and current. This dissertation highlights the problems international students face adjusting to the norms and practices they encounter on their academic courses and as such provides knowledge for the institution.

1. The dissertation is well organised and well written.
2. ELC is a multinational company that provides service to the higher education sector. The pre-sessional courses at ELC are not run by the university.
3. Most pre-sessional courses are concerned with language entry not academic entry requirements.
4. I think you could have addressed the importance of passing the ELC test. This is used as an entry requirement yet is not subjected to the rigorous consideration of validity and reliability as tests such as IELTS. The ELC test is an in-house test.
5. Another thing that could have been discussed is the role pre-sessional course plays in generating revenue for the university. Perhaps some discussion of the numbers of students enrolling on the pre-sessional course might have been interesting.
6. The literature review covers a wide range of up to date and relevant sources which support the study. The literature review shows synthesis and a critical stance. The main argument is very clear throughout.
7. ESAP and EGAP are referred to. These terms should have been defined in light of the approach of the pre-sessional course.
8. The research design is good.
9. The methodological approach is well articulated.
10. The main shortcoming of the design is the number of participants. However, this is understandable in such a short-term project.
11. All of the respondents were Chinese. This should have been discussed and justified in more detail, was this a deliberate strategy?
12. The analysis of the data is appropriate.
13. I was unsure about the discussion of reliability and validity. Reference was made to transcripts being made available to the reader. I wonder who this refers to? Were the transcripts available to the participants? This could be considered an aspect of reliability. If the reader is the dissertation examiner, then the issue of reliability is not addressed.
14. The findings are interesting and would be useful for the pre-sessional course designers.
15. I think the results could have been synthesised more across the data sources and linked to the literature in more depth.
16. The suggestions to improve practice on the pre-sessional course were good.
17. I would have liked to have seen more discussion concerning the implications for future research.

In sum, this is a very good and valuable piece of research.

FIGURE 15.2 Example of a dissertation examiner's report

15.2 The viva

A viva is an oral examination of the dissertation that usually occurs after the written dissertation has been assessed. The viva involves two or more examiners who ask the student questions about the study. Not all course-work master's include a viva for every student, some departments only conduct vivas with outstanding and/or failing students, or when there is a discrepancy between grades.

Usually, the examiners will have decided whether the dissertation is a pass or fail before the viva, but the viva can bring a fail grade up to a pass or a borderline pass down to a fail. The viva usually has a question-and-answer format about sections of the dissertation' however, it is not a mere descriptive exercise. It should be assumed that the examiners have read the dissertation and will ask more probing questions about the research perspective and the significance of the dissertation. However, it is possible that the examiner has not read the dissertation in great detail and may need the student to give a brief overview of the dissertation. Table 15.3 shows the stages a viva may follow.

15.2.1 Before the viva

One of the most common mistakes is not to prepare for the viva. The best way to prepare is by re-reading the dissertation in a questioning way using the assessment criteria as guiding principles. It is useful to practice summarising the major points in the dissertation, particularly the important findings. It should be possible to anticipate most of the viva questions. It is also useful to know who the examiners will be and to look at their research profiles on the internet. If there have been further publications in the field, these can be referred to during the viva.

The questions in the viva will adhere to the dissertation sections – that is, literature, method, results and discussion – although these may not be dealt with in a linear fashion. Figure 15.3 presents a list of possible questions that can be asked during the viva.

In some departments it may be possible to have a mock viva. This is a practice run with the supervisor and another academic. This is extremely useful; however, in large departments with around 100 students submitting dissertations, this will

TABLE 15.3 Stages for viva oral examination

Stage 1	Marking	Examiners mark the dissertation individually and decide on a provisional grade.
Stage 2	Pre-viva	Examiners have pre viva discussion.
Stage 3	Viva	Student makes short presentation of research. Examiners ask questions.
Stage 4	Post viva	Examiners discuss the viva and agree on a final grade.
Stage 5	Feedback	Examiners prepare report for student with the outcome.

Can you summarise your work in one or two sentences?

Why did you choose to research this topic?

What are your research objectives?

Who would you say are the main scholars in this area?

Can you summarise your theoretical framework?

Why did you choose a quantitative/qualitative approach to your research?

Can you explain your procedure?

Why did you choose your methods?

Why did you choose your particular sample?

To what extent do you think your sample is representative?

What do you think is the most significant finding in you research?

What do you think is your contribution to knowledge?

What are the limitations of your research?

What are the practical implications for the findings in your research?

What scope is there for further research in this area?

FIGURE 15.3 Some typical questions asked during oral examinations

probably not be possible, as academic staff are extremely stretched during this period.

TASK 15.3

Using the questions in Figure 15.3, practice asking and answering questions about your dissertation with a fellow student.

15.2.2 During the viva

The student should try to be as relaxed and confident as possible; dwelling on negative thoughts and catastrophising can diminish performance. Such anxiety can be helped by counteracting negative thoughts with positive self-talk prior to the viva. Self-talk is internal dialogue; in other words, talking to oneself. It is important to remember that the student has a good knowledge of the study topic after spending a lot of time thinking, reading and investigating the area. After conducting the

TABLE 15.4 Some examples of positive and negative self-talk

Negative self-talk	*Positive self-talk*
I'm stupid. It was a fluke I got on this course.	I got on this course based on my qualifications and experience. I'm going to maximise my experience and achieve my goal.
I'm an imposter! The examiners will find out how stupid I really am.	The examiners will see I have worked very hard and have something to offer. They will learn from my talk.
My talk is so boring.	My study is very interesting and I'm sure the examiners will be interested too.
I don't know anything about the topic.	I've spent six months thinking about this topic. I'm an expert.
I'll fail the viva.	The viva is something I haven't done before. The experience will be interesting. I'm going to make the most of it.
I'll make a mess of my talk. I'm so anxious.	This is not my first talk. I'm a teacher and I have the skills needed. It'll be a good talk.
My research is not valuable.	I'm very proud of myself for achieving this difficult task.

research, the student should feel confident they have a deep knowledge about the subject area. During the viva it is important not to view the examiners as adversaries trying to find fault, but rather supportive colleagues that are interested in the project. Table 15.4 lists some examples of positive and negative self-talk. During the viva students should be polite and not confrontational or defensive. The examiners will undoubtedly have useful feedback that can be used to improve the dissertation if necessary or that can be used in future research or publication.

15.3 Oral presentations

Instead of a viva, some programmes require students give a presentation to staff and students in the department after the submission of their dissertation as a way of sharing knowledge. The presentation is likely to be very short depending on the number of presenters, for example, a ten-minute presentation is not unusual. This can be a very satisfying activity for the student as it marks completion and highlights personal achievement. It can also be helpful as a preamble to preparing a plan for a journal article based on the study. Unlike the viva, the presentation is a descriptive process that summarises the study in terms of aims and results. The audience is non-expert and is interested in the findings, so very detailed descriptions of the literature and methodology would be out of place. It is better to communicate well at a somewhat shallow level than fail to communicate complex content. Table 15.5 presents a possible template for an oral presentation based on a master's dissertation.

TABLE 15.5 Template for a short oral presentation about the dissertation

Stage	*Include*
Introduction to research	Topic outline
	Why you chose the topic
	Motivation for study
Background to topic	Very brief literature background underpinning research
	Theoretical framework
	Researching area
	Research questions
Procedure	Selection of data
	Process of data collection
Results	Include simple graphics if needed
	Answers to research questions
Significance of research	In relation to current research
	In relation to practice
	Limitations
	Problems encountered
Reflection	On research experience

15.4 After the dissertation

15.4.1 Resubmission

In some circumstances students do not achieve a high enough grade to warrant a pass. The two most frequent reasons for failing a dissertation are plagiarism or lack of effort. In terms of plagiarism, sometimes the student runs out of time and thinks copying others' work can help, or they may seek the help of an online dissertation writing service. Both of these are classed as academic dishonesty and usually result in a fail grade. Failing the dissertation through lack of effort means the student has not devoted enough time to the study, sometimes as a result of taking a holiday during the dissertation period. A dissertation that receives a fail grade usually means that an overall pass on the master's degree cannot be achieved because the dissertation carries a large proportion of the final grade. In most universities students are given the opportunity to resubmit the dissertation in a given time frame. Usually examiners will provide detailed comments and advice for revising the dissertation. Dissertations usually fail on substantive shortcomings, such as a lack of a theoretical framework, rather than surface level shortcomings, such as lack of sub-headings. It is essential that all areas identified by the examiners are addressed rather than just those that are easy to fix. By following the examiners' advice, it should be possible to avoid a final fail grade.

15.4.2 Using the dissertation as a pathway

Some students use the dissertation as a pathway to enrolling on a PhD or another research degree. The dissertation should demonstrate research skills and as such can be regarded as a basic qualification in doing research. The dissertation grade and feedback can be useful when applying for funding for further study. However, competition for funding for a PhD is fierce so, realistically, only those dissertations that have achieved a distinction or higher stand a chance of securing funding. If the student manages to publish from the dissertation, this will greatly enhance the chances. If the student is planning on further study, it is a good idea to build on the research in the dissertation. For example, the master's dissertation could be validation of instrumentation that may be used in the PhD project. The PhD proposal can then build on the implications for further research raised in the discussion chapter of the dissertation.

One area that needs consideration in using the master's as a pathway to a higher research degree is that of timing. In many cases the assessment and final grade of the dissertation is not available until after the closing date for PhD and funding applications. This can be inconvenient, particularly for international students.

Dissertation supervisors can play an important role in supporting applications for further study and funding, as they can attest to the research expertise and potential of the student by being a referee. The choice of referees in further study is very important. Some students try to choose high ranking academics as referees; while this is a good idea it should not be done at the expense of using the supervisor. The supervisor is the person who is most familiar with the research and can make the best assessment of the student's potential for research. It is also important to seek the permission of the referee prior to the application and to give the referee plenty of time to complete the task rather than leaving it to the last minute. To get the most appropriate reference it is a good idea to send the application and application requirements to the referee when requesting a reference.

References are usually submitted online by the referee. It is unusual for applicants to submit references themselves, as these should be confidential. Non-confidential references are not usually acceptable. A typical format is for the referee to complete two sections for the reference: a questionnaire section and a text section. In the quantitative section there may be questions that focus on abilities that are viewed as important for doctoral research. This often includes a comparative element. Figure 15.4 presents a sample form sent to a potential referee for an application for PhD programme or funding application. In the text section the referee is required to write a short piece on the strengths of the applicant and the suitability of the applicant for higher research.

15.4.3 Disseminating knowledge

After the dissertation, particularly if the student wants to continue to a higher research degree, the findings of the dissertation need to be disseminated. There are a range of methods of doing this. Initially, a department presentation is a good way of doing this. Subsequent methods are through conference presentations and publishing a journal article. Some students are lucky enough to publish with their supervisor as a co-author, which is an excellent way of learning the procedure, with the supervisor mentoring the student through the process.

Please rank the candidate in terms of students in the cohort:

Ability	Top 5%	Top 15%	Top 25%	Top 50%	Bottom 50%
Intellectual skills					
Research skills					
Critical ability					
Oral English communication					
Written English communication					

Please give your opinion on the candidate's suitability for this award:

FIGURE 15.4 Example of a referee form

15.4.4 Giving a conference presentation

Presenting at a conference is an excellent choice for students who hope to continue with their research. At a conference, the research is made public and the presenter may get valuable feedback on their work. Conferences are excellent places for networking and establishing contact with experts in the field. Potential higher research degree supervisors can be approached personally, and the intended project discussed. The further advantage of presenting at a conference is the opportunity to publish in the conference proceedings. These are often peer reviewed, which means they can be classed as a peer reviewed publication on a CV.

15.4.5 Publishing a journal article

Getting an article published based on a master's project would greatly enhance the chance of getting on a funded higher research degree programme. There are several steps in writing and getting a journal article published in an academic journal that should be followed. These are presented in Table 15.6.

The choice of journal is very important. There are two main types of journal in TESOL and applied linguistics: those with an academic focus and those with a

TABLE 15.6 Publishing a journal article

Steps	*Comments*
Choose an appropriate journal	Choose a journal that publishes articles in your research area. Is the journal practically oriented or academically oriented? Do not choose a high-ranking journal unless research findings are groundbreaking.
Read aims, intended readership and technical requirements of the journal	Use these to tailor the article. Do not go over the word count.
Write article without cutting and pasting from original dissertation	Journals usually do not publish dissertations in their entirety.

professional focus. The readership of these journals differs, with academic journals targeting researchers and professional journals targeting teachers. Realistically it is unlikely that top journals will publish a small-scale study such as a master's study unless the findings are ground-breaking. Students often find local journals more appropriate for their research. This might be a university journal or a regional journal, such as *Asian EFL Journal.*

TASK 15.4

Does your department/university have its own journal?
Does it publish articles based on master's research?
What are the requirements for articles in this journal? Eg, word length, readership etc.

Willy Renandya has published an excellent guide to journals in TESOL and applied linguistics. In this guide he refers to 'bogus journals'. These are unscrupulous journals that are run exclusively for profit. The warning signs of such journals, according to Renandya, are requesting publication fees, high frequency of publication, very high acceptance rate, obscure editorial board members and a poor quality of research published. Publishing with such journals gives a poor impression on the student's CV, but importantly, the journal can take over the copyright, making it impossible for students to publish from the study elsewhere in the future. Along similar lines, sometimes student are approached via email by unscrupulous publishers to publish their dissertation as is in a book format. The turnaround promised is very quick, but again the student runs the risk of losing copyright.

15.4.6 Differences between a dissertation and an article

Writing a journal article is very different from writing a dissertation, so the text needs to be changed completely. Table 15.7 outlines some of the major differences between writing a dissertation and writing a journal article.

TABLE 15.7 Differences between a dissertation and journal article

Dissertation	*Article*
Word length	
Around 15,000	5000 upwards, based on journal requirements
Focus	
Academic	Academic and/or professional
Readership	
Examiner, supervisor, academic in department, may be known	Academics, students and teachers – unknown
Language	
Very explicit to demonstrate expertise and understanding or research processes;	Audience more expert so can omit much detail
a great deal of meta-text structuring organisation eg, "In this section . . ."	Omit most of the meta-text
Referencing style of department	Referencing style of journal – often different from the department style
Organisation	
Sections dictated by department	Sections dictated by journal
Uses headings and sub-headings	Headings and sub-headings less prolific
Includes large appendices	May only have one or no appendices

Journals vary in the length of time from submission to publication. Usually a submitted article is quickly reviewed by the desk editor. Then, if the article shows potential, it is sent out for peer review. Two or three reviewers conduct the review. They are usually given around one month to do this, although this can take much longer than this. Once this is done the reviews are sent back to the author. In most cases there is a need for revision, and this may take some time. Realistically it will take around six months to one year from submission to publication. Writers should try not to feel despondent with the comments in the review and try to view them in a positive light. The comments are designed to help the writer improve the paper.

15.4.7 Dissertation awards

Another way of easing the pathway to a higher research degree and subsequent funding is to get an award for the dissertation. Many of the examples used in this book are taken from award winning ELT dissertations made available online by the British Council. The British Council ELT dissertation award is given to several excellent dissertations every year. Details of entry and the availability of dissertations can be found at https://englishagenda.britishcouncil.org/research-publications/elt-masters-dissertations/elt-masters-dissertation-award.

Summary

This chapter has addressed issues that may arise after the submission of the dissertation. This includes failing and resubmission of the dissertation and using the dissertation as a pathway to a higher research degree. Participating in a viva is addressed, and some guidelines for disseminating knowledge – for example, through publishing in an academic journal – are presented. Chapter 16 includes a list of academic journals in the field of TESOL and applied linguistics.

Common mistakes after the dissertation

- In cases of failure, not adhering to the examiners' advice
- Not preparing for the viva
- Attempting to get onto a PhD programme with a totally different topic
- Using high ranking academics unfamiliar with the dissertation as referees for funding or research degree application
- Missing the deadline for higher research degree or funding applications
- Not asking permission of referees to provide recommendations

FAQs

1. *Can I take a holiday after my course-work and lectures are finished?*
   It is not advisable to do this. Most students underestimate the demands of doing the dissertation and struggle to finish on time. As mentioned in this chapter, a lack of effort is one of the major reasons for failure of the dissertation, and taking a holiday during the dissertation period greatly reduces the time spent on the project.
2. *Will I have to have a viva?*
   Departments vary in their requirements for oral examination. In some universities every dissertation student needs to have a viva; in some universities only borderline distinction and fail cases need to do this. The procedure will be clear in the department guidelines, and the student will be advised if there is a need to take part in a viva.
3. *Can I publish my dissertation?*
   Dissertations, journal articles and book chapters differ widely in terms of writing and content. Publishers do not usually publish a dissertation as is, so it will take quite some time for the dissertation to be changed into a publishable format.
4. *Where can I get funding for a PhD?*
   There are a number of types of funding available for PhD research. These may be university based, national or international. A good starting point is the following link: www.findaphd.com/funding/guides/phd-funding-guide.aspx (accessed 24 May, 2019).
   The university will usually have links for funding research. An example of university-based funding can be viewed here: www.ncl.ac.uk/postgraduate/funding/searchfunding/ (accessed 24 May, 2019).
5. *Do I need a distinction or high distinction to go on to a PhD?*
   Not necessarily. Some students wait several years after their master's degree before applying for a PhD. In the interim they might generate a good academic

record of conference papers and publications; this will help with the PhD application. However, the overall grade for the master's degree and, in particular, the grade for the dissertation and the research methods module are very important in determining suitability for higher degree research and for funding.

Further reading

Biggam (2016) has a good section on assessment criteria of dissertations and also has a good section on the viva. (2019) have an interesting book that focuses on writing for publication that addresses the process of writing as well as the process of getting published. Willy Renandya (2014) addresses issues in choosing the most appropriate journal to send an article to. Jeffrey Bealle used to keep a list of questionable open access journals; while this is no longer available, the following link can be used to check whether a journal or publisher is appropriate: https://beallslist.weebly.com (accessed 14 May, 2019). The British Council have ELT masters' dissertations available to download.

References

Biggam, J. (2016). *Succeeding with your master's dissertation: A step-by-step handbook.* Maidenhead: Open University Press.

British Council. (2018). *Research publications.* Retrieved from https://englishagenda.britishcouncil.org/research-publications/elt-masters-Britsh dissertations/elt-masters-dissertation-award (Accessed 14 May, 2019)

Paltridge, B., & Starfield, S. (2019). *Getting published in academic journals: Navigating the publication process.* Ann Arbor, MI: University of Michigan Press.

Renandya, W. (2014). Choosing the right international journal in TESOL and Applied Linguistics. *ELT World Online, 6*(June), 1–17. Retrieved from https://cpb-us-w2.wpmucdn.com/blog.nus.edu.sg/dist/7/112/files/2014/06/Choosing-the-Right-International-Journal-in-TESOL-and-Applied-Linguistics_editforpdf-10fy3c2.pdf (Accessed 14 May, 2019)

16
RESOURCES

This chapter includes examples and links to facilitate the dissertation writing process.

16.1 Dissertation guides

It is important that the dissertation guide issued by the department is adhered to closely, but sometimes these can be rather brief or even not available. Below are links to dissertation guides that may provide useful insights into the process of doing a master's dissertation. Some of these guides do not focus specifically on TESOL and applied linguistics master's degrees, but the general principles will apply.

- Graduate Institute, Geneva. (n.d.). *Guidelines for a master's dissertation.* Retrieved from http://graduateinstitute.ch/files/live/sites/iheid/files/sites/students/documents-master/en/MINT_Dissertation_Guidelines.pdf (Accessed 9 April, 2019).
- Heriot-Watt University. (2012). School of management and languages (UD) *A guide to writing your master's dissertation.* Retrieved from http://www2.hw.ac.uk/sml/postgraduate/downloads/dissertations/dissertationguide.pdf (Accessed 10 April, 2019).
- Kings College London. (n.d.). *Dissertation guidance.* Retrieved from www.kcl.ac.uk/artshums/depts/trs/study/handbook/assessment/taught/dissguide.aspx (Accessed 9 April, 2019).
- SOAS University. (n.d.). *London Postgraduate taught degree guidelines.* Retrieved from www.soas.ac.uk/registry/degreeregulations/file123478.pdf (Accessed 9 April, 2019).
- University of Leeds, School of Management and Languages. (2012). *A guide to writing your master's dissertation.* Retrieved from http://www2.hw.ac.uk/sml/postgraduate/downloads/dissertations/dissertationguide.pdf (Accessed 9 April, 2019).

- University of Leicester. (2009). *Study guide for writing the dissertation*. Retrieved from https://www2.le.ac.uk/offices/ld/resources/writing/writing-resources/writing-dissertation (Accessed 9 April, 2019).
- University of Reading. (2018). *School of literature and languages MA programmes in TESOL and applied linguistics student handbook*. Retrieved from www.reading.ac.uk/web/files/english-language/2018_19_MATESOL_MAAL_Handbook_update_2_10_18.pdf (pp. 55–59) (Accessed 9 April, 2009).
- University of San Francisco, International and Multicultural Department. (2017). *MA Field project/thesis writing guide*. Retrieved from https://myusf.usfca.edu/sites/default/files/Field_Project_Thesis_Guide_2017-18_FINAL.pdf (Accessed 27 May, 2019).
- University of Sheffield. (n.d.). *MA in applied linguistics with TESOL handbook*. Retrieved from www.sheffield.ac.uk/polopoly_fs/1.463811!/file/Sample-MAALHandbook.pdf (Accessed 9 April, 2019).
- University of Southampton Writing Centre. (2016). *Writing skills: The dissertation*. Retrieved from https://writingatsouthampton.files.wordpress.com/2016/10/dissertations.pdf (Accessed 9 April, 2019).

16.2 Proposal writing guides

The following are publications that address the process of writing a research proposal. The guides are general and not specific to TESOL and applied linguistics but should be useful.

- University of Edinburgh (n.d.) www.ed.ac.uk/files/imports/fileManager/HowToWriteProposal090415.pdf (Accessed 14 May, 2019).
- University of Sydney, Learning Centre (2012) *Writing a thesis proposal: Independent learning resources*. https://sydney.edu.au/stuserv/documents/learning_centre/Thesis_Proposal_2012.pdf (Accessed 10 April, 2019).
- University of New South Wales (n.d.) *Guide for writing thesis proposals*. https://student.unsw.edu.au/thesis-proposals (Accessed 10 April, 2019).
- University of Manchester (n.d.) *How to write a research proposal*. www.manchester.ac.uk/study/postgraduate-research/admissions/how-to-apply/research-proposal/ (Accessed 14 May, 2019).

16.3 List of Routledge Handbooks on TESOL and applied linguistics

Up-to-date, edited, state-of-the-art volumes can provide a good overview of a topic area with links to further reading. Routledge Handbooks are edited volumes of papers on different subjects in TESOL and applied linguistics. These handbooks are a very good starting point for learning about a dissertation topic and finding links to recent research in the field.

Barron, A., Gu, Y., & Steen, G. (Eds.). (2017). *Routledge handbook of pragmatics*. Abingdon: Routledge.

Bhatia, V., & Bremner, S. (Eds.). (2016). *Routledge handbook of language and professional communication*. Abingdon: Routledge.
Bigelow, M., & Ennser-Kananen, J. (Eds.). (2018). *Routledge handbook of educational linguistics*. Abingdon: Routledge.
Farr, F., & Murray, L. (Eds.). (2016). *Routledge handbook of language learning and technology*. Abingdon: Routledge.
Flowerdew, J., & Richardson, J. F. (Eds.). (2017). *Routledge handbook of critical discourse studies*. Abingdon: Routledge.
Fulcher, G., & Davidson, F. (Eds.). (2016). *Routledge handbook of language testing*. Abingdon: Routledge.
Garton, S., & Copland, F. (Eds.). (2018). *Routledge handbook of teaching English to young learners*. Abingdon: Routledge.
Gass, S. M., & Mackay, A. (Eds.). (2013). *Routledge handbook of second language acquisition*. Abingdon: Routledge.
Gee, J. P., & Handford, M. (Eds.). (2013). *Routledge handbook of discourse analysis*. Abingdon: Routledge.
Hall, G. (Ed.). (2016). *Routledge handbook of English language teaching*. Abingdon: Routledge.
Hyland, K., & Shaw, P. (Eds.). (2016). *Routledge handbook of English for academic purposes*. Abingdon: Routledge.
Jackson, J. (Ed.). (2012). *Routledge handbook of language and intercultural communication*. Abingdon: Routledge.
Jenkins, J., Baker, W., & Dewey, M. (Eds.). (2017). *Routledge handbook of English as a Lingua Franca*. Abingdon: Routledge.
Kirkpatrick, A. (Ed.). (2012). *Routledge handbook of world Englishes*. Abingdon: Routledge.
Leow, R. (Ed.). (2019). *Routledge handbook of second language research in classroom learning*. Abingdon: Routledge.
Loewen, S., & Sata, M. (Eds.). (2016). *Routledge handbook of instructed second language acquisition*. Abingdon: Routledge.
Mann, S., & Walsh, S. (Eds.). (2019). *Routledge handbook of English language teacher education*. Abingdon: Routledge.
Martin-Jones, M., Blackledge, A., & Creese, A. (Eds.). (2015). *Routledge handbook of multilingualism*. Abingdon: Routledge.
Mickan, P. (Ed.). (2019). *Routledge handbook of language education curriculum design*. Abingdon: Routledge.
O'Keefe, A., & McCarthy, M. (Eds.). (2010). *The Routledge handbook of corpus linguistics*. Abingdon: Routledge.
Preece, S. (Ed.). (2016). *Routledge handbook of language and identity*. Abingdon: Routledge.
Simpson, J. (Ed.). (2011). *Routledge handbook of applied linguistics*. Abingdon: Routledge.
Vine, B. (Ed.). (2017). *Routledge handbook of language in the workplace*. Abingdon: Routledge.

16.4 List of academic journals in TESOL and applied linguistics

The following is a list of academic journals widely used in TESOL and applied linguistics. Those that may be likely to publish master's research are starred.*

Annual Review of Applied Linguistics
www.cambridge.org/core/journals/annual-review-of-applied-linguistics (Accessed 10 April, 2019)

Applied Linguistics
https://academic.oup.com/applij (Accessed 10 April, 2019)
*Asian EFL Journal**
www.asian-efl-journal.com/ (Accessed 10 April, 2019)
*Asian ESP Journal**
www.asian-esp-journal.com/ (Accessed 10 April, 2019)
Assessing Writing
www.journals.elsevier.com/assessing-writing/ (Accessed 10 April, 2019)
Bilingualism: Language and Cognition
www.cambridge.org/core/journals/bilingualism-language-and-cognition (Accessed 10 April, 2019)
Chinese Journal of Applied Linguistics
www.degruyter.com/view/j/cjal (Accessed 10 April, 2019)
ELT Journal
https://academic.oup.com/eltj (Accessed 10 April, 2019)
English for Specific Purposes
www.journals.elsevier.com/english-for-specific-purposes/ (Accessed 10 April, 2019)
English Language and Linguistics
www.cambridge.org/core/journals/english-language-and-linguistics (Accessed 10 April, 2019)
*English Teaching Professional**
www.etprofessional.com/home (Accessed 10 April, 2019)
*English Today**
www.cambridge.org/core/journals/english-today (Accessed 10 April, 2019)
English World-Wide
www.benjamins.com/catalog/eww (Accessed 10 April, 2019)
International Journal of Applied Linguistics
https://onlinelibrary.wiley.com/journal/14734192 (Accessed 10 April, 2019)
International Journal of Bilingual Education and Bilingualism
www.tandfonline.com/toc/rbeb20/current (Accessed 10 April, 2019)
International Journal of Linguistics
www.macrothink.org/journal/index.php/ijl (Accessed 10 April, 2019)
International Review of Applied Linguistics in Language Teaching
www.degruyter.com/view/j/iral (Accessed 10 April, 2019)
*Internet TESL Journal**
http://iteslj.org/ (Accessed 10 April, 2019)
*Japan Association for Language Teaching (JALT) Journal**
http://jalt-publications.org (Accessed 10 April, 2019)
Journal of English as an International Language Journal
www.eilj.com (Accessed 10 April, 2019)
Journal of English for Academic Purposes
www.journals.elsevier.com/journal-of-english-for-academic-purposes/ (Accessed 10 April, 2019)
Journal of Language, Identity and Education
www.asu.edu/educ/sceed/JLIE/ (Accessed 10 April, 2019)

Journal of Second Language Writing
www.journals.elsevier.com/journal-of-second-language-writing/ (Accessed 10 April, 2019)
Language, Culture and Society
https://benjamins.com/catalog/lcs (Accessed 10 April, 2019)
Language Learning
https://onlinelibrary.wiley.com/journal/14679922 (Accessed 10 April, 2019)
Language Learning and Technology
www.lltjournal.org/ (Accessed 10 April, 2019)
Language Teaching
www.cambridge.org/core/journals/language-teaching (Accessed 10 April, 2019)
Linguistics and Education
www.journals.elsevier.com/linguistics-and-education/ (Accessed 10 April, 2019)
Modern Language Journal
https://onlinelibrary.wiley.com/journal/15404781 (Accessed 10 April, 2019)
*RELC Journal**
https://journals.sagepub.com/home/rel (Accessed 10 April, 2019)
Second Language Research
https://journals.sagepub.com/home/slr (Accessed 10 April, 2019)
Studies in Second Language Acquisition
www.cambridge.org/core/journals/studies-in-second-language-acquisition (Accessed 10 April, 2019)
System
www.journals.elsevier.com/system/ (Accessed 10 April, 2019)
TESL-EJ
http://tesl-ej.org/wordpress/ (Accessed 10 April, 2019)
TESOL Quarterly
www.tesol.org/read-and-publish/journals/tesol-quarterly (Accessed 10 April, 2019)

16.5 Sources for the literature review

The following are useful links for conducting and writing a literature review.

16.5.1 Referencing software

Before choosing a programme to manage references and citing, it is best to check what is available to students through the university, as there will probably be free access and guidelines on how to use the software.

The following are the main programmes for referencing:

- EndNote https://endnote.com/ (Accessed 10 April, 2019)
- Zotero www.zotero.org/ (Accessed 10 April, 2019)
- Mendeley www.mendeley.com/?interaction_required=true (Accessed 10 April, 2019)

The University of Manchester library has a good guide that compares the features of the main referencing software: http://subjects.library.manchester.ac.uk/c.php?g=64326&p=413447 (accessed 10 April, 2019).

16.5.2 Referencing guides

The following provide links to referencing guides.

- The University of Auckland has an excellent site that deals with all matters relating to referencing, including 'quickcite', which is a guide for the major styles for types of literature in referencing. www.cite.auckland.ac.nz/1.html (Accessed 10 April, 2019).
- The University of Bath has a PDF and an electronic guide to APA 6th. Electronic guide: https://library.bath.ac.uk/referencing/apa (Accessed 11 April, 2019). PDF guide: www.bath.ac.uk/publications/library-guides-to-citing-referencing/attachments/american-psychological-association-style-guide.pdf (Accessed 11 April, 2019).
- Purdue University's Online Writing Lab (OWL) has some excellent resources for referring in APA and other styles. https://owl.purdue.edu/owl/research_and_citation/apa_style/apa_formatting_and_style_guide/general_format.html (Accessed 11 April, 2019).

16.5.3 Guides to the literature review

The following guides focus on the process of writing the literature chapter.

- The Writing Center, University of North Carolina at Chapel Hill. https://writingcenter.unc.edu/tips-and-tools/literature-reviews/ (Accessed 11 April, 2019)
- University of Leicester. https://www2.le.ac.uk/offices/ld/resources/writing/writing-resources/literature-review (Accessed 11 April, 2019)
- University of Reading video guide. www.screencast.com/t/RdY4lwEW (Accessed 11 April, 2019)

16.5.4 Digital object identifiers (DOIs)

Some publishers require DOIs for articles. The following can be used to find the DOI if this is available for any publication:

www.crossref.org/guestquery/ (Accessed 11 April, 2019)

16.6 Sources for research methodology

The following are useful links for learning and writing about research methodology.

- The University of Birmingham has a good site that gives advice on the choice of methodologies. www.socscidiss.bham.ac.uk/methodologies.html (Accessed 14 May, 2019).
- The University of Huddersfield has advice on writing the methodology chapter. www.socscidiss.bham.ac.uk/methodologies.html (Accessed 14 May, 2019).
- Gabriella Runblad has a good site that features videos about statistical methods in applied linguistics. www.appliedlinguistics.org.uk/ (Accessed 14 May, 2019).

The following books are useful for research methods used in TESOL and applied linguistics.

Dörnyei, Z. (2007). *Research methods in applied linguistics*. Oxford: Oxford University Press.
Dörnyei, Z., & Csizér, K. (2012). How to design and analyze surveys in SLA research. In A. Mackay & S. Gass (Eds.), *Research methods in second language acquisition: A practical guide* (pp. 74–94). Malden, MA: Wiley-Blackwell.
Lincoln, Y. S., & Guba, E. G. (1985). *Naturalistic inquiry*. Newbury Park, CA: Sage.
Litosseliti, L. (Ed.). (2010). *Research methods in linguistics*. London: Continuum.
Mackay, A., & Gass, S. (2005). *Second language research: Methodology and design*. Mahwah, NJ: Lawrence Erlbaum.
Paltridge, B., & Phakiti, A. (Eds.). (2015). *Research methods in applied linguistics*. London: Bloomsbury.
Punch, K. (2016). *Developing effective research proposals* (3rd ed.). London: Sage.
Richards, K. (2003). *Qualitative inquiry in TESOL*. Basingstoke: Macmillan.
Richards, K. (2009). Trends in qualitative research in language teaching: State-of-the-art article. *Language Teaching*, *42*(2), 147–180.
Silverman, D. (2017). *Doing qualitative research* (5th ed.). London: Sage.

16.6.1 Statistical analysis software

The following links have information about data analysis software. SPSS and SAS need to be purchased, R is free.

- SPSS www.ibm.com/uk-en/analytics/spss-statistics-software (Accessed 11 April, 2019)
- SAS www.sas.com/en_us/software/stat.html (Accessed 11 April, 2019)
- R Available to download from various institutions: https://cran.r-project.org/mirrors.html (Accessed 11 April, 2019)

16.7 Finding dissertations

The following are links to sites that can be used to access master's dissertations. Your university may have a similar portal for dissertations through the university library.

- Dissertation abstracts. https://linguistlist.org/pubs/diss/index.cfm (Accessed 14 May, 2019).
- University of San Francisco (n.d.). *International and multicultural education department MA field project/thesis writing guide*. https://repository.usfca.edu/ime/ (Accessed 28 May, 2019)
- University of San Francisco (n.d.) *TESOL MA Theses and projects*. https://repository.usfca.edu/tesol/ (Accessed 9 April, 2019).
- Asian EFL Journal theses. www.asian-efl-journal.com/thesis/ (Accessed 14 May, 2019).
- British Council ELT dissertations. https://englishagenda.britishcouncil.org/research-publications/elt-masters-dissertations (Accessed 14 May, 2019).
- Proquest dissertations. www.proquest.com/products-services/dissertations/ (Accessed 14 May, 2019).

16.8 Setting up a writing group

Writing the dissertation can be a lonely time for the writer; working with others during the dissertation process can be very useful. By setting up a writing group, participants can discuss their goals and obstacles to achieving these, can get feedback on writing and ideas and can spend some uninterrupted time writing.

Lee and Golde have published an excellent PDF booklet on setting up and maintaining a writing group. While this targets PhD students, master's dissertation students can also benefit. They propose ten questions that need to be addressed when setting up a writing group; some examples of the types of questions that may be asked are presented in Table 16.1. There are no right answers to these questions, but it is essential that group members agree on the answers. They suggest writing groups should comprise four or five writers, otherwise the feedback process becomes too lengthy.

Links for guidelines on setting up a writing group:

- Lee, S., & Golde, C., Starting an Effective Dissertation Writing Group [PDF document]. Stanford University. https://unmgrc.unm.edu/writing-groups/documents/starting-an-effective-group.pdf (Accessed 11 April, 2019).
- Getting the support you need: Starting a writing group. University of Nebraska. www.unl.edu/gradstudies/connections/getting-support-you-need-starting-writing-group (Accessed 11 April, 2019).

16.9 Academic writing links

The following are useful links for general academic writing.

- Reading University has a series of pages devoted to academic writing. Topics covered include styles of writing, grammar, punctuation and editing. https://libguides.reading.ac.uk/writing/home (Accessed 11 April, 2019).
- Purdue University Online Writing Lab (OWL) has an excellent site that provides advice on a range of academic writing topics; the site includes videos. https://owl.purdue.edu/owl/purdue_owl.html (Accessed 11 April, 2019).

The Academic Phrasebank is a useful resource for expressing a range of functions in the following types of writing:

Introducing work
Referring to sources
Describing methods
Reporting results
Discussing findings
Writing conclusions

www.phrasebank.manchester.ac.uk/ (Accessed 11 April, 2019).

TABLE 16.1 Questions to ask when setting up a writing group

	Question	*Example*
1.	How often, how long and where will the will the group meet? How long will each meeting be? Where will the meeting be held?	Once a week for 60 minutes in a library meeting room.
2.	How big will the group be?	Four or five members; that allows time for feedback.
3.	What are the rules for membership?	Similar topics? Similar class groupings? How will they be approached?
4.	What will the format of the meetings be?	How many minutes should be spent on updates, feedback, goals, discussion, quiet writing?
5.	What are the formal roles for the group?	Possible roles: Convenor who sets up meetings and places. A facilitator who keeps the meeting discussion on track. Note taker who records major points of the meeting. Time keeper who monitors the timing of the discussion. These positions might rotate.
6.	What types of writing will the group read?	Outlines Drafts Proposals Dissertation chapters
7.	When, how and how much writing to submit to members?	Where these will be dropped off? Electronic submission to group? How many pages?
8.	What types of feedback is given?	How much time can be allocated to feedback? At what level – ideas, structure, proof-reading?
9.	How will feedback be given?	In writing? Verbally during meeting?
10.	What is the commitment?	It would be reasonable to set up an initial period of three months for a group of master's students.

Source: Based on Lee and Golde. https://unmgrc.unm.edu/writing-groups/documents/starting-an-effective-group.pdf

- The University of Sydney Learning Centre provides an interactive site that focuses on grammar, using sources and structuring an academic text. https://writesite.elearn.usyd.edu.au/ (Accessed 11 April, 2019).

16.10 Example of a research proposal with analysis

Table 16.2 shows an example of master's dissertation research proposal with an analysis of the sections.

TABLE 16.2 Sample proposal with comments

Text	*Comment*
1. Provisional Title: Online Language Learning: Using Conversation Analysis to Uncover the Affordances of 'Zoom' Videoconferencing.	For this proposal a provisional title is required. This may change during the research.
2. Research Focus and Rationale It is now a commonly held belief that people develop their second language skills through instances of interaction with others. Interaction is therefore a collaborative activity, allowing interlocutors to develop communicative competence which is the foundation upon which language development is built (Wells, 1981)[1] With recent developments of Web 2.0 tools such as blogs, chat rooms and videoconferencing applications, opportunities for language learners to interact with others have grown1. With this in mind, it is vital that language learners and teachers have a thorough understanding of the role technology has to play in language development.[2] *This study aims to investigate interactions between a teacher and a learner by using conversation analysis (CA) to micro-analyse video-based data.*[3] The interactions will be on videoconferencing software 'Zoom' which is widely-used and, due to previous employment, familiar to the researcher, who currently has 10 students who have expressed willingness to participate.[4] This research is needed in order to add to the interaction-based research from a conversational analytic perspective, as current research in this area is heavily weighted in favour of other areas of online learning.[5] A study using conversation analysis for second language acquisition (CA-SLA) is necessary here for a number of reasons, firstly CA-SLA affords the opportunity to micro-analyse interaction, by using detailed recordings and transcriptions (Ten Have, 2007) which are needed to fully understand Zoom's affordances and limitations. Secondly, CA-SLA studies' aims are "not to explain *why* people act in the way they do, but rather to explicate *how* they do it" (Ibid: p. 20 original emphasis). Finally, CA-SLA's inductive and emic epistemological position permits its point of departure to be an insider, participant's perspective, which should provide deeper understandings of interaction.[6] These deeper understandings are also aided by CA-SLA's use of naturally occurring data "because {CA-SLA} considers talk-in-interaction as a 'situated' achievement rather than as a product of personal intensions . . ." (Ibid: p. 20). A number of studies have looked at perceptions and attitudes students and learners have towards online learning, some performing comparative, statistical analyses of pre/post-test scores from online/blended learning and offline/face-to-face courses. These studies are undoubtedly important for the online-learning field as a whole, however, studies like this ignore the micro-details of interaction which need to explored in detail if we are to fully understand online learning environments. There are some studies that have looked at interaction in online settings, however, the number of these using video-based data and multimodal analyses is limited, which is the gap this study intends to fill.[7]	The focus and rationale deal with why the research is important. 1. This introductory sentence sets the scene for the research with a general background statement. 2. This refers to why the study is important. The importance of the study. 3. The statement of purpose of the study. 4. Information about the methods in the study. 5. The significance of the study. 6. Further explanation and justification for the study. 7. More detail and justification referring to the literature

(*Continued*)

TABLE 16.2 (Continued)

Text	*Comment*
3. Literature Review **3.1 Overview** Multimodal studies of online language learning have fast become an area of a great significance in the computer-assisted language learning (CALL) field (Lamy, 2013).[8] This study aims to narrow focus to desktop videoconferencing (DVC), which is a relatively new medium of interaction in CALL research. DVC has attracted research from a variety of areas, from teacher and healthcare training, to intercultural development.[9] A number of researchers have explored videoconferencing in general, looking at areas such as its affordances (for example Krutka & Carano, 2016; Dey-Plissonneau, 2017; Lino et al., 2016), and learners' attitudes (for example Istifci, 2017; Gyamfi & Sukseemuang, 2017; Chakowa, 2018). These studies, although providing some useful data, focussed solely on the *results* of online and offline courses, which skips the actual learning event itself. CA studies making use of multimodal aspects of video-based data and detailed transcriptions, which are key to giving readers access to the details of a study's findings (Rapley, 2007), could uncover a much deeper understanding of DVC interactions during language learning.[10] **3.2 Text-Based and Voice-Based Interaction Studies**[11] There are studies analysing online interactions via text-chats (for example Lamy, 2004; Simpson, 2005; Yanguas, 2010; Yu & Zeng, 2011; Coyle et al., 2017), however, the majority of these studies are not totally relevant here for two main reasons. Firstly, they did not adopt emic epistemologies key to conversation analytic approaches and secondly, although text-based and voice/video-based interactions share the trait of being highly organised, they differ in very significant ways (for a detailed description see Jenks, 2014). One text-based study worth mentioning is a case-study by Gonzalez-Lloret (2011). The study used CA to micro-analyse interactions between a Spanish L2 and a Spanish L1 speaker, which revealed that over the 8-week period of the study, the learner was able to develop her use of resources around areas of 'trouble-talk', highlighting that CA-SLA is a suitable approach to the study of online interactions in general. Additionally, there are many voice-based online interactions (for example Jenks, 2009a; Jenks, 2009b; Jenks & Firth, 2013; Brandt & Jenks, 2013; Jenks and Brandt, 2013) which are more relevant to this study. Chris Jenks's studies looked at voiced-based interactions using Skype, the qualitative approach to his studies and the use of detailed transcriptions provided an in-depth understanding of interaction. Jenks (2009a) analysed 'overlap' in multi-participant voiced-based chat rooms highlighting how pauses act as a source and interactional resource with regards to overlapping talk, again signalling CA's usefulness in this area. The present study, however, intends to dig even deeper into language learning in online interactions with the addition embodied actions afforded by video-based interactions, which is much more widely used today.[12]	8. A general introduction to the rationale of the study. 9. The aims of the study. 10. General literature background. 11. The writer has used sub-headings to organise the literature review. 12. The writer uses a wide range of sources to support claims. The argument is structured first, and the literature sources are combined to support the view.

3.3 Video-Based Interaction Studies There are few video-based, CA studies encompassing the use of semiotic resources into their analyses, however, two are worth mentioning here. Firstly, in her study of 'meaning making' conducted via desktop videoconferencing, Satar (2016) used multimodal interaction analysis, which has its roots in CA, with screenshots and detailed multimodal transcriptions which provided rich data with significant findings and conclusions. Some of Satar's findings included highlighting how non-verbal features can be used to express emotions, and how learners can complete a task by using gesture, which eliminates the need to answer in complete sentences. Secondly, a study by Kazar (2016), showed more successful interactions in videoconferencing than audio-based interaction. Kazar used CA to compare audio and videoconferencing with regards to 'wait time' and found that in audio interactions, teachers took the conversational floor faster than videoconferencing. Showing that videoconferencing "resulted in smoother turn-taking and fewer overlaps of students' and teachers' turns" (p. 60), due to the number of visual ques available – thus indicating videoconferencing's greater usefulness for online learning. The studies of Satar (2016) and Kazar (2016) are the most closely related to the proposed area of study here, however, they certainly indicate that there is a gap in the research which needs to be addressed. The findings from these studies indicate that there are unique aspects to videoconferencing worth investigating.[13] Based on the combined findings of Gonzalez-Lloret (2011) indicating the usefulness of CA to the microanalysis of online interaction and Satar (2016)[14] indicating the importance of embodied actions, a study combining the two seems like the most appropriate and effective way to uncover the details of how videoconferencing interaction is organised and negotiated. **4. Research Questions**[15] 1. What are the pedagogical affordances of 'Zoom'? 2. How do instances of learning arise in videoconference language learning on 'Zoom'? 3. How do interlocutors utilise multiple modalities to maintain interactional order on Zoom?	13. Signals gap in current research. 14. The writer uses recent sources in the proposal. 15. In this proposal the research questions are positioned at the end of the literature review.

(Continued)

TABLE 16.2 (Continued)

Text	*Comment*
5. Methodology **5.1 Data Collection and Participants** The data will be desktop screen recordings of teacher-student interactions via the videoconferencing software 'Zoom' created by Zoom Video Communications, Inc. There will be 10–12 recordings, each approximately one hour in length consisting of two participants, one learner and one teacher.[16] The learners will be 5 Thai, CEFR level B2-C2 English language learners, the youngest is 23 and the oldest is 34. There will be 5 qualified English as a Second Language (ESL) teachers with a range of 3–10 years of teaching experience, with each teacher teaching two separate hour-long classes. The participants will be selected based on their willingness to participate.[17] The interactions are entirely naturalistic in that they would have occurred even if this study did not take place as they are part of course that the students and teachers signed up for prior to the start of this study. They will, however, need to complete an ethics form prior to data collection. **5.2 Theoretical Frameworks**[18] **5.2.1 Overview** Videoconferencing interactions were selected because they allow interlocutors to deploy a range of modes for communication, which can provide very 'deep' data. Video-based interactions' scope of analysable modalities is vast, from aural to visual, including but not limited to; volume, intonation, tempo, pitch, facial expression, gesture and proxemics (Cappellini & Azaoui, 2017), which should provide the most useful and in-depth data possible. This array of modalities affords more opportunities to discover recurring events in the data, which should allow the substantiation of an observation with reference to other modalities. These benefits do, however, create the issue of highly complex data, therefore, calling for a methodology capable of making sense of highly complex situations, which is why this study will adopt a qualitative approach, supported by Dornyei's assertion that "Qualitative methods are useful for making sense of highly complex situations" (2007, p.39).	16. Information about the data. 17. Information about the participants. 18. This proposal includes a theoretical discussion about the methodological approach to the project and includes references relevant to the specific methods.

5.2.2 Conversation Analysis

Conversation Analysis (CA) was first introduced in the works of Harvey Sacks on telephone calls to the Suicide Prevention Center, which has since developed into a qualitative methodology for the analysis of 'talk-in-interaction'. CA studies need not focus on the linguistic aspects of interaction but on the social act itself, which can also make use of semiotic resources, such as embodied actions, to understand how order is maintained in interaction. Norris (2004), argued that embodied actions are an important part of interaction and stated that different modes are utilised holistically in the process of meaning-making, which is why they will be analysed here. Sacks was inspired by the early work on 'ethnomethodology' by Garfinkel (1967), in which he developed an approach to deal with a problem in sociology – How is social order possible? Garfinkel argued that the methods people use to interact are not standardised, rather, they are context dependent. With this argument in mind, it is clear that CA's ontological beliefs lie in 'contextual idealism', which argues that the social world consists of constructed representations which are shared by people in particular contexts (Ritchie et al., 2014). The assertion of the importance of 'context' is key to the principles and assumptions of CA. CA has also been chosen for this study as it gives preference to an inductive approach and is built on an emic epistemology with regards to the analysis of data (Markee, 2008). This epistemological position aims to use observations of the world to build knowledge from the bottom up by starting with the data (Ormston et al., 2014), which should provide greater opportunity to uncover microdetails of the interactions.

CA should also allow this study to avoid encountering problems caused by a number of challenges researchers face while conducting online, multimodal studies. One of these challenges is the shortage of useable theoretical frameworks designed specifically to explore online multimodal interaction in a language learning context (Satar, 2016). There are theories for face-to-face communication, however, this may not be suitable for online multimodal communication due to the differences between them. Semiotic resources used in online communication are used in ways not seen in face-to-face and thus create new patterns and interpretative systems (Sindoni, 2013), which would make theories of face-to-face interaction redundant. Using theoretical frameworks to understand online multimodal communication could, therefore, cause difficulty in drawing useful conclusions from the data. Although, even if there were frameworks for online interaction, they might still create problems for this study because semiotic resources are not always understood in the manner in which they were intended (Norris, 2004), thus making findings somewhat unreliable. Because of this, Satar (Ibid) asserts that "When collecting, transcribing, analysing and interpreting online multimodal data, it is crucial to bear [the possible lack of mutual understanding] in mind." (p. 306). CA's ability to focus on the microdetails of interaction, should minimise this risk and should clearly highlight if the use of a semiotic resource was understood as intended.

(Continued)

TABLE 16.2 (Continued)

Text	*Comment*
5.3 Ethics[19] A university ethics approval form will be submitted prior to the start of this study (Appendix 1) and participants will receive a 'Participant Information Sheet' (Appendix 2). The 'Participant Information Sheet' ensures participants give 'voluntary informed consent' prior to the collection of the data. Punch (2014) defines this as "... agree[ing] freely to be part of research ... understand[ing] what their participation entails and how it will be reported, and ... feel[ing] free to withdraw their agreement at any time ..." (p. 44). To do this, participants will have their faces blurred and their names changed during transcriptions in order to ensure privacy.	19. The proposal refers to ethics and includes the ethics application form, a participant information sheet and consent sheet in the appendix.
6. Data Analysis[20] When conducting a study using CA, it is very important for a researcher not to forget that the actual recordings themselves remain the primary source of data. However, in order to illustrate to readers what you (the researcher) were able to observe, a transcription will be needed (Rapley, 2007; Hitchby & Woofit, 2008). Unfortunately, a written transcription will likely involve the loss of some detail regardless of the depth of transcription used (Liddicoat, 2011). This is something that is unavoidable and is a necessary sacrifice when conducting a conversation analytic study, but there are ways in which a researcher can minimise the loss of detail during transcription. One such way is to choose the most suitable transcription convention specific to each study. This study will use the conventions of Mondada (2014) as the conventions "are conceived to annotate all possibly relevant embodied actions, such as gesture, gaze, body posture, movements, etc. that happen simultaneously to talk or during moments of absence in talk" (p. 1). It is hoped that these conventions will help to minimise the loss of detail during transcription, which should provide a more thorough understanding of the interactions. When the transcriptions are finished, there is the common issue CA studies face – where to begin the data analysis? There is the possibility of starting the analysis from a preconception based on a literature-inspired question. This approach, however, is "generally looked upon with some suspicion in CA" (Ten Have, 2007, p. 119) due to CA's emic and inductive epistemological beliefs. It is therefore important to analyse find how interlocutors socially organise their interaction with 'unmotivated looking'. Liddicoat (2011, p. 70) defines 'unmotivated looking' as "a process of ... reading through the transcribed text to obtain a feel for the data [, which] is a process of immersing oneself in the data in order to see what is happening in it". There is the paradoxical issue of sticking to 'unmotivated looking', when in reality all looking is motivated (Psathas, 1990b), which is an impurity of CA that just has to be acknowledged and worked around as best as possible.	20. This proposal has a separate section for data analysis, justifying this with evidence for the literature.

7. Timetable

	April	*May*	*June*	*July*	*August*
Research Proposal	X				
Literature Research	X	X			
Data Collection		X			
Literature Review		X	X		
Data Analysis (Including MARG session)			X	X	
Findings and Discussion				X	X
Conclusion and Abstract					X
Proof-reading and Revision					X
Submission					X

8. References[21, 22, 23]

Brandt, A., & Jenks, C. J. (2013). Computer-mediated spoken interaction: Aspects of trouble in multi-party chat rooms. *Language@Internet*, Article 4, 1–18.

Cappellini, M., & Azaoui, B. (2017). Sequences of normative evaluation in two telecollaboration projects: A comparative study of multimodal feedback through desktop videoconference. *Language Learning in Higher Education*, 7(1), 55–80.

Chakowa, J. (2018). Enhancing beginners' Second Language learning through an Informal Online Environment. *Journal of Educators Online*, *15*(1). Retrieved from https://files.eric.ed.gov/fulltext/EJ1168942.pdf (Accessed 16 April, 2018).

Coyle, Y., & Reverte Prieto, M. J. (2017). Children's interaction and lexical acquisition in text-based online chat. *Language Learning & Technology*, *21*(2), 179–199.

Dey-Plissonneau, A. (2017). Emerging affordances in videoconferencing for language learning and teaching. In K. Borthwick, L. Bradley, & S. Thouesney (Eds.), *CALL in a climate of change: Adapting to turbulent global conditions – Short papers from EUROCALL 2017*. Southampton, 23–26 August, 2017. Research-publishing.net, pp. 92–98.

21. The reference list includes a great deal of sources. These sources include seminal theoretical works, relevant research articles and up-to-date sources.
22. The reference list is presented in the department style.
23. Internet sources provide link and date accessed.

(*Continued*)

TABLE 16.2 (Continued)

Text	*Comment*
Dornyei, Z. (2007). *Research methods in applied linguistics*. Oxford: Oxford University Press.	
Dörnyei, Z., & Taguchi, T. (2009). *Questionnaires in second language research: Construction, administration, and processing* (2nd ed.). New York, NY: Routledge.	
González-Lloret, M. (2011). Conversation analysis of computer-mediated communication. *CALICO Journal*, *28*(2), 308–325.	
Gyamfi, G., & Sukseemuang, P. (2017). EFL Learners' perceptions, practices and achievement with the online learning program "Tell me more". *Contemporary Educational Technology*, *8*(4), 338–358.	
Hutchby, I., & Wooffitt, R. (2008). *Conversation Analysis, 2: Principles, Practices and Implications*. Cambridge: Polity.	
Iino, A, Yabuta, Y., & Nakamura, Y. (2016). Effects of task-based videoconferencing on speaking performance and overall proficiency. *Research-Publishing. Net* (Accessed 17 April, 2018)	
Istifci, I. (2017). Perceptions of Turkish EFL students on online language learning platforms and blended language learning. *Journal of Education and Learning*, *6*(1), 113–121.	
Jenks, C. J. (2009a). When is it appropriate to talk? Managing overlapping talk in multi-participant voice-based chat rooms. *Computer Assisted Language Learning*, *22*(1), 19-30.	
Jenks, C. J. (2009b). Getting acquainted in Skypecasts: Aspects of social organization in online chat rooms. *International Journal of Applied Linguistics*, *19*(1), 26–46.	
Jenks, C. J. (2014). *Social interaction in second language chat rooms*. Edinburgh: Edinburgh University Press.	
Jenks, C. J., & Brandt, A. (2013). Managing mutual orientation in the absence of physical co-presence: Multi-party voice-based chat room interaction. *Discourse Processes*, *50*(4), 227–248.	
Jenks, C. J., & Firth, A. (2013). Interaction in synchronous voice-based computer-mediated communication. In S. Herring, D. Stein, & T. Virtanen (Eds.), *Handbook of the pragmatics of computer-mediated communication* (pp. 209–234). Berlin: Mouton de Gruyter.	
Kazar, O. (2016). Teachers' reaction to silence and teachers' wait time in video and audioconferencing English lessons: Do webcams make a difference? *System*, *62*, 55–62.	
Krutka, D., & Carano, K. (2016). Videoconferencing for global citizenship education: Wise practices for social studies educators. *Journal of Social Studies Education Research*, 7(2), 109–136.	

Lamy, M. N. (2004). Oral conversations online: Redefining oral competence in synchronous environments. *ReCALL, 16*(2), 520–538.

Lamy, M. N. (2013). Distance CALL online. In M. Thomas, H. Reinders, & M. Warschauer (Eds.), *Contemporary computer-assisted language learning* (pp. 141–158). London: Bloomsbury.

Liddicoat, A. J. (2011). *An introduction to conversation analysis*. London: Continuum International Publishing Group.

Markee, N. (2008). Toward a learning behavior tracking methodology for CA-for-SLA. *Applied Linguistics*, *29*(3), 404–402.

Mondada, L. (2014). *Conventions for multimodal transcription*. Retrieved from https://mainly.sciencesconf.org/conference/mainly/pages/Mondada2013_conv_multimodality_copie.pdf (Accessed 10 April, 2018).

Norris, S. (2004). *Analysing multimodal interaction: A methodological framework*. New York, NY: Routledge.

Ormston, R., Spencer, L., Barnard, M., & Snape, D. (2014). The Foundations of qualitative research. In J. Richie, J. Lewis, C. McNaughton Nicholls, and R. Ormston (Eds.), *Qualitative research practice: A guide for social science students & researchers* (pp. 1–25). London: Sage Publications.

Psathas, G. (1990b). Introduction: Methodological issues and recent developments in the study of naturally occurring interaction. In G. Psathas (Ed.), *Interactional competence* (pp. 1–30). Washington, DC: University Press of America.

Punch, K. (2014). *Introduction to social research: Quantitative & qualitative approaches*. London: Sage Publications.

Rapley, T. (2007). *Doing conversation, discourse and document analysis*. London: Sage Publications.

Satar, M. (2016). Meaning-making in online language learner interactions via desktop videoconferencing. *ReCALL*, *28*(3), 305–325.

Simpson, J. (2005). Learning electronic literacy skills in an online language learning community. *Computer Assisted Language Learning*, *18*(4), 327–345.

Sindoni, M. G. (2013). *Spoken and written discourse in online interactions: A multimodal approach*. London: Routledge.

Ten Have, P. (2007). *Doing Conversation Analysis*. London: Sage Publications.

Wells, G. (1981). *Learning through interaction: Vol. 1: The study of language development*. Cambridge: Cambridge University Press.

Yanguas, I. (2010). Oral computer-mediated interaction between L2 Learners: It's about time! *Language Learning & Technology*, *14*(3), 72–93.

Yu, L., & Zeng, G. (2011). Managing CMC-based task through text-based dialogue: An exploratory study in a Chinese EFL context. *English Language Teaching*, *4*(4), 221–233, 22, 23.

Source: Spencer, M. (2018). Synchronous online learning via Zoom Videoconferencing: A multimodal conversation analytic study of teacher-student Interaction (Unpublished master's dissertation). Newcastle University, Newcastle.

16.11 Examples of dissertation abstracts

This section shows some of master's dissertation abstracts, highlighting study design. Some of these dissertations are freely available to download online through the links listed.

16.11.1 Study using ethnography, text analysis, observations, interviews

Research has established that many non-native speaking graduate students and faculty in EFL settings need language support to write for publication in English and are under increasing pressure to do so. However, the research is less clear on exactly how such support can be delivered effectively. This study seeks to better understand the writing practices of a single engineering lab to determine how materials and support could better scaffold the apprenticeship characteristic of co-authored research in engineering lab environments. The motivation is to improve the writing consultations, workshops and materials support at an English Writing Lab service for graduate students at a research university in Korea (www.hanyangowl.org).

Ethnographic data was gathered from texts, interviews, informal interaction, and participant observation of meetings between graduate students and their advisor. Given that the apprenticeship process is the most valuable form of graduate study but that students must also develop independent research skills, it is argued that programme responses and materials in the emerging field of English for Research Publication Purposes (ERPP) must be more innovatively designed to accommodate the distinct characteristics of graduate study, particularly in non-English speaking settings. The findings distinguish between skills that urgently need to be addressed through required elearning diagnostic quizzes checked by senior students and faculty, such as proper paraphrasing, and other needs such as computer skills and knowledge of writing principles that could be efficiently delivered through elearning materials. Observations and interviews also revealed the need for simpler, more concise print and online searchable materials designed to be used by students while writing, rather than textbooks. Most significantly, observation also made clear the need for heuristics and checklists to facilitate the interaction and mentoring between senior and novice students, and between students and their advisor. The paper concludes by arguing that ERPP research-practitioners should expand the boundaries of the field by including support for all facets of research writing including facilitating mentoring, peer learning, and the writing process but to do so in responses embedded within existing lab practices rather than traditional teaching. Therefore, greater use of participant observation research is suggested to formulate such innovative responses.

Turner, A. (2012). *Participant observation of the interaction in an engineering lab to improve materials design and writing support for graduate students and faculty publishing in English at a research university in Korea*. (Master's Dissertation), Aston University. www.baleap.org/wp-content/uploads/2016/03/Adam-Turner.pdf (Accessed 15 May, 2019).

16.11.2 Study using existing quantitative questionnaires and interviews utilising descriptive and inferential statistics

The study examines the role of culture and the role it plays in mediating learners' responses to culturally divergent reading materials. This investigation is motivated by three research questions: (1) Do students have a preference for culturally relevant instructional materials? (2) What influence does faith have on student's responses to culturally divergent reading materials? (3) Which topics do students prefer to read? To examine these questions, this study employed an adapted version of Leak's parametric Faith Development Scale, the Materials Appropriation Preference Scale, the Willingness and Response Scale and one-to-one follow up interviews. The participants were Gulf students studying on a pre-sessional English course. Previous studies have shown that faith has played a crucial role in the way learners have responded to culturally divergent materials. Literature on the way that learners have responded to culturally divergent materials has focused almost exclusively on learners from the outer and expanding circle countries with no similar incidents reported, for example, in the UK or between Arab learners. The findings suggest that students have a strong preference for culturally relevant instructional materials and reinforce the wider picture that materials must reflect the lives of their users. Finally, the study offers an uncharted area for further study in the inquiry of faith in SLA.

Alzalam, A. (2018). *Culturally relevant materials: An inquiry into the role of faith*. (Master's Dissertation). University of Hull. https://englishagenda.britishcouncil.org/sites/default/files/attachments/alaa_dean_alzalam_university_of_hull_dissertation.pdf (Accessed 15 May, 2019)

16.11.3 Study using a case study design

It has become increasingly common for practitioners of extensive reading (ER) to incorporate the use of language learning tasks into their lessons. The links between tasks for ER and the principles of task-based language teaching (TBLT), however, have not been fully explored. It is suggested that research on task design and task evaluation can provide insights to teachers about how to effectively utilize graded readers for various types of meaning-focused language learning. This case study presents a micro-evaluation (based on Ellis, 1997) of five tasks for extensive reading with a class of intermediate-level first-year students at a Japanese university. The evaluation consisted of observation by the teacher, analysis of spoken and written work, and student feedback through questionnaires and interviews. The purpose of the study was to utilize the principles of TBLT to systematically and empirically evaluate each task in practice. Based on the results of the evaluation, conclusions are reached about the benefits of tasks for ER and how tasks can be implemented effectively in an ER context. The findings suggest that, through the use of well-designed tasks, ER and TBLT can function together as mutually supportive forms of meaning-focused pedagogy.

Van Deusen, B. (2011). *A micro-evaluation of five tasks for extensive reading*. (Master's Dissertation). University of Birmingham. http://asian-efl-journal.com/wp-content/uploads/mgm/downloads/30882500.pdf (Accessed 15 May, 2019)

16.11.4 Study based on classroom discourse and observations

Investigation into the relationship between what teachers say, intend, and do can help improve overall teacher effectiveness. Reviews of teacher belief systems and classroom discourse helped base this study on the relationship between beliefs and class practices. This small-scale study of three native-English speaking conversation teachers at a Korean university consisted of a triangulated methodology integrating a teachers' beliefs survey, classroom observations, and a retrospective interview. Analyzing the follow-up move in whole-class discourse using a modified version of the Sinclair and Coulthard IRF model, discoursal and evaluative teaching strategies were examined to determine if inferences could be made regarding teachers' beliefs and classroom behaviors. Aside from a few inconsistencies, it was found that these teachers' educational beliefs were manifested in their class actions in the observed and analysed portions of their classes. Unanticipated study problems and limitations in discourse analysis were acknowledged and recommendations for further research made. Additional studies of how teachers use teacher talk in their follow-up move could further support the findings in this study.

Jones, S. (2011). *Investigating the F-move in teacher talk: A South Korean study on teachers' beliefs and classroom practices*. (Master's Dissertation). University of Birmingham.www.birmingham.ac.uk/Documents/college-artslaw/cels/essays/matefltesldissertations/Jonesdiss.pdf (Accessed 15 May, 2019)

16.11.5 Action research study using an intervention

In the 21st century meta-cognitive skills are recognised as one of the key competences in learning a foreign language. However, a lot of opportunities throughout the world in English language teaching are being missed. This is especially so in Asian contexts because such skills are not taught and as the text books and published materials do not encourage such skills. This research, thus, attempts to describe an intervention where these skills could flourish.

In attempting to describe an intervention where such skills can flourish this research outlines a small-scale study on implementing meta-cognitive strategies for students of English as a foreign language (EFL). These students range from 10 to 12 years of age and are also referred to as the 'middle aged group'. The dissertation discusses the value of reflection and teaching within a reflective framework. For this purpose, four Iranian children were chosen to participate in an 8 hour intervention, which was especially designed to enhance their reflective skills. The intervention consisted of three stages. These three stages were planning, monitoring and evaluating learning tasks. The students were then invited to incorporate the three stages into their collaborative activity, which included the making of a project and performing a written task.

The results indicated that throughout this small intervention the learners grew an explicit awareness of the reflective process or the reflective cycle. Furthermore, they demonstrated knowledge of self-evaluation and some signs of self-regulated behaviour. After these 4 hours the students reported on how they had benefited from the reflective process. The feedback also reflected their enthusiasm and interest in the project.

Finally, this research highlights the limitations of this study and suggests the implications that may arise for teachers. It then recommends the type of further research needed in the field of meta-cognition.

Hazari, S. (2014). *Equipping young learners with learning to learn strategies by developing their meta-cognitive skills through reflection*. https://englishagenda.britishcouncil.org/sites/default/files/filefield_paths/sami_warwick_diss_2014.pdf (Accessed 27 July, 2019).

16.11.6 Study using existing textual data

This study explores the vocabulary learning opportunities that may be provided to the English language learner through the study of a commercial English Language Teaching (ELT) coursebook. The recent recognition given to the importance of vocabulary learning in both first and second language acquisition has led to a rise in studies investigating the vocabulary demands and vocabulary learning opportunities in different types of texts such as novels and newspaper articles using computer-generated data based on word frequency lists. However, to date no such research has been conducted on popular ELT coursebooks widely used in English language teaching contexts. Therefore, it was the aim of this study to shed light on the vocabulary learning potential of one of the most popular coursebooks on the global market today, New Headway Student's Book for upper-intermediate learners, using a computer programme designed for vocabulary analysis of texts. The results of the present study indicate that: 1) the learner would require knowledge of the 1st and 2nd 1,000 most frequent words in English in order to be familiar with a sufficient proportion of the words in the text to comprehend the coursebook text and to guess the meaning of unknown words from context, 2) the coursebook provides opportunities to deepen the knowledge of the 2nd 1,000 most frequent words through its repetition of these words and its presentation of various forms, meanings and collocations of these words throughout the text, and 3) the coursebook offers few opportunities to expand vocabulary knowledge beyond the 1st and 2nd 1,000 most frequent words. The study offers insights into how the main findings may inform English language pedagogy and provides implications for future research.

Matsuoka, W. E. (2009). *Vocabulary learning opportunities in a commercial ELT coursebook* (Unpublished master's dissertation). University of Sydney, Sydney.

16.11.7 Study trialling a pedagogical technique – story telling

As an English teacher, it is a tough job to provide enjoyable and efficient English classes for students, especially for young learners. Being different from adults, children have their own characteristic ways of learning a foreign language. Teachers can use many activities, such as storytelling, singing, playing games, and so on to arouse their interest. One of the interesting activities to use in class is telling stories. This is a worthwhile English teaching method in Chinese primary school classrooms. It is important for English learners to master the main points of stories, identify characters, and summarise content. Through storytelling skills, the classroom can be transformed from a boring environment into a warm one where students are paying attention, participating, and producing. In this study, the researchers attempted to ascertain whether the use of storytelling could stimulate children's motivation to learn English and which aspects of it were affected. This research project was conducted using a storytelling approach with 40 students from a grade five class in a Chinese primary school, to evaluate whether their motivation had been stimulated. Over the course of one month, the teacher applied a storytelling approach in one class. The Attitude/Motivation Test Battery (AMTB), which was invented by Gardner (2004), was conducted at the beginning and the end of the one-month experiment in order to collect the data. By analysing the data, it was concluded that the motivation for students to learn English did improve when the storytelling approach was used, though not significantly. Moreover, the students did display a greater interest in learning vocabulary and speaking, and their initiative for learning was strengthened.

This paper aims to explore the use of story teaching in Chinese primary school English classes so as to stimulate students' motivation in learning (Chen, 2017).

Chen, Y. (2017). *The impact of storytelling on young learners' motivation in English classes in primary school in China* (Unpublished master's Dissertation). Newcastle University, Newcastle.

16.11.8 In-depth qualitative study using a small sample

Access to professional development opportunities is important in any sector. However, as some EFL teaching programmes, for example the CELTA, are for one month only new English L2 teachers need the skills for 'bottom up' professional development. This study aims to investigate how three experienced EFL teachers engage in collaborative dialogic reflective practices that create a professional development learning space in their staffroom in Madrid, Spain. The multimethod approach adopted, discursive analysis supported by interview data, has provided both an emic and etic perspective to produce a fine-grained analysis. This study is viewed from a sociocultural theory epistemological stance and investigated how the interactants utilize their peers as a source of professional knowledge. The findings suggest that the participants actively engage in co-constructing collaborative dialogic reflective spaces that positively impact their professional knowledge. Therefore, further research is warranted to gain a deeper understanding of teacher learning in relation to informal EFL teacher learning.

Forde, R. (2018). *How can I teach this? Examining collaborative dialogic reflection and its impact on teacher learning*. (Unpublished master's dissertation). Newcastle University, Newcastle.

16.11.9 Study using a pre- and post-test design

This dissertation investigated the influence of pre-writing strategies on essay writing structure amongst English as a Second Language (ESL) learners enrolled in an English for Academic Purposes (EAP) programme. Pre-writing strategies are said to assist in lightening the cognitive load experienced by writers, during the writing phase, and thus contribute to improving elements of the final written product, such as essay structure. This four-week study adopted a quasi-experimental, pretest, posttest research design with two treatment groups. Participants were assigned to either the Outlining Group ($N = 46$) or the Concept Mapping Group ($N = 43$) based on the intact classes in the EAP programme. The study sought to answer the following two research questions: (1) What is the nature of ESL students' writing as measured before and after pre-writing strategy intervention? (2) What are students' perceptions of pre-writing strategies before and after pre-writing strategy intervention? Data collection instruments for these questions included: Research Question 1 – (1) a pre-intervention paragraph, (2) a delayed post-intervention essay; Research Question 2 – (3) Pre-Intervention Questionnaire, (4) Immediate Post-Intervention Questionnaire, and (5) Delayed Post-Intervention Questionnaire. Regarding Research Question 1, significant within-group increases in structure scores for both groups were revealed and a non-significant difference in between-group delayed post-intervention structure scores. Regarding Research Question 2, paired-samples t-test results indicated a significant effect for time in perceptions for the Outlining Group for a conclusion and all essay sections combined compared to non-significant within-group differences in perceptions for the Concept Mapping Group. Furthermore, non-significant between-group differences in perceptions were also found. Limitations of the study include a lack of qualitative data to complement the quantitative data as well as a lack of teachers' perceptions towards the influence of pre-writing strategies on writing structure. Finally, methodological implications are discussed regarding future research, with the dissertation concluding with pedagogical implications in light of the findings, which could be of benefit to students and teachers in ESL settings.

Steinhoff, A. (2018). *The influence of pre-writing strategies on the quality of essay structure and topic sentences in ESL academic writing*. (Master's Dissertation), University of Sydney.

16.12 Further weblinks

16.12.1 How to get published

TESOL Convention & Exhibit (TESOL, 2015 Toronto)
www.tesol.org/docs/default-source/books/how-to-get-published-in-applied-linguistics-serials.pdf?sfvrsn=4

16.12.2 The linguist list

The Linguist List is a website that has a wide range of resources freely available. Resources include lists of journals, current news in applied linguistics, syllabuses and dissertation abstracts. The site has old and new links here:

https://linguistlist.org/

https://new.linguistlist.org/

The old site provides links to dissertation abstracts. These abstracts include those at undergraduate, postgraduate and higher research degree levels.

16.12.3 Time management apps

- Any.do www.any.do/
- Get it done https://getitdoneapp.com/
- Trello https://trello.com/?truid=trbf098b-f460-2c5b-205a-931be112039c

16.12.4 Blogs

- Andy Gillet has an excellent blog about academic English that includes a section on academic reading strategies with exercises: www.uefap.com/reading/readframnote_sum.htm.

16.13 Dissertation checklist

Table 16.3 provides a detailed checklist that needs to be completed before the final submission of the dissertation.

TABLE 16.3 Checklist for editing the dissertation

Area		✓
Organisation	Included preliminary pages with Roman numerals, i, ii, iii, iv etc	
	Title page with university logo	
	Declaration of originality	
	Ethics approval	
	Acknowledgements	
	Abstract	
	Table of contents	
	List of tables/figures	
Presentation	Uses recommended font (eg Times New Roman 12 point)	
	Uses recommended spacing (eg double)	
	Uses headings and sub-headings	

Area		✓
	Uses no more than three levels of numbering (eg 3.1.2)	
	Dissertation has page numbers	
	Each chapter has an introduction	
	Each chapter has a conclusion	
	Every table and figure has a number and a title	
	Every table and figure is referred to in the text	
	Tables and figures are prepared by student rather than cut and paste from statistical output	
Language	No informal or emotional language used (eg really, unfortunately)	
	No abbreviations (eg isn't, don't)	
	No run on sentences (she is interested in linguistics she is doing some research on this topic)	
	All subjects and verbs agree	
	Tense is used correctly	
	Each sentence has a capital letter and a full stop	
	Punctuation is correct	
Literature review	Uses academic rather than professional references	
	References are up to date	
	Uses appropriate referencing style	
	All citations match reference list	
	Literature review chapter structured around an argument	
	Does not include too many secondary citations	
Methodology	Includes research questions	
	Explains and justifies research approach (quantitative, qualitative, mixed methods)	
	Explains and justifies data collection methods	
	Explains and justifies data collection instruments	
	Includes discussion of ethics	
	Explains sampling procedure	
	Includes information about participants	
	Addresses reliability and validity	
Results	Results ordered in logical fashion	
	Results linked to research questions	
	Use of graphics appropriate	
	Results includes some interpretation	
Discussion	Research questions answered explicitly	
	Linked to literature (theory and previous research)	
	Claims supported by research evidence	
	Includes discussion from theoretical and practical perspectives	

(*Continued*)

TABLE 16.3 (Continued)

Area		✓
Conclusion	Addresses aims of research	
	Summarises findings	
	Discusses limitations of study	
	Makes suggestions for further research	
	Makes suggestions for practice	
Appendices	Each appendix has a title and a number or letter	
	Includes required material (eg interview transcripts)	
	Does not include material central to the dissertation	
	Includes ethic approval and consent form	
References	As for literature review above	
	Ordering of list is alphabetical	
	Authors listed by family name, not given name	
	Reference list is in same font and spacing as the rest of the dissertation	

GLOSSARY

Abstract Dissertations usually need an abstract. This is a succinct description of the study, including the results. The abstract may need to be submitted before the dissertation and is used to choose the most appropriate examiners for the dissertation. The abstract will usually include key terms, which will make the dissertation more searchable.

Academic literacies Academic literacies is a theoretical view of English for Academic Purposes that views academic literacy as being plural. Literacies vary according to the context of the communication and the members of the discourse community in which they occur.

Acknowledgements At the beginning of the dissertation it is usual to thank people who have helped with the dissertation both academically and emotionally. Typically, the funding body, the supervisor, editor and family are thanked.

Action research Action research is the term used for classroom-based enquiry that involves the teacher and the class and focuses on an aspect of teaching. Changes to teaching are trialled, and these are reflected upon in a formal manner.

ANOVA This refers to analysis of variance and is a statistical method used to investigate differences in means of two or more sets of scores. Different types of ANOVAs are independent samples, repeated measures, one way, two way and factorial.

Appendices The appendices in a dissertation may contain extra material relevant but not central to the study, such as full questionnaires, results and consent forms.

Assessment criteria Assessment criteria are the guidelines provided to examiners for the assessment of academic work. They are based on the aims and objectives of the academic course. The criteria usually take the form of a set of descriptors of academic performance grades at different levels, for example, pass, high distinction.

Capstone activity A capstone activity is an academic activity that will enable the student to reach his or her academic ceiling. It is designed to push the student intellectually. The dissertation is usually classed a capstone activity.

Chi-square Chi-square is a statistical method used to investigate the relationship between two categorical variables.

Codebook A codebook is produced when conducting quantitative analysis. This provides information of all the coding in the analysis and the procedures applied to the data.

Databases When writing a literature review it is helpful to consult databases in the fields of language and linguistics to generate a list of sources to consult. These are usually available through the university library. An example of a useful database in TESOL and applied linguistics is LLBA.

Data screening This is the process in quantitative analysis whereby the data set is examined for entry errors, inconsistencies and outliers. Data must be screened before commencing the analysis otherwise the results could be distorted.

Declaration In most dissertations, the student is required to sign a declaration of academic honesty. This typically refers to confirming that the research has ethics approval and may include a statement regarding plagiarism.

Descriptive statistics This refers to statistics to describe the findings, for example, the scores on a questionnaire. Typically, the mean, mode and median are produced. Descriptive statistics are usually contrasted with inferential statistics that use analyses to generalise findings beyond the sample.

Digital object identifier (DOI) The DOI is a unique alpha-numeric code assigned to a text. This does not change over time. Some universities and publishers insist on these being included in reference lists of texts such as dissertations and journal articles.

Discussion chapter The discussion chapter relates the study findings to theory and research in the area. It is in this chapter that the research questions are answered.

Dissertation A dissertation in UK English refers to the document produced as part of a master's degree. This is usually a small-scale research project. Master's dissertations are usually between 10,000 and 20,000 words. In the US a dissertation refers to the document produced as the result of a PhD project.

Ethics Most universities require researchers to have ethics approval for research using participants. This is a procedure whereby the student gets approval for the research prior to collecting data. Central to the ethics approval process is the notion of informed consent. This means that all participants need to be informed of the nature of the research and that participation is voluntary. Most departments have ethics templates comprising an application form, a participant information sheet and a participant consent form.

Examiner This is the person who assesses the dissertation. Usually a dissertation will have at least two examiners who mark the work independently. Where the examiners differ in the final grade a third examiner may be used. The examiners may be the supervisor, internal to the department or external from other universities.

Factor analysis This is a statistical method that explores relationships among variables to indicate underlying groupings. It is often used to validate questionnaires.

Higher research degree The term 'higher research degree' refers to all research degrees. These include Master's by Research, PhDs and MPhils. The term does not usually refer to a course-work master's that includes a research component.

Informed consent All participants need to be informed of the nature of the research and what is required of them before giving consent to participate in the research. Informed consent is usually collected by giving the participant an information sheet and a consent form. The consent form needs to be signed before participation. Both the information sheet and the consent sheet need to be approved by the relevant ethics committee prior to the commencement of data collection.

Inferential statistics This reflects a set of analyses that can generalise findings beyond the sample used. Typical examples of inferential statistics in master's dissertations are t-tests, ANOVA, correlations, regression and Chi-square.

Interviews Interviews can be used to collect data from individuals or groups. They can be conducted face to face or they can be facilitated using technology, for example, video interviews using Skype. There are three types of interview: structured, semi-structured and unstructured. Structured interviews ask the participants the same questions; semi-structured interviews have a set of questions to ask but may deviate from these; unstructured interviews rely on broad topic areas without set questions.

Introduction The introduction to the dissertation should situate the study describing the research purpose and objectives. It does this by providing some background information to the study and outlines the research purpose and objectives. The research questions may be included in the introduction.

Limitations A dissertation will usually include a section on the limitations of the study. This refers to any shortcomings of the study, perhaps due to time and access to participants. In this section it is common to refer to the need for further research to address these limitations.

Literature review A literature review is the basis of a dissertation. The review should include both theory and research and should be evaluative. The literature chapter in a dissertation should reflect an argument concerning the research problem and be the basis for the research questions.

Methodology The methodological approach to a research project refers to the underlying view of knowledge research. This may be constructivist, which is the basis for a qualitative perspective to research, or positivist, which is the basis for a quantitative perspective to research. A mixed methods approach is classed as a pragmatic approach.

Mean, median and mode These are descriptive statics that describe the central tendency of data. The mean (M) refers to the average; the median (Md) refers to the exact middle score and the mode refers to the most frequently reported score.

Methods Research methods are those techniques chosen to collect data. These may be qualitative, for example, interviews, open ended questions and focus groups. Or they may be quantitative, for example, Likert scales and can-do questionnaires.

Non-parametric tests Non-parametric tests are used when the data violate the assumptions of parametric tests in terms of distribution and sampling.

Parametric tests Parametric statistics is the default in quantitative inferential statistics. For parametric tests, data should be interval or continuous and be normally distributed. If this is not the case, non-parametric tests should be used.

Plagiarism Plagiarism refers to using another person's ideas and passing them as one's own. This can be accidental, as is the case with inaccurate referencing, or intentional, where the writer intends to deceive.

Procedure In a dissertation and dissertation proposal it is usual to have a section on the procedure of the research. This reflects a step-by-step description of how the data will be collected, where, when and from whom.

Process of writing Writing is viewed as a process rather than a product. The dissertation should go through several cycles of drafting and redrafting before the finished version is produced.

Proposal Most dissertations are preceded by a research proposal that outlines the project. This is a document or between 1000 and 3000 words. Often this is an assessed task. The student can get feedback on the research design and feasibility. The proposal is often used to allocate a suitable supervisor.

Rationale The rationale of the dissertation is a statement or section that justifies the research. It provides a reason why the project is important.

Reference list The reference list is positioned at the end of the dissertation before the appendices. This list should contain every reference cited in the text rather than all the works consulted. Usually the academic department has a preferred referencing style, for example, APA 6th edition or Harvard.

Reliability Reliability refers to the consistency of the results of a research project. A reliable study would produce the same results if the study was replicated.

Research design The research design of a project refers to the approaches and methods used for a study, for example, in a qualitative design case study or action research. Examples in a quantitative design are experimental and quasi-experimental designs.

Research diary A research diary is a day-by-day account of all activities connected with the research project. This may be paper based or electronic.

Research questions All research projects need at least one research question, usually more. The research questions need to be answered by the research project, and assessment will be based on this. The questions need to be detailed and precise.

Results chapter This chapter in the dissertation presents the findings of the study. Usually the chapter also includes a brief interpretation of the findings, but the main significance of the results is discussed in the discussion chapter. Sometimes the results and discussion chapter are combined.

Sampling Sampling is the technique used to select the sample of participants. Random sampling refers to selecting participants on an entirely random basis, purposive sample refers to looking at specific groups of participants, snowball sampling refers to getting a small group of participants who suggest or recruit further participants.

Standard deviation (SD) This is a descriptive statistic that reflects the difference of a collection of scores from the mean (M).

Supervisor The supervisor is the person who is responsible for a student's research project. Usually students are allocated one supervisor, but in some situations there may be more than one supervisor. Supervisory sessions are usually one to one, where the student gets feedback on the project and is given the opportunity to clarify issues.

Title The dissertation title usually does not need to be finalised until the submission of the dissertation. Titles need to reflect the content of the study accurately and should contain descriptors, which make online searching for the dissertation easier.

Topic A dissertation topic refers to the general area of the research. Topics are chosen very early in the dissertation process and are refined during the development of the study; finalisation of the topic usually occurs with the research proposal.

T-tests This is a statistical method used to examine two sets of scores. There are two main types of t-tests: independent samples using different groups of participants and repeated measures using the same group on two occasions.

Validity The validity of a research project refers to whether the research measures what it intends to measure. For example, a reading test measures reading and not writing.

Viva A viva is an oral examination of the dissertation involving at least two examiners. It usually takes the form of a question-and-answer exam based on the dissertation, which has already been marked. Upon completion of the viva the final grade is awarded.

INDEX

Note: Page numbers in *italics* indicate a figure and page numbers in **bold** indicate a table on the corresponding page.

abbreviations 186, *187*
abstracts 52, 179–180, **181–182**, **182–183**, 217–231
academic journals 210–212
academic writing: audience 112; expectations 112; grammar 113; punctuation types **114–115**; purpose of 112; style 112–115; vocabulary **113**; weblinks 215
acknowledgements 183
action research 38, 49, 228–229
analysis 42–44
appendices 59, 186–189, *188*, *189*, 191–192
articles: differences between dissertations and 204–205, **205**; publishing 203–204, **204**
assessment 19, 59–60, 64
assessment criteria 194, **194**, **195**
assignments: differences between dissertations and 2, **2–3**; topic selection from modules/assignments 11–12; topic selection from previous dissertations 12
audience 112
awards 205

Bealle, Jeffrey 207
Beile, Penny 129
Bell, Judith 87
bias 12
bibliography 59
Biggam, John 62, 207
Bitchener, John 161, 174
Blaxter, Loraine 87
blogs 232
Bloomer, Aileen 19
Boote, David N. 129
British National Corps (BNC) 42
Bui, Yvonne N. 19

'capstone' activity 1–2
case studies 39, 227–228
citation management software 26–27, **27**
citations 126, *127*, 129
claims *159*
classroom discourse analysis (DA) 42, 228
codebooks 93–95
conference presentations 202, 203
Conhoto, Ana Isabel 102
consent 46, 49, 87
contact time 64–65
corpus analysis 92
corpus linguistics 42
correlational studies 37, *150*
critical reading 28, 124
critical writing 124
Cronbach's Alpha 48

data analysis: assistance 100–101; common mistakes 101–102; FAQs 102; methods of 137–138; qualitative analysis 43;

quantitative analysis 43, **44**, 92–98; software 214; use of research diary 89–91; writing about *137*
databases 25–26
data collection: common mistakes 86; FAQs 86–87; methods of 137; recruiting participants 75–76; sites 83, 85; types of 87; types of participants 73–75; unforeseen circumstances 84–86
data collection methods: corpus linguistics 42; discourse analysis 42; focus groups 41; interviews 40–41; observations 41; questionnaires 39, *40*, 49, 79–82; textual data 78–79
declaration page 186, *187*
Denscombe, Martyn 192
Denzin, Norman K. 103
descriptive statistics 43, 49, **149**, 227
diary 5, 89–91, 107, **108**
Dickson, Ben 42
Digital Object Identifier (DOI) numbers 29, 172, 174, 213
discourse analysis (DA) 42, 99
discussion chapter: common mistakes 160; conclusion to *156*; examples of descriptors *153*; FAQs 160–161; implications of study 158; language in 158; limitations section 156; organisation of 155–156; purpose of 152–154; referring to previous research *153*; structure of *157*; template for relating results to literature **154**; writing 152–161
dissertation: abbreviations 186, *187*; abstracts 52, 179–180, **181–182**, **182–183**, 217–231; acknowledgements 183; alternatives 2; appendices 59, 186–189, *188*, *189*, 191–192; checklist **232–234**; common mistakes in completing 191; declaration page 186, *187*; definition 1; differences between article and 204–205, **205**; differences between assignments and 2, **2–3**; disseminating knowledge 202–203; editing 189; examination 193–207; examples of organisation *109*, *110*; FAQs on completion 191–192; guides 208–209; managing process 4–6; methodology chapter 131–143; organisation 109; post-dissertation 201–205; proof-reading 189; purpose of 2; table of contents 183–185, *185*; term list 186; title page 179, *180*; titles 16–18; use of proposal 62; using as pathway 201–202; weblinks 214–215
documentation 98–100
Doing a literature review (Hart) 129
Doing a literature search (Hart) 31
Dörnyei, Zoltán 49

editing 189–190, **190**
Edley, Nigel 41
Educational Resources Information Center (ERIC) 26
email 65
ethics approval 14, 46, 49, 59, 86, 140, 142
ethnographic research 38–39, 217–227
Everett, Euris 70
examination process: assessment criteria 194, **194**, **195**; dissertation marking 193–194; feedback 195–196
examiners 193–194
examiner's report *196*
expectations 112
experimental research 36
extensions 191

Feak, Christine B. 161, 174, 192
feedback 19, 52, 59–60, 65, 195–196
feedback form *196*
Field, Andy 102
figures *150*
focus groups 41
funding 206
Furseth, Inger 70

Gillet, Andy 28, 31, 232
Google 25
grades 117
grammar **113–114**
graphics 148–149, 160
Guba, Egon G. 46

handbooks 22–23, 209–210
Hart, Chris 31, 62, 129
Harwood, Nigel 70
How to write a master's thesis (Bui) 19
Hughes, Christina 87

'imposter syndrome' 5
inferential statistics 43, 49, 227
informed consent 46, 49, 87
Institute for Scientific Information (ISI) 25
interventions 228–229
interviews 40–41, 82–84, 98–100, *151*, 217–227

journals 210–212
JSTOR 26

Language Teaching (journal) 23, 49
Larson-Hall, Jenifer 102

limitations section *157*
Lincoln, Yvonna S. 46, 103
Linguist List 232
literature guide, The (Ridley) 31
literature review: broad review 22–25; characteristics of **120**; citations 126, *127*; common mistakes 30, 128; criteria for selecting sources **27**; critical reading and writing skills 124; as dissertation alternative 2; dissertation proposal 55; FAQs 30, 128; finding sources 25–27, 30; gap in knowledge reference 125, *125*, *126*; organisation of 120, *121*, 122, *122*; plagiarism 29; process 21–31; purpose of 22, *22*, 119; reading skills 27–29; sources 121, 212–213; stages 22–29; structure of *122*, *123*; template for initial **24**; types of literature 24–25; writing 119–129
Litosseliti, Lia 41, 49
Locke, Lawrence F. 62

marking scheme 115–116
Mehdi Riazi, Abdol 103
mixed methods research design 32, 33, 39, 132, 142
modules 11–12

observations 41, 217–227, 228
oral examination *see* viva
oral presentations 200, **201**

Pallant, Julie 102
Paltridge, Brian 42, 49, 70, 161, 174
participants: describing and selecting *136*; fellow students 73–74; friends 74; from home institution 74; minimum number for data collection 87; recruiting 75–76, 85, 134–135; sources of **75**; types of 73–75; unforeseen circumstances 84–86; from university language centre 74; using intact classes 74
pedagogical techniques 230
peer review 25
permission 85
personal interest 12
Petric, Bojana 70
Phakiti, Aek 49
plagiarism 29, 128
post-dissertation: awards 205; common mistakes 206; conference presentations 202, 203; disseminating knowledge 202–203; FAQs 206–207; publishing 202, 203–204, **204**, 206, 232; resubmission 201
post-test design 231
pre-test design 231
primary sources 26
procrastination 107, **108**
proof-reading 189–190
proposal: assessment 59–60; checklist **60–61**; common mistakes 61–62; FAQs 62; feedback 59–60; guides 209; introduction 53–54; literature review 55; methodological approach 57; methodology 57; procedure/timeline 58; purpose of 51; purpose statement 54; research questions 55–57, **58**, 132; sample 217, **218–226**; use in dissertation 62
ProQuest 26
PsycInfo 26
Publication Manual of the American Psychological Association (APA), 6th edition *29*, 59, 148, 160, 171
publishing 202, 203–204, **204**, 206, 232
Punch, Keith F. 62
punctuation 114
purpose statements *167*

qualitative data analysis: common approaches to 100; data preparation 98–100; interviews 98–100; research design 43; stages *99*
qualitative research design methods 33, 37, **37**, 39, 49, 82–83, *139*, 142, 227, 230–231
quantitative data analysis: codebook preparation 93–95; data description 95; data preparation 92–98; data screening 95; further analysis 96; research design 43; stages *97*
quantitative research design methods 32–37, 39, 49, 82–83, *138*, 142, 148
quasi-experimental research 36
questionnaires 39, *40*, 49, 227

readers 64
reading: background 22; critical 28; keeping track of 26–27; skills 27–29; strategies **28**, 28–29; topic selection 14
recording devices 86
referee form *203*
reference list 170–173, **171**, *172*
reference styles 28–29, 59, 173–174, 213
referencing software 172, 212–213
reliability 46–48, 138, *138*, 142
Renandya, Willy 207
research: bias 12; doable 14–15; methodology 32–33; questions 55–57; role of 29; types of literature 24–25
research design: approaches 32–37; common mistakes 48; data analysis 42–44; data collection methods 342;

ethics approval 14, 46, 49; FAQs 48–49; qualitative methods 33, 37, **37**, 39, 48–49, 82–83; quantitative methods 32–37, 39, 48–49, 82–83; reliability 46–48; sampling 45; types of 37–39; validity 46–48
research diary 5, 89–91
researcher 133
research methodology: analysis 42–44, 137; characteristics of 57; ethics approval 46; reliability 46–48, 142; research design 33–42; sampling 45; sources 213–214; validity 46–48, 142
research methodology chapter: characteristics of **131–132**; common mistakes 142; data analysis 137–138; data collection 137; ethics approval 140, *140*; FAQs 142; language in 140–141; methodological approach 132–133, *135*; organisation of *134*, *135*; participants 134–135, *136*; purpose of 131; reliability 138, *138*, *139*; research questions 132; research setting 133–134; role of researcher 133; validity 138, *139*; writing 131–143
research questions 55–57, **58**, 96, 119, 132
research setting 133–134
results chapter: common mistakes 159–160; criteria for selecting results *145*; FAQs 160; introduction *147*, *148*; language in 158; organisation by cases *147*; organisation of 146–147; purpose of 145; reporting qualitative results 149, 152; reporting quantitative results 148; use of tables and graphics 148–149, 160; writing 144–152
Richards, Keith 103
Ridley, Diana 31
role-perception scale 70
Rose, Susan 102
Routledge handbook of applied linguistics (Simpson) 22–23
Routledge handbook of English language teaching (Hall) 23

sampling 45
screening process 95, 102
secondary sources 26, 30
self-talk **200**
Silverman, David 103
software: data analysis 214; referencing 172, 212–213
sources 25–27, 59
Spinks, Nigel 102
Starfield, Sue 70, 161, 174
statistical package for the social sciences (SPSS) 92, 93–95, 102
statistics 43, 49, 92, *97*, **97–98**
student roles 65–66
style guides 118
summaries 67–68
supervision: by committee 64; common mistakes 69; contact time 64–65; FAQs 70; group 65; online 64–65; problems with 68; supervisory meetings 66–68
supervisors: allocation of 63–64; data analysis assistance 102; expertise 13, 18; role 65–66; role in topic selection 18–19, 62, 70; role of student 65–66
support networks 70
survey research 37–38, 49
Swales, John 161, 174, 192

table of contents 183–185, *185*
tables 148–149, *150*, 160
term list 186
text analysis 217–227
textual data 78–79, 229–230
theory 29
Tight, Malcolm 87
time management 4–5, 232
title page 179, *180*
titles: construction **18**; dissertation 16–18; examples *17*
topics: based on career trajectory 13–14; based on supervisor expertise 13; changing 16, 62; choosing 11–19; common mistakes 18; development 15–16; FAQs 18–19; focusing **15**, **16**; informed by personal interest 12; informed by professional need 13; researchable 14; role of supervisors 18–19, 62, 70; selection from modules/assignments 11–12, 19; selection from previous dissertations 12
transcription 84, 98–100, 102
'trustworthiness' 46

validity 46–48, 138, *139*, 142
verbs 126, **127**
viva 64, 198–200, 206
vocabulary 113

Waters, Stephen 87
weblinks: academic writing 215; for dissertations 214–215; resources 232
Wikipedia 22, 25
word length 191–192
Wray, Alison 19
writing: academic 112–115; common mistakes 116; conclusion 166, **168–169**, **170**, 173; diary 107, **108**; discussion chapter 152–161; dissertation

organisation 109; examples of dissertation organisation *109*, *110*; FAQs 117, 174; general guidelines 107–118; general requirements of dissertation 111, *111*; introduction 163, 163–166, **164–165**, *166*, 173; literature review 119–129; marking scheme 115–116; process 116, *117*; procrastination 107, **108**; research methodology chapter 131–143; results chapter 144–152
writing/editing services 191
writing groups 215, **216**

Printed in Great Britain
by Amazon

65588347R00151